WHAT PEOPLE ARE

THE TWO FACES OF CHRISTIANITY

This is a book that every Christian, post-Christian, and anti-Christian should read. It leads all sorts of readers to see the New Testament with new eyes. It shows how the Gospels and the letters of Paul shape people today, for better or for worse. It makes a case for the teaching of Jesus as psychologically healthy, as well as deeply spiritual. It also argues that Paul was a flawed human being, whose teachings can be dangerous if readers do not reflect on them critically.

Professor Adela Collins, Buckingham Professor of New Testament Criticism and Interpretation at Yale University Divinity School

The world is full of authoritarian versions of religion, including Christianity. In this lucid work Richard Oxtoby argues for a non-authoritarian version of the Christian faith, open and liberal-minded. All the churches would benefit from hearing what he has to say.

Professor John Barton, Oriel and Laing Professor of the Interpretation of Holy Scripture, Oxford University

This book is a valuable guide to authentic Christianity and to where it has gone wrong. Clear, courageous and challenging, it rests on thorough research, rich psychological insight and deep spiritual experience. It deserves to be widely read and above all, heeded.

Martin Prozesky, Emeritus Professor of Comparative and Applied Ethics at the University of Natal, South Africa

Dr Oxtoby provides a valuable opportunity for the reader to reflect anew on the teachings of Jesus rather than the teachings about him. "Separating the wheat from the chaff", scripturally speaking (Matthew 3 :12), the author enables a more focussed fluency of faith on the part of those seeking to understand the core teachings of Jesus. Dr Oxtoby has done the cause of Christianity a world of good in writing this book.

Rev Gordon Oliver, Minister-Emeritus, Unitarian Church, Cape Town, and Mayor of Cape Town 1989 - 1991

The Two Faces of Christianity

The Two Faces of Christianity

Richard Markham Oxtoby

CHRISTIAN
ALTERNATIVE

Winchester, UK
Washington, USA

First published by Christian Alternative Books, 2014
Christian Alternative Books is an imprint of John Hunt Publishing Ltd.,
Laurel House, Station Approach,
Alresford, Hants, SO24 9JH, UK
office1@jhpbooks.net
www.johnhuntpublishing.com
www.christian-alternative.com

For distributor details and how to order please visit the 'Ordering' section on our website.

Text copyright: Richard Markham Oxtoby 2013

ISBN: 978 1 78279 104 1

A CIP catalogue record for this book is available from the British Library.

Design: Stuart Davies

Printed in the USA by Edwards Brothers Malloy

We operate a distinctive and ethical publishing philosophy in all
areas of our business, from our global network of authors to
production and worldwide distribution.

CONTENTS

Progress in truth – truth of science and truth of religion – is mainly a progress in the framing of concepts, in discarding artificial abstractions or partial metaphors, and in evolving notions which strike more deeply into the root of reality. – A. N. Whitehead. *Religion in the Making.*

Learn from yesterday, Live for today, Hope for tomorrow. The important thing is to not stop questioning. – Albert Einstein

To a visitor who described himself as a seeker after Truth the Master said, "If what you seek is Truth, there is one thing you must have above all else." "I know. An overwhelming passion for it." "No. An unremitting readiness to admit you may be wrong." – Father Anthony de Mello, SJ

The only thing necessary for evil to flourish is for good men to do nothing. – Edmund Burke

We know what happens to people who stay in the middle of the road. They get run over. – Aneurin Bevan

With grateful thanks
To the memory of my parents,
The quality of whose lives
Influenced my spiritual development
More than all the books I have read,
And more than all the sermons I have ever heard
On that subject.

Introduction

The teacher who walks in the shadow of the temple, among his followers, gives not of his wisdom, but rather of his faith and his lovingness. If he is indeed wise he does not bid you enter the house of his wisdom, but rather leads you to the threshold of your own mind.[1]
– **Kahlil Gibran** *The Prophet*

There is a wide diversity of views among those who think of themselves as Christians as to what constitute the core beliefs of that religion. I am writing this book in the belief that, as the profound philosopher and mathematician A. N. Whitehead asserted in his *Religion in the Making*, "You cannot shelter theology from science, or science from theology. There is no short-cut to truth."[2]

One fundamental difference between science and theology is that, in theory at least, scientists regard all conclusions drawn from the application of scientific method to any subject matter, as provisional truths. They fully expect these will be modified in the course of further research, and indeed welcome such developments. The scientific enterprise is all about finding ever better ways of understanding different aspects of the universe in which we live.

By contrast, generally speaking theology is about the search for eternal, absolute, unchanging truths: What is the 'right way' to understand the spiritual world, and its relationship with the material one? Such a search is often marked by dogmatic intolerance, and the belief that certain 'truths' of a particular religion are unalterable, defining beliefs of that religion. In the case of Christianity, prominent among those 'truths' is a belief in the existence of God as a being who is, in the words of the Concise Oxford English Dictionary (hereinafter referred to as the COED), "entitled to obedience, reverence, and worship". Also widely believed to be defining characteristics of Christianity are the beliefs that Jesus was 'the Son of God', both fully God and fully man,[3] that he was born of a virgin, and after his death was resurrected and now sits on the right hand of God. Perhaps most importantly for the majority of Christians, Jesus' death was set up by God as a substitute punishment for the sins of humanity.

Potential readers of this book should be warned that I do not accept any of those dogmatic statements as true, and believe there are powerful psychological reasons for rejecting them. It is my considered opinion that they have nothing to do with the teachings and beliefs of Jesus. The idea of God as a despotic creator-ruler was around long before the birth of Jesus, and has been simply taken over by most of the Christian Church (and that other great monotheistic religion, Islam). Beliefs about the conception, birth, divine status, and resurrection of Jesus, originated in the early Christian Church. Whether intentionally developed for that purpose or not, the supernaturalist, magical thinking underlying these ideas has for many people the effect of putting them and the religion built around them out of the realm of rational debate. Jesus' status as an atonement sacrifice for the sins of humanity is simply an expression of sadistic and masochistic authoritarian psychopathology, and has nothing whatsoever to do with spirituality. At the same time it feels appropriate to call myself a Christian because of the way in which the ethical principles taught and demonstrated by Jesus of Nazareth, resonate within me.

In this regard I find myself very much in the same position as Thomas Jefferson, the third President of the United States (1801-1809), and the principal author of the American *Declaration of Independence* of 1776. Jefferson believed that Jesus' ethical principles provided the "most sublime and benevolent code of morals which has ever been offered to man". He produced a much-reduced version of the New Testament, containing only what he believed to be those truths. When taken to task by more conservative Christians, he responded by saying that the work he had done on the New Testament, far from disqualifying him from describing himself as a Christian, was "proof that I am a Christian".

There is no way of proving that my views (many of them shared by a minority of other Christians) on the nature of God, and the significance of Jesus' life and death are either right or wrong. In any case the extent to which my views are right or wrong is really a matter of little importance to anyone except myself. What is important is the effect that contact with those ideas has on the religious thinking and spiritual experience of those who encounter them. I believe very strongly in the truth contained in the lines from Kahlil Gibran quoted at the beginning of this introduction.

I am under no illusion that I have said the last word on any of the topics I deal with in this book, but it is my earnest hope that those who read what I have written will find it has brought the whole question of Christian Ethics more clearly to their attention, and that they will find that that experience has liberated them into developing for themselves, "notions which strike more deeply into the root of reality".[4]

Chapter I

The Two Faces of Christianity

Christmas 1924
"Peace upon earth," the angels sang.
We pay a thousand priests to ring it.
And after 2000 years of Mass
We've got as far as poison gas.
– Thomas Hardy

Thomas Hardy's bitter post-World War I reminder of the Christian Church's failure so far to get anywhere near bringing in the era of the Kingdom of God on earth must be thought-provoking to the more reflective and honest of those of us who are prepared to call ourselves 'Christians'. Unless engaging in the psychological defence mechanism of denial on a grand scale, Christians must be aware that beyond those towering monuments to the good which has been done in the name of their religion, are some horrendous examples of 'man's inhumanity to man'.

The work of Albert Schweitzer (1875 – 1965), who abandoned a promising career as an academic philosopher, theologian, and musician in Germany to study medicine and bring the medical expertise of Western Europe to people in Africa (many of whose physical sufferings in the years before the establishment of the World Health Organisation and other international humanitarian bodies would otherwise have been ended only by their death), is but one example among many, of Christians who have made massive humanitarian contributions to making the world a better place.

But a very different picture of the influence of the Christian religion appears when we think of the brutal attacks on Islam undertaken 'in the name of God' under the banner of the Crusades, the persecution and mass killings of Jews which branches of the Christian Church were at times actually complicit in, and at others turned a blind eye to, the appalling barbarities of the Inquisition, and the torture and the killing of heretics and witches. Tragically, recent examples of such religiously inspired (and often sanctioned) cruelties are not hard to find. From the way in which the 'Born Again Christian' George Bush, aided and abetted by the 'devout Christian' Tony Blair, suppressed whatever stirrings of Christian compassion they may at times have felt in their acquiescence in, and responsibility for the use of waterboarding and other forms of torture of terrorist suspects (many of whom have since been released without the finding of any evidence that they present a danger to humanity), to the recent kicking to death of a Catholic peace worker by Protestant vigilantes in post-'Civil War' 21st-century Ireland, the story of the Christian Church's involvement in the infliction of pain, suffering, and death, is not an inspiring one. Despite the heroic humanitarian efforts of some saintly individuals (many of them unknown and unsung), overall the Christian Church as a whole must be regarded as a dismal failure in effectively promoting those humanitarian ideals which lie at the heart of what most people regard as Christian ethics.

Can this failure of the Christian Church be simply put down to the weaknesses of fallible humans whose ability to live up to the ideals of their religion leaves much to be desired? In this book I want to suggest that that is far too facile an explanation, and one which leaves little hope of the situation ever improving. I believe, however, that there is a better explanation, and a fairly simple one at that. It is, moreover, one that points the way to the possibility of ridding the Christian Church of the psychopathology that has marred the thinking (and therefore behaviour) of many of the adherents of the religion throughout its history. Insofar as we are successful in doing this, we shall see even more of the actualisation of the potential of those powerful positive forces contained within Christian Ethics to make the world an unambiguously better place for all.

It has been said that a compulsive desire to analyse everything as falling into one or other of two categories is so prevalent among academics as to almost warrant describing that behaviour as an 'academic disease'. Pathological habit or not, the multifarious divisions within Christianity seem to almost beg for some fundamental simplification of the bewildering variety of different religious systems claiming the mantle of Christian orthodoxy. Of course there has in the past been no shortage of two-category analyses within Christianity – Roman Catholic versus Protestant, Established Church versus Non-conformist, Mainstream versus Evangelical Church or Fringe Sect, True Believer versus Heretic, Born Again versus Spiritually Dead, those destined to experience the joys of Heaven for all eternity versus those damned to eternal suffering in Hell, are only a few of the 'us versus them' analyses that have long been commonplace within the Christian Church. However, none of these two-category divisions seems to take us further than a simple labelling of relatively superficial differences between the various Christian Churches in terms of belief and practice. Even the differentiation between fundamentalist and more rational approaches to biblical interpretation, which takes us closer to the heart of the issue, is not a significantly helpful distinction to make without deeper analysis.

Almost all religious systems are, to a greater or lesser extent, wracked by internal conflicts. Is it possible to stand outside the narrow confines of any one religious system and find amongst the plethora of competing views within it, any broad trends which do make sense of what is going on between the warring factions? Psychology is obviously one discipline whose insights ought to have something valuable to offer in this respect. That being so it is surprising how few publications appear each year offering any sort of psychological analysis of religious issues. The reason is doubtless the pervasiveness of atheistic beliefs among academic psychologists. Whilst the fact that an atheistic psychologist will inevitably view any religious system as a delusional one does not in itself rule it out as a legitimate object of study, it probably does mean that he or she is less likely than an open- and spiritually-minded psychologist to find it an interesting and important field in which to work.

Why the extremely high rate of atheism among psychologists in Christian and post-Christian societies? I believe there are at least two important reasons. One is probably the very influential rejection by Sigmund Freud of religion as an illusion based on wish-fulfilment. The growth in influence of the psychoanalytic movement seems to have paralleled the decline of Christianity at least in Western Europe, and indeed acceptance of orthodox psychoanalytic dogma does imply that there is something intellectually disreputable about the holding of a religious point of view. As Richard Webster in his *Why Freud was wrong: Sin, Science and Psychoanalysis*[5] has pointed out, however, Psychoanalysis itself has many of the characteristics of a religious movement and it will be interesting to see whether the decline in influence of its increasingly shaky claims to intellectual respectability leads to any resurgence of interest in questions of religion among academic psychologists.

There is another significant reason for the high atheism rate among psychologists, however, and that is the very real intellectual disreputability, Freud aside, of certain viewpoints perceived by many to be a necessary part of Christianity. I shall argue later in this book that these viewpoints, inevitably unacceptable to the majority of psychologists, are not intrinsic to a religious outlook, Christian or otherwise. One immediately striking example of this is the belief that we are all 'miserable sinners', rotten at the core, and need to be 'saved' from the consequences of all the wrongdoing with which we fill our lives.

It is unfortunate, but understandable, that so many intellectually able and emotionally intelligent people, repelled by such an unkind and unhelpful view of the human condition, want nothing more to do with a religion that espouses such views. To react in this way seems to me, to draw on an overworked metaphor, to be throwing the baby out with the bathwater. The first step in avoiding such a waste of the resources available to us to live a happy and meaningful life is to clearly identify what is baby and what is bathwater, and it is to contribute to such clarification that this book has been written.

Two religions, one label

Much of the malaise around religion in post-Christian societies, I believe, exists because of a lack of awareness that under the cloak of Christianity two very different religious and psychological systems of thought exist. There is considerable evidence that a very similar two-fold division exists within other major world religions (certainly in at least Islam, Judaism, and Buddhism), but I shall restrict myself in this book to Christianity, it being the only religion I know well enough to speak about with some authority. Christianity, however, is certainly not unique in having not merely two different religions, but two distinctly different *types* of religion sharing the same verbal label.

The starting point for my own enlightenment in this matter was the discovery some years ago of an all-too-little-known book by Eric Fromm, a leading figure in the Neo-Freudian movement, called *Psychoanalysis and Religion*.[6] In this book, first published in 1950, Fromm differentiates between authoritarian religions (in which an all-powerful, all-good God is seen as having ultimate control over dependent, weak and sinful human beings) and humanistic religions (in which God is seen in a non-personified way as the good within each human).

In authoritarian religions God is seen as existing in an adversarial relationship with humankind, over whose eternal destiny either in heaven or hell he has absolute control.

In humanistic religions God is seen as existing in an intimately integrated, co-operative relationship with humankind, as a power, a source of positive energy within each human being, but having an objective existence as a spiritual being: God is both immanent in nature and transcends it, having an existence beyond that of the individual living creatures of which 'he' is a part.

Fromm draws attention to how strongly our conception of what constitutes 'religion' is influenced by what is in fact only one type of religion – the authoritarian type. He notes that the *Oxford Dictionary* definition of religion is "a rather accurate definition of authoritarian religion." It reads: "[Religion is] recognition on the part of man of some higher unseen power as having control of his destiny, and as being entitled to obedience, reverence, and worship." No wonder that those to whom such a disempowering and abusive view of humankind is unacceptable should reject not just authoritarian religion but religion as a whole, or at least Christianity, if their experience of religion has been restricted to the authoritarian form of that religion.

As Fromm points out, it is not just "the recognition that man is controlled by a higher power outside of himself" that defines an authoritarian religion. It is the further belief that "this power, because of the control it exercises, is *entitled* to obedience, reverence, and worship."[7] This is where the disempowering of the human being comes in. Humankind has no rights to autonomy, to independent thinking or action. The deity is "*entitled* to obedience, reverence and worship." It is this, I believe, more than any other aspect of Christianity, which sticks in the gullet of enlightened thinkers in general, and psychologists in particular, as a destructively demeaning and belittling view of the nature of the human being.

And of course such a concept has no necessary relationship to religion and one's conception of spiritual realities at all, the Oxford Dictionary notwithstanding. What such a view of the nature of religion does have a necessary connection with is authoritarian systems in general, in which submission of each layer of a power hierarchy to the layer above is demonstrated through unquestioning obedience to its expressed or implied demands. Recognition of a "higher power as having control ... and as being entitled to obedience" is not a necessary component of a religious point of view, but it is a necessary part of an authoritarian one. Such an authoritarian viewpoint can be imposed on our understanding of spiritual things, but it cannot thereby monopolise the field. Unfortunately though, it can and often does have considerable success in its monopolistic attempts. The extent to which it has done so varies throughout history, due to a complex interaction of many political, economic, educational and cultural factors.

It is my aim in this book to examine key elements of Christian thinking and belief in terms of Fromm's concept of the distinction between humanistic and authoritarian religions. The more I have thought about this subject the more light this way of looking at things has shed for me on the fundamental psychological reasons why the Christian Church today (as it has been ever since its inception) is a house divided against itself, and why probably almost as much evil as good has been done in its name.

Christianity is not a single religion. It contains within itself two very different systems of thought, which reflect something far more fundamental than the differences between Catholicism and Protestantism, or between either of these and the Eastern Orthodox churches. In this book I have tried to clarify the often incompatible and even contradictory views which comprise Christianity as it exists in the world today. In identifying these conflicting streams of thought as the humanistic and the authoritarian faces of the religion it is not my intention to suggest that the population of all Christians can be divided into just one or other of two rigid categories – humanistic or authoritarian. Most Christians will hold views (consciously or unconsciously) which belong predominantly to one or other of these categories, but also some views which belong to the other. My own belief is that those ideas belonging to the humanistic face of Christianity are profoundly true and of immense potential power to make the world a better place for all living creatures. In so far as anyone holding these views also holds some beliefs stemming from the authoritarian face of Christianity it is my firm conviction that if they were able to recognise the psychopathologies from which those views spring, and let go of them, they would be contributing in a significant way to making the world a better place.

Chapter 2

The Human Condition

If we attend to the general principles which regulate all endeavours after clear statement of truth, we must be prepared to amplify, recast, generalize, and adapt, so as to absorb into one system all sources of experience.[8]
– Alfred North Whitehead. *Religion in the Making*

1. What is the fundamental motivator of human behaviour? What do we all constantly seek in life?

To feel OK about ourselves; to feel that whatever faults we may possess as the inevitable result of being human, at least deep down inside each of us is a good and beautiful person, more sinned against than sinning. Feeling guilty is a miserable state to be in, and we will go to great lengths, whether by becoming ill, the use and abuse of alcohol, street-drugs, prescription medication or religious conversion to eliminate, or at least dull the pain of feeling guilty.

2. How do we preserve and enhance our self-esteem?

- By doing 'good works', in other words by doing things that will earn us the approval of at least some other people.
- By seeking to live in the company of other people who generally approve of the way we live our life and will give us positive feedback about what a valuable member of the human race we are.
- By using a number of mental mechanisms with which our nervous systems are equipped.

3. What innate mechanisms of the mind exist to protect us from psychological hurt?

One of the most important of several mechanisms that serve this function is what Sigmund Freud, the twentieth-century Austrian neurologist turned psychoanalyst, called 'Defence Mechanisms'. These are ways in which our mind distorts its picture of reality to exclude from consciousness any thoughts or feelings which we believe it is wrong for us to have, and whose presence in us cause us anxiety when we become aware of them.

So far as religious thinking is concerned, the most important of the defence mechanisms that Freud identified are Denial, Repression, Projection, Reaction Formation, and Rationalisation. An extension of Freud's thinking in this respect is the concept of our 'Shadow self', developed by the twentieth-century Swiss Psychiatrist Carl Gustav Jung, who early in his career was a member of Freud's inner circle.

Denial

Underlying all the defences we shall consider here is the kingpin defence mechanism of *denial*. This involves a refusal to face facts, either those about the external situation in which we find ourselves, or about our own feelings. Refusing to become aware of the telltale signs of the impending break-up of a relationship, or that a developing relationship is not going to be good for one, or one parent not allowing themselves to become aware of the probability that the other is sexually abusing a child, are all-too-common examples of denial.

Repression

Denying the reality of a feeling does not of course make that feeling go away, no matter how hard we try to keep it out of our consciousness, and denied reality has a nasty habit of constantly rearing its ugly head and intruding itself into our lives, often at the most unexpected times and in the most unexpected places.

The presence of repression shows itself by the arousal of anxiety when certain issues or topics are broached. When someone becomes agitated and perhaps very judgemental if a conversation should get around, however light-heartedly to, for example, something like the issue of extra-marital affairs, it might be because that individual has been experiencing some temptation to get involved with someone in just that way. If they are struggling to repress that thought, being part of a conversation in which such a topic is discussed reminds them of something they are trying very hard to forget, and the thought may well make them anxious and even agitated. There are of course also other reasons why people might find a conversation about any particular topic uncomfortable.

Projection

Projection is the defence mechanism whereby we deny responsibility for those of our own thoughts and feelings which are unacceptable to us, and attribute them to others. The defence mechanism of *Projection* always goes hand in hand with that of *Denial*. The desire to feel good about ourselves, to feel that 'I'm OK', is a universal and most powerful motivator of human behaviour. The less confident we are that we really are 'a good person', the more having any thoughts or feelings that cast doubt on how good a person we are will tempt us to deny the reality of those feelings. If the mechanisms of denial and repression alone are not sufficient to make our awareness of any unwanted feelings disappear completely, then one of the other mechanisms that may come into play is Projection, whereby we admit the presence of troublesome feelings but deny that they are ours, and accuse someone else of being the source of them. "Yes there is anger around, but it's not me that is so angry, it's you who is getting angry with me." The process of projection develops early in life – the semi-playful attribution in childhood of the doing of 'naughty' things to the activities of 'Mr Nobody' is widespread.

Projection can be applied in an attempt to get rid of *any* unwanted feelings, but it is those two particularly important emotions – anger and sexual desire – which are the most frequent targets of this defence mechanism. The denial of the presence of these emotions in oneself, and their projection onto others, is one of the key processes in a host of human psychological problems, from jealousy (where the individual projects his or her own interest in exploring wider sexual experience onto their partner, or onto others they believe are seeking such experiences with them), to full blown psychotic disorders in which the individual's contact with all aspects of their reality becomes tenuous in the extreme.

One of the sad things about the effects of the operation of the defence mechanism of Projection is that it plays into the effects of another powerful psychological process – the Self-fulfilling Prophecy. If we attribute certain of our own feelings to someone else, even if initially they did not have them, we shall behave towards that person as though they did, and that almost guarantees that they will indeed develop such feelings towards us.

If that happens, of course we are likely to feel that we were right all along and that the source of the upsetting anger really is the other person. In this way a self-justifying closed system is set up which protects us from having to take any responsibility for the unhappy situation which has developed. This situation of being at the mercy of someone else's negative feelings is a very disempowered state to be in, and likely to generate its own set of extremely unhappy, negative emotions in us.

Reaction Formation

Reaction Formation refers to a process whereby we unconsciously 'put on an act' which creates the feeling in outside observers (and to at least some extent in ourselves) that our emotional state is exactly the opposite of what it really is; for example, smiling when one's heart is breaking. One striking example of the operation of the defence mechanism of Reaction Formation in literature is to be found in Charles Dickens' wonderful pen portrait of the "ever so 'umble" Uriah Heep, in his novel *David Copperfield*. The scene in which Uriah finally drops his mask of sickly obsequiousness and reveals his true feelings of bitter envy and anger towards those whom he had been treating with nauseatingly excessive humility, is one of the outstanding examples of the expression of penetrating psychological insight in literature.

How do we know when someone is not being authentic, not acting in an entirely honest and straightforward way, and where the mechanism of Reaction Formation is probably operating? One telltale giveaway is when we start to feel about someone, "Methinks the lady (or gentleman) protesteth too much". A very different way in which Reaction Formation manifests itself is to be seen in some of the most damaging cases of childhood sexual abuse, where the older person not only seeks sexual gratification in their interaction with a child, but also treats him or her in a verbally and/or physically abusive way – for the older person it is a way of denying the presence of any love interest, but for the poor child it is a case of insult being added to injury.

Rationalisation

An amusing, presumably fictitious story which perfectly captures the essence of the defence mechanism of Rationalisation is told by Amy Tan in her novel *Saving Fish From Drowning*.[9] The story in question is about a pious man who explained to his followers, "It is evil to take lives and noble to save them. Each day I pledge to save a hundred lives. I drop my net in the lake and scoop out a hundred fishes. I place the fishes on the bank, where they flop and twirl. 'Don't be scared', I tell those fishes. 'I am saving you from drowning.' Soon enough the fishes grow calm and lie still. Yet, sad to say, I am always too late. The fishes expire. And because it is evil to waste anything, I take those dead fishes to market and I sell them for a good price. With the money I receive, I buy more nets so I can save more fishes."

Rationalisation is to be observed when someone is making a not-entirely-convincing attempt to explain in purely rational terms their reasons for doing something they feel they ought not to have done, or for having failed to do something they feel they ought to have done. When we are rationalising we are giving an explanation for our behaviour in terms of pure reason, suppressing reference to any emotional considerations. The logic may be unassailable, but logical considerations may not have been the most powerful motivator of our actions, and at least to the emotionally intelligent, it shows! Although to describe *Rationalisation* as 'telling rational lies' may be a bit harsh, when the mechanism is in operation we are certainly suppressing part of the truth about why we behaved as we did – the anxiety we were spared by not acting in a certain way or the emotional satisfaction we gained from what we did.

Most smug moralistic explanations for behaviour are at least partly rationalisations. Oscar Wilde captured the essence of the situation perfectly when he wrote, "In cases like this it becomes more than a duty to speak one's mind: it becomes a positive pleasure." The motivation for most psychological acts has both rational and emotional components. When we rationalise we are reporting only the intellectual component (real or created specially for the occasion) of our motivations. There may or may not be some truth in what we are saying, but even if we are telling the truth and nothing but the truth we are certainly not telling the *whole* truth. And very often that untold part of the truth is the most relevant part. One of St Paul's less endearing habits, as we shall examine in Chapter 7, is of from time to time assuring readers of his epistles that in saying what he is saying to them, he is only motivated by concern for their welfare, when it is abundantly clear to a dispassionate observer that his real motivation is a much less noble one, like consolidating his position as the pre-eminent apostle to the Gentiles, or making his life of 'service to the Lord' more comfortable.

Our Shadow

Another related mechanism which is often used to protect our sense of self-worth, and is closely related to Freud's concept of Projection, is the creation of our Shadow, a process which Jung brought to our attention. According to Jung, in splitting off from consciousness and repressing what we regard as unacceptable parts of our mind, we create a Shadow-self which as far as possible we keep tucked out of sight. The part of our personality which we show to the world Jung called our Persona, but what the world usually sees is only part of who we really are.

Extremely important in understanding human behaviour are the disowned parts of our personality which we have projected into our Shadow, where they lurk, banished from consciousness, but every now and then emerging into some uncharacteristic behaviour which sometimes shocks and horrifies us and anyone we are interacting with at the time. We find ourselves saying something like, "How could I have said that?" or, "It's not like me to ..." These intrusions of untypical thoughts and behaviours by repressed parts of the personality of religious people are frequently attributed to the presence of the Devil or some other 'evil spirit' – an unhelpful way at looking at things, but one that, given an appropriate definition of 'the devil', is not without some truth in it. The more successfully we disown the parts of ourself which we believe to be bad and wicked, the more our Shadow feels like an invading foreign force which is 'not me'. However foreign those disowned parts of ourselves may feel though, they *are* parts of ourselves and unless we take responsibility for having them we shall never be able to control them.

4. How do we minimise the distress our Shadow sometimes causes us?

What sort of a picture we have of the person we want to be is partly determined by our genetic inheritance, but even more strongly by all the life experiences that have come our way. Some life experiences make it relatively easy to live up to the ideals we set for ourselves; others make it very difficult indeed to do so, and tempt us to deny more and more of the (to us painful) reality of who we are, pushing that into our Shadow. The more of ourselves we have shovelled into that Shadow, the more frequently will parts of it erupt into consciousness and cause us anxiety when they do. The best way to minimise that distress is to empty our Shadow of as much of its content as possible by allowing ourselves to become fully conscious of those aspects of ourselves which we had previously been denying; in other words to accept ourselves for what we are, warts and all. None of us are 'bad' just because we have the potential for bad behaviour, and sometimes engage in it. We all have the same potential in that respect. But all praise to us when we do not actualise that potential, when we do not become cruel and hurtful when others become that way towards us. Full self-acceptance is a fundamental requirement for that self-love which Jesus' ethical principles urge upon us if we are to become a blessing to all living things, as discussed in Chapter 5 of this book.

One of the grave disservices which St Paul has done to many people who have read those of his letters which are recorded in the Christian Bible, is to help create in their minds the same deep splits as he had between his Persona and his Shadow, between the biological reality of who he was as a human being (his 'carnal mind'), and the spiritual side of his being.

5. How can we identify what lies in our Shadow?

This can be a lengthy process, perhaps inevitably a lifelong one, requiring much ruthlessly honest soul-searching. There is, however, one very quick and simple technique to help us to find at least some of our Shadow qualities, and that is succinctly captured in the snappy sentence, "If you can spot it, you've got it!". It is not always a totally reliable indicator of what is going on in ourselves, but it is a fairly safe bet that when some behaviour or characteristic of someone else really gets under our skin and annoys us more than we might reasonably expect it to, it is because our Shadow contains the potential for engaging in just such behaviours, and expressing in various ways the very attitudes whose presence in someone else annoys us so much.

6. Is it always a bad thing to make a mistake?

There are at least three different fundamental learning processes, through the mechanism of which experience changes our behaviour. The most important of these is trial-and-error learning, in which the probability of our repeating any particular behaviour is influenced by the consequences of that behaviour.[10] Broadly speaking, if anything we do brings us pleasure (short-term or long-term) then we shall be more likely to do that same thing again when we are in the same or a closely similar situation. If the consequences of any behaviour we engage in are unpleasant, we are less likely to engage in that behaviour again in the future.

For trial-and-error learning to occur, two things are essential: the one is to sometimes do something right and the other thing is to sometimes do something wrong, to make a mistake. We rarely make a perfect job of our initial attempts at doing the things we later become skilful at. Making a mistake can sometimes be a disaster but it can also be an invaluable learning experience. It all depends on what happens after we have made the mistake; what happens in terms of the behaviour of other people who witness our mistake, and what we think and do after making that mistake. Even the great Einstein lived with the experience of frequently making mistakes. He wrote, "I think and think for months and years. Ninety-nine times the conclusion is false. The hundredth time I am right." Fortunate indeed are those who have learned to view adult life not as an examination to assess how thoroughly they have learned the lessons they have been taught in earlier life, but rather as a continuous learning experience.

Trial-and-error learning has the experience of failure, of 'making an error', at the very heart of its structure. Failure does not mean we have reached the end of the particular road we have been travelling on; it is a stage in the learning process towards eventual success. In this frame of mind one can sometimes even laugh at one's failures – they are not the end of the world, and life will go on regardless of them. Whether we go on to ever-greater heights of achievement or to an old age of bitterness and despair depends entirely on our attitude towards that failure. Was it a valuable, albeit painful, learning experience which clarified for us what we needed to do to succeed, or was it a discouraging slap in the face that confirmed all our worst fears about how fundamentally useless we are?

7. How can we influence behaviour? The differential effects of reward and punishment

Many people have a very simplistic understanding of this subject, an understanding which usually boils down to, "If you want to encourage a certain behaviour (which you regard as good), reward it. If you want to discourage a certain behaviour (which you regard as 'bad') punish it." But a huge amount of research work has resulted in the very clear understanding that the effects of reward and punishment are by no means equal and opposite. Reward, in the form of praise and acknowledgement and/or something more tangible, does indeed reliably increase the probability that any rewarded behaviour will be repeated in the future. The effects of punishment are, however, very variable, depending only in part on the severity of that punishment. Many aspects of the punished individual's prior history and the nature of their relationship with the punishing person affect the outcome of the punishment. As the behaviour of political activists and religious martyrs reminds us, the level of commitment the individual feels to the cause they are working for is also a highly significant factor in determining the effects that any punishment they receive has on their subsequent behaviour.

What is punishment? It is any unpleasant consequence that follows anything we do. It is not the same thing as constructive negative feedback which builds up the confidence, optimism and sense of self-worth of the person being communicated with, rather than breaking them down. Pointing out what we see as someone's faults in a gentle, kindly, encouraging-of-improvement way when we feel that they have done something wrong (to someone else or to themselves) is a loving behaviour. Reacting with moral outrage in a way which makes the person feel bad about themselves is a punishing behaviour and anything but loving. Very often if love is flowing strongly enough and bringing significant affirmation of the individual's good qualities, wrongdoing will disappear of its own accord even without any constructive negative feedback, although such guidance is often necessary.

On the other hand, whether punishment succeeds in permanently getting rid of undesired behaviour or not depends on whether anything constructive is learnt when the punishment ceases. Punishment itself teaches nothing. When it starts it suppresses the preceding behaviour but it is what the person was doing, thinking, and feeling when the punishment stopped that is the learned behaviour the individual takes away from the experience of punishment. They *may* learn to do something virtuous, which is very different from the thing they were being punished for and which is incompatible with it, in which case the punishment is deemed to have been successful. The process whereby the termination of punishment strengthens immediately-preceding behaviour is technically known as negative reinforcement.

But it is often the case that all the punished person learns is to keep their wrongdoing more effectively hidden from disapproving eyes. Lying, cheating, and hypocrisy are often the qualities that people acquire from punishment, and the more successfully they have learned this, the more unaware the punishing agent will be that the punishment has not produced the desired result, whatever superficial appearances may suggest to the contrary.

The idea that without careful attention to the encouragement of good behaviour, punishment may in fact produce a situation which from an ethical point of view is worse than it was before the punishment started, is closely parallel to the insight which Jesus demonstrated in talking about (using the only concepts that were available to him 2000 years ago), the potential downside of the 'driving out of devils' (as reported in Matthew 12:43-45 and Luke 11:24-26), ending in, "and the last state of that man is worse than the first".

Many of the experiences, both rewarding and punishing, which have shaped our lives did not come our way because of anyone's express determination that they should. For example, the amount of time as a child and as a young person we experienced being nurtured, having our good qualities affirmed and receiving clear signs of the fact that those closest to us were glad that we existed, as opposed to the amount of time we spent feeling unwanted and more of a nuisance than a pleasure (which will have significantly influenced how kind or cruel we are towards others) was usually not carefully planned to achieve a clearly-defined future goal; most of the time, in interacting with us, our parents were just living out their lives, unconscious of the forces that had moulded them in the past. For example, nobody set out to ensure that we developed the use of certain defence mechanisms to protect our self-esteem, but our parents may well have provided a model for us in that respect – a process of which both they and we were most probably completely unconscious.

But from time to time our parents and other important people in our lives did take active steps to shape our behaviour, thoughts and attitudes, either to make their own lives more comfortable and satisfying, or because they genuinely believed such shaping was in our own best interests. The more they encouraged us (as opposed to trying to force us) into the patterns of behaviour they wanted to see in us, the more they respected our right to be ourselves, and the more nurturing love they showed towards us, the more successful they will have been in achieving their objectives.

8. The Male-Female dimension

The biological differences between the sexes are so significant that it would be almost unbelievable if there were no corresponding differences in the psychological make-up of those mind-body-spirit unities we call 'man' and those we call 'woman'. The widespread interest in John Gray's best-selling *Men are from Mars, Women from Venus* is indicative of the fact that it deals with issues which are a matter of common observation which sometimes cause significant distress and anxiety. The similar success of Rob Becker's one-man play, *Defending the Caveman*, and the uninhibited laughter it provokes in audiences is further testimony to the fact that the presumed male/female psychological differences it makes much of are a matter of common observation, and of considerable interest to the 'man or woman in the street'.

One of the most regrettable corollary beliefs of the view that the psychology of men and women are in some ways quite different, is the idea that the 'battle of the sexes' is a painful but inevitable part of human experience. This in turn then becomes the justification for a host of prejudiced and destructive views about the negative qualities of men just because they are men, and of women just because they are women. Such a view is attractive to some people because it lets them off the painful hook of exploring whether it is not their own behaviour which is responsible for any difficulties that arise in their relationships, rather than any endemic weakness or inadequacy that the other person possesses just because they are biologically a man or a woman.

However much or little truth there may be in any specific generalisation about the psychological nature of men and women, such generalisations are generally crudely simplistic. Far more helpful in promoting joyful relationships between the sexes is a view put forward by Jung to the effect that in addition to whatever differences there may be in the psychology of men and women rooted in their biological differences, each person, male or female has both a Masculine Principle and a Feminine Principle within them, and at any one time is functioning predominantly in one or other of these modes.

This is hardly surprising. Since every individual is the product of the joining together of a male sperm and a female ovum, half our genetic inheritance comes from a man and half from a woman. How could it be otherwise than that psychologically as well as biologically we all carry both male and female qualities within us? The Feminine Principle in a man Jung termed his *Anima* (the feminine form of the Latin word for mind) and the Masculine Principle in a woman Jung called her *Animus* (the masculine form of the Latin word for mind).

To the extent that an individual's Masculine Principle is in control (whether they are a man or a woman), rationality and down-to-earth practicality prevail. Everything is either black or white, no shades of ambiguous grey being allowed to confuse any issues under consideration. All that is needed to solve any problem is to apply the cast-iron laws of logic to it.

To the extent that an individual's Feminine Principle is in control (whether that person is a man or a woman), rationality and logic take second place to issues of feeling and emotion. Concern for people's emotional state, feelings of love, of compassion, the desire to nurture, the enjoyment of beauty, and the experience of contact with the spiritual world are the sorts of things which occupy our minds in this state. Intuitions are taken seriously and not regarded as something to be ignored because they are sometimes unsupported by, or even in conflict with the outcome of logical analysis.

The concepts of Masculine and Feminine Principles are quite closely similar to the neuropsychological concepts of Left- and Right-brain functioning. The idea here is that in roughly 95% of the general population who are right-handed (as 90% of them are), the left and right sides of the Cerebral Cortex, (the outermost and most recently evolved layer of the brain – 'cortex' being the Latin word for 'bark') are specialised for different types of information processing; the left-hand side for verbal, mathematical and logical analysis and synthesis, the right-hand side for the processing of spatial, aesthetic, and emotional information. Although the detailed elaborations of this idea that some neuropsychologists have made are over-simplistic, the theory is not without merit and some empirical support, and certainly the parallels with Jung's thinking about the Animus and the Anima are intriguing.

No one ever stays in one of these Animus/Left-brain or Anima/Right-brain states for ever, and there is no suggestion that one of them is better than the other. For optimal mental functioning we, both men and women, need to be using each of these different types of data analysis from time to time, and to be able to move freely between them as circumstances require.

In the Western world at least, the huge benefits to humanity which have accrued from the painstaking, Left-brain, Masculine Principle type of work of hard-nosed scientists (both male and female) has often led to a massive over-valuing of that aspect of mental functioning at the expense of Right-brain, Feminine Principle functioning in life as a whole. Even in the scientific realm all the great advances in our understanding of the universe have been made not only because of the application of rigidly logical thinking to one way of looking at a problem, but equally because Right-brain thinking has provided creative new ways of looking at the issue under investigation. These new ways have led to the questioning of some of the (often unconscious assumptions) to which Left-brain thinking has been applied. Even outside the scientific realm, in the increasingly technologically sophisticated modern world the dangers of a one-sided intellectual approach to life are being increasingly recognised, and the 'soft skills' mediated by Right-brain, Feminine Principle psychological functioning are acquiring greater importance and respect. The professional work of engineers, actuaries, accountants and such people used to be regarded as requiring almost nothing but Masculine-Principle functioning, but the realisation of the impact of the ever-accelerating changes in society and the conditions of human life, is leading to a reassessment of the importance of Right-brain, Feminine Principle ways of being, in which the emotional content of relationships and the spiritual side of life is being seen in many quarters as having ever-greater importance.

In matters of religion, as in those of mental health, pigeon-holing people and ideas as belonging to one rigid category or another is never helpful. The categories of humanistic and authoritarian religions, Left- and Right-brain functioning, and Masculine and Feminine Principles are simply ways of thinking which bring into focus some of the essential psychological characteristics of different individuals. They are mentioned here because readers may find it enlightening to toy with the idea that humanistic Christianity can be seen as to a significant extent a Right-brain/Feminine Principle religion, and authoritarian

Christianity a much more Left-brain/Masculine Principle one.

9. Language and communication

Language obviously plays a huge role in the communication of what people believe to be spiritual truth, and what they believe to be religious error. The steady flow of new translations of the Bible text, partly in response to the discovery of additional manuscripts, particularly those dating from earlier than any previously known, and partly in response to changing habits of language use, is testimony to the importance quite rightly attached to the dictionary meaning of words. But the dictionary meaning of words is by no means the only source of the information we obtain from verbal communication and from communications about religious and spiritual matters in particular. In fact the conclusion to be drawn from the many psychological research studies that have been conducted on this topic is that *on average* in face-to-face verbal communications only about 7% of the meaning which listeners extract from such conversations comes from the dictionary meaning of the words used. Even when the communicator is not physically present (as in telephone conversations, and the reading of written or printed documents, text messages and e-mails) the contribution of the dictionary meaning of the individual words falls far short of 100%. Where does the rest of the message received come from?

There are many different factors at play, and the concepts of Left- and Right-brain, and Masculine- and Feminine-Principle functioning provide one useful framework within which to try to understand these. In extracting meaning from a verbal communication, Left-brain, Masculine-Principle functioning is crucial. It is by that means that the dictionary meaning of the words used in a message and the fundamental grammatical and logical structures of phrases and sentences are discovered.

But the brain always works as a whole, and its right hemisphere does not go to sleep while the left hemisphere is going about its specialised work. The Right-brain, our Feminine-Principle, is simultaneously active, and it is here that our Emotional Intelligence operates to supplement our Left-hemisphere processing of the dictionary meanings of the words we see or hear. In the case of face-to-face conversations, Right-hemisphere analysis of (amongst other things), the tension or relaxed gentleness of the communicator's body posture, their facial expressions and tone of voice can tell us much about the speaker's state of mind, and feelings towards us. This Right-hemisphere processing sometimes alerts us to the fact that the strict dictionary meaning of some of the words used is *not* the meaning the speaker or writer wishes to convey, indeed it may be the exact opposite, as in the sarcastically sneered comment, "That's very clever" or, "That's very funny".

It is as a result of the supplementary help of Right-brain processing that we either come to largely trust the integrity and good intentions of the communicator, or begin to feel that something doesn't quite add up in what someone is saying to us. We may then begin to feel that perhaps what we are observing is the operation of defence mechanisms interfering with the completely honest expression of thought and feeling. If this feeling becomes very strong we shall probably want to exclaim with that eminent nineteenth-century philosopher, essayist, and Unitarian minister Ralph Waldo Emerson, "Who you are shouts so loudly in my ears that I cannot hear what you are saying." This is particularly the case where religious language is concerned. Even people whose emotional intelligence is not particularly highly developed are sometimes quick to spot a lack of harmony between the dictionary meaning of the words used and the body language of the individual using those words. The greater the discrepancy between the two, the less persuasive the individual's communication is likely to be.

Verbal subtleties

Obviously body language is a source of information about what is going on in a speaker's mind which is available to us only when we have visual contact with them. But there are some relatively subtle aspects of language use which also convey information to us, in addition to that contained in the dictionary meaning of words, even when we are not receiving any relevant visual input. One of the most readily noticed of these factors is that some words carry a significant emotional charge. Many words exist which in addition to supplying us with factual information about somebody's race, gender, sexual orientation or religious allegiance leave us in no doubt about the individual's prejudice against members of the particular group to which any person thus described belongs.

On the positive side, some words have the power to conjure up powerful positive emotional states within us. Skilled writers of both prose and poetry are adept at choosing their words and the way they connect them in such a way as to arouse in us far more than just a knowledge of the facts contained in the dictionary definition of the words they have used.

One example of this which I find particularly striking is from one of A. A. Milne's timeless Winnie-the-Pooh stories. I could paraphrase the seven lines in the quote below as, "Rabbit's clever and has brains, and that is the reason why he seems to never really understand anything", and that does reasonably accurately convey the essential meaning of A. A. Milne's words, but it does so in a boring, matter-of-fact way, which seems to be anything but wise and profound, if not downright stupid. The original reads,

"Rabbit's clever," said Pooh thoughtfully.
"Yes," said Piglet, "Rabbit's clever."
"And he has Brain."
"Yes," said Piglet, "Rabbit has Brain."
There was a long silence.

"I suppose," said Pooh, "that that's why he never understands anything."[11]

Why does that quotation hold our attention, leave us thinking and wondering, and feels to be imparting some profound truth about the limitations of intellectual intelligence? It is partly because there is something about A. A. Milne's choice of words and the way they are put together which takes us back into that world of imaginative make-believe we inhabited as a child, when we felt to be part of some magical wonderland which lies beyond the iron rules of logic and the simple hard-nosed facts of material existence.

Much more could be said on this subject but this is probably not the place to do it. What it all boils down to is that there is more to verbal communication (especially when it comes to dealing with emotionally-rich issues) than simply supplying information about the bare bones of a situation captured in the dictionary meaning of the words used to describe it. One aspect of this which is of particular importance where emotional and spiritual issues are concerned is the power of beautiful things and beautiful experiences to rearrange our mental furniture in a way which increases our awareness of the goodness which abounds in the universe and can inspire us to redouble our efforts to make the world a better place for all living creatures.

Goodness, Beauty, and Truth have long been recognised as a trio of intimately inter-related concepts which are of great relevance where matters of religion and spirituality are concerned. Truth is important, but goodness and beauty are aspects of the total truth of any situation. Whatever the gain in intellectual precision may have been, beauty is something which has often been lost in modern English translations of the Bible. For many Christians who are sensitive to the powerful emotional effects and spiritual experiences beautiful language can produce, listening to bible readings from many of the modern translations of the English Bible is rather like attending a church service in a disused warehouse. The same service held in a beautiful church or cathedral might have communicated the same Left-brain intellectual content, but our experience of spiritual things might have been immeasurably enhanced by the things of beauty which would speak wordlessly to our hearts and minds through the Right-brain processing of visual and auditory beauty. The power of words is immense, but the whole setting in which verbal communication takes place can significantly affect the overall message we receive from any verbal communication. Fortunate indeed are those whose earliest experiences with the printed word occurred while sitting cuddled on the lap of a loving parent.

Many people in many parts of the Christian Church are far too attached to the idea that communication must necessarily involve the use of words. But anyone who has interacted with a much-loved pet knows that such a creature can communicate powerfully with us although not being able to speak a single word. There is much truth in the saying of the nineteenth-century Czechoslovakian composer Bedřich Smetena, "Words – the language of ideas. Music – the language of feeling." Music and all other forms of art, as well as the beauties of nature, can be powerful communicators of many aspects of spiritual truth. The importance of beauty as a spiritual concept seems to be being increasingly neglected in many parts of the Christian Church in recent years.

Alexander Solzhenitsyn spent many years in prison under the Soviet regime. In his acceptance speech for his Nobel Prize for literature in 1970, expanding on a thought ("Beauty will save the world") expressed by the Russian author Dostoyevsky in his novel *The Idiot*, said,

Perhaps, then, the old trinity of Truth, Goodness and Beauty is not simply the dressed-up, worn-out old formula we in our presumptuous, materialistic youth thought it was. If the crowns of these three trees meet (as most scholars have asserted) and if the too obvious, too straight sprouts of Truth and Goodness have been knocked down, cut off, not let grow – perhaps the whimsical, unpredictable, unexpected branches of Beauty will work their way through, rise up to that very place, and thus complete the work of all three.

It is because of the power of the right words used in the right way to create a particular emotional and intellectual state within us that the increasing abandonment of any use of the 1611 King James Version of the English Bible by Christian Churches is so regrettable. In some cases, by throwing out the truths communicated by the aesthetic beauty of beautiful language, the unacceptable triviality and ugliness of some of the ideas conveyed by the basic dictionary meaning of some of the words used is starkly revealed. The loss of the more subtle aspects of the impact of the original wording of the King James Version (KJV) sometimes means a real loss of spiritual value.

Perhaps there is even more going on when we listen to, or read the KJV than what we have discussed above. It has been suggested that some of the language used in that version of the English Bible was already 'old-fashioned' when that translation was made, and that it was deliberately used rather than the more 'modern' words then current because of the special emotional atmosphere those 'old-fashioned' words created, even in the seventeenth century.

Perhaps it is significant that one of the ways, powerful for many people, of facilitating entry into a hypnotic trance state is to suggest to them that time is running backwards, and that they are entering a mental state that they used to be in in the past. Perhaps it is also worth pondering in this connection, Jesus' belief that, as reported in Matthew 18:3, "Unless you change and become like children, you will never enter the kingdom of heaven".

A further thought worth considering in this context relates to the very widespread use of candles in various rituals across a wide range of different religions. Focussing attention on a candle flame is for many people a powerfully effective way of entering a hypnotic trance state, and one of the striking characteristics of being in a hypnotic trance, is the sidelining of intellectual analysis in favour of pure unanalysed raw experience. This fact is an important part of the reason why in the trance state, a subject is much more highly suggestible than they are when in a state of normal consciousness, in which suggestions are generally subjected to some careful analytical thought before they are either acted on or rejected.

Fundamentalism

One of the obstacles which has historically stood in the way of humanity extracting the maximum benefit from the many, many words which have been written on spiritual and religious matters has been the widespread human tendency to adopt a fundamentalist interpretation of such texts. So far as Christianity is concerned, the Concise Oxford English Dictionary (COED) defines fundamentalism as, "a form of Protestant Christianity which upholds belief in the strict and literal interpretation of the Bible".[12] Such a view ignores the historical realities of the origins of the Bible. The final form of the Christian Bible (whichever of the variant forms of it are accepted as the 'True Bible') was arrived at as a result of a number of very human decisions as to just which of the many religious texts circulating at the time should be regarded as containing 'the Word of God'. There was no clap of thunder and the sudden appearance of a beautifully bound copy of 'The Holy Bible' in their home language on everyone's dining room table; nor did anyone ever descend from a mountain top communion with God with a newly-received copy of the Christian Bible tucked under their arm.

The decisions as to what the final form of the Christian Bible should be were made by committees of old men (perish the thought that any woman's opinion should be sought!) whose main qualification for making such far-reaching decisions was that they had succeeded in satisfying their desire for a position of power and control within the Christian Church. To regard such people as uniquely fitted to 'know the mind of God' in respect of the final form of the Christian scriptures beggars belief.

Another problem is that it is very rare for *any* piece of writing of any significant length to use all the words in it in a completely literal way to describe only the simple concrete reality of any situation. Religious texts particularly, are often written rich in metaphor and allegory, and the Christian Bible and other respected religious writings are no exception to this general habit. The COED defines metaphor as "a figure of speech in which a word or phrase is applied to something to which it is not literally applicable: a thing regarded as symbolic of something else," and allegory as "a story, poem, or picture which can be interpreted to reveal a hidden meaning".

If someone says, "I was in heaven listening to her beautiful singing," no one would think for a moment that the person who was experiencing such ecstatic pleasure thought they had actually died and gone to heaven. They would instinctively know that the word 'heaven' was being used metaphorically. It is a short-cut to saying, "It was so beautiful that it was as though I was in heaven," and yet so often when a fundamentalist Christian encounters sentences like, "I know a person in Christ who fourteen years ago was caught up to the third Heaven," (II Corinthians 12:2) they immediately assume that, out of respect for the biblical record, they must believe that the person thus described had entered some different physical place.

Strangely, those who hold such a view, and who probably feel obliged to believe that God created all the plants and animals in the world on the day before he created the Sun and Moon (as reported in Genesis I:11-19), can sometimes go to extraordinary lengths to avoid interpreting as literally true the verse in which Jesus is reported to have said that, "There be some standing here, which shall not taste of death, till they see the Son of man coming in his kingdom". (Matthew 16:28. Similar reports are to be found in Matthew 23:36; Matthew 24:34; Mark 9:1; and Luke 9:27). If those words of Jesus, reported in all three of the Synoptic gospels, are a reasonably accurate reflection of something Jesus actually said, (and how many fundamentalists would doubt that they are?), and are taken literally (as fundamentalists are apt to do) as referring to an imminent apocalyptic event, then it is clear that Jesus was simply wrong when he made that prediction – an almost unthinkable possibility for most, if not all fundamentalists.

For the really strict fundamentalist the precise dictionary definition of every word is precisely what the writer meant to convey. If somewhere in the Bible it is said that the sun and moon suddenly appeared out of nothing on the fourth day of God's sudden burst of intense creative activity, (which is precisely what is communicated to us in Genesis 1:14-19), then that is exactly what happened. The fact that according to that Genesis account (Genesis 1:9-13) God had created dry land and all the grasses and herbs and fruit trees that grow upon it, not only in the space of 24 hours, but 'on the third day', in other words 24 hours before the sun and moon even existed, then that must be exactly, literally what happened, notwithstanding the apparent absurdity of that idea from what we know about the biology of plant growth.

Whether or not that seemingly muddled-up dating of the creation of the sun and the creation of vegetation is the most unbelievable aspect of the Creation story in the first chapter of the book of Genesis is a moot point. Genesis 1:6-8 tells us that God spent the day before he created all the world's vegetation, in creating "a dome" to "separate the waters from the waters. So

God made the dome and separated the waters that were under the dome from those that were above the dome. And it was so. God called the dome Sky." Genesis is silent about what happened to the waters that were above the sky. Perhaps there is water on Mars after all! The scientists' objections to the fundamentalist Christian's way of looking at the development of the universe are irrelevant to the fundamentalist, because although such amazing feats of creationism are impossible for humans, "with God all things are possible". (Matthew 19:26). In other words no possible claim about the extent of God's power, no matter how absurd that claim may be, can ever be refuted on practical grounds.

The issue of whether or not the first Genesis account is to be regarded as a statement of historical and scientific fact has generated enormous controversy, and the Fundamentalists among the Christian community have dug themselves in very strongly to defend their position. It is interesting to note that even the puritanical Calvin, whom most would regard as by no means a liberal theologian, in fact as probably one of the most rigidly narrow-minded of Protestant reformers, believed that the Bible was not the place to look for historical and scientific facts.

Those who do not share Calvin's views in that respect, must however find it very difficult to stick to their position of believing in the literal truth and absolute veracity of everything the Bible contains when they move into some other areas remote from the Genesis Creation story. Presumably few sexually active fundamentalists believe in the absolute God-ordained truth of Paul's views on sex which we shall look at in some detail in Chapter 7, and presumably few of them would countenance anything other than a metaphorical interpretation of the flights of poetic fantasy in that beautiful, passionate love poem, *The Song of Solomon*, through every chapter of which breathes a joyful celebration of the physical and psychological manifestations of human sexuality. One wonders whether Paul, with his very different attitude to sexuality, had ever read this particular book which is to be found in both the Hebrew and the Christian bibles.

While reflecting on the account of the Creation of the universe to be found in the first book of Genesis it is worth noting that there is a second Creation story in the first book of the Bible (in Genesis 2:4-23) which does not specify any time-periods during which any particular part of the creation process occurred, except for that which elapsed between the creation of men and women. This ought to create problems for those who cling to a literal interpretation of the first Creation account. According to that first, date-specific Creation story, God created man and woman simultaneously ("So God created man in his *own* image, in the image of God created he him; male and female created he them"[13] Genesis 1:27), whereas in the second Creation story, God created woman as an afterthought some time after he had created man, as something to comfort him in his loneliness, perhaps to share his workload, and doubtless to provide an acceptable outlet for his sexual appetites lest he be tempted to indulge in the appalling sins of masturbation, homosexuality, or bestiality. ("And the Lord God said, It is not good that the man should be alone; I will make him an help meet for him." Genesis 2:18). What role man was to play in the woman's life is not specified, being presumably seen as of no great importance in comparison with her obligations and duties towards the dominant male.

The ignoring of the complex variety of sources from which we extract the full meaning of verbal communications, spoken or written, is only part of the problem with fundamentalism – the belief that every word in the Bible has to be taken literally as the truth, the whole truth, and nothing but the truth about certain simple historical facts. It is problematic enough that those who adopt a fundamentalist interpretation of scripture grant an absolute validity to every statement made by the dozens of writers whose work has been collected together to form the Bible (a validity which most of us would never dream of granting to the writings of historians in any other field), but there is a further problem to which the fundamentalist approach is prone, and that can make it misleading in our attempts to understand spirituality. This problem, which is not manifest by every fundamentalist, but occurs all too frequently, is that side by side with the consciously held belief that every word in the Bible is literally true, often goes a belief (conscious or otherwise) that not only did Jesus (or Moses or Isaiah, or John the Baptist, or whoever) say exactly what the Bible says they said on a particular subject, but that was *all* they said on it.

This is manifestly absurd on every count, and it is doubtful whether anyone other than the most rigid fundamentalist believes that the four gospels provide a comprehensively detailed account of *everything* Jesus said during his ministry, or at least that that is all he said on any particular subject which is of importance to us today, even if that ministry was only nine or ten months long, as Geza Vermes in his *The Authentic Gospel of Jesus*[14] suggests it probably was. For most Christians those words of the writer of John's gospel, "And many other signs truly did Jesus in the presence of his disciples, which are not written in this book" (John 20:30), are self-evidently true. Nevertheless some of those Christian fundamentalists who believe that every word in the Bible is the word of God, quite illogically seem to view any proclaimed truth which is not to be found in the Bible with grave suspicion – their default position apparently being that any spiritual insight must be viewed as false unless and until it is proved true by an assemblage of biblical texts. In fact, wherever it is to be found, whatever is claimed to be a spiritual truth must be subjected to critical evaluation using all the relevant resources of modern historical, theological, linguistic, and psychological scholarship as well as our 'gut feel', if we are to get anywhere near the profound understanding of all aspects of life through which the world will slowly but surely become a better place for all.

The case of the Ten Commandments provides another object lesson in this respect. The two versions of these injunctions in the Bible (at Exodus 20:2-17 and Deuteronomy 5:6-21) cover the same topics, but with slightly different emphases. The last verse of both these statements, which provide a listing of the things we must not covet, end with the words, "or anything that belongs to your neighbour". Interestingly, however, although both the biblical versions of the Ten Commandments specifically prohibit the coveting of either a male or a female slave, it is only the coveting of a neighbour's wife (presumably by anyone, male or female), and not of a neighbour's husband which is specifically forbidden.

The rigid fundamentalist ought to conclude from this that it is a sin to covet a neighbour's wife, but not a sin for them to covet a neighbour's husband, since this case is very specifically not mentioned in the detailed listing of the people whom we are not allowed to covet. Most fundamentalists of course do not conclude from this that God doesn't care one way or the other whether someone's husband is being coveted or not, but gets very angry if a wife is being coveted by her neighbour – after all, so some people's thinking runs, she is her husband's property isn't she? They generally prefer to deal with this problem by arguing it away as this special case being covered by the clause, "or anything that belongs to your neighbour", conveniently ignoring the fact that some explanation is required as to why it was necessary to specifically mention both male and female slaves, but only wives, and not husbands.

A non-fundamentalist reading of the texts would lead to an exploration of what this very specific exclusion of husbands from the list of those who must not be coveted tells us about power relations between men and women, and the attitudes to the relative unimportance of what a woman wants as opposed to what a man wants which prevailed in the society and at the time that the Ten Commandments were written down. After all, so such thinking runs, why shouldn't a man be flattered by the knowledge that he is desired by more than one woman, but heaven help any woman (and her admirers!) who experiences an ego-boost from knowing that she is desired by more than one man? Consistency in the application of fundamentalist principles is not the most striking characteristic of those who demand that the Bible be interpreted in this way.

The most obvious disservice a fundamentalist interpretation of the Bible does to earnest attempts to get a better understanding of spiritual things is to treat the written statements of fallible human beings as being, 'the word of God'. This many of them most certainly are not. Every word in the Bible was written by human beings, and those words and the way they are assembled represent the best they could do to communicate what they believed to be important truths. As in every field of human endeavour, some of those writers made a better job of it than others, and often their output was of uneven quality. As we shall see in Chapter 7, this is particularly true of St Paul, who is the acknowledged author of more biblical books than any other writer.

Trevor Ling in his book, *A History of Religion East and West*[15] (already referred to in the notes to this chapter) has a valuable discussion which applies as strongly to the Christian New Testament as to any religious text.

Religious thought gets into (difficulty) when a prophet's words have become canonised as sacred scripture and the original situation to which they were addressed has passed away, leaving only the words themselves which, while they had an immediate relevance and vitality in that original situation, have now lost it, but have gained an independent existence and are being cogitated upon, and systematised, and shaped into dogmas.

To fall down in awe before what one believes to be the absolute truth of any piece of religious writing or preaching is to worship an idol. Much the same applies to the 'truths' proclaimed by scientists which, as most of them would be the first to acknowledge, are all provisional rather than absolute.

10. Our developmental history

Each human life starts within our mother's womb, and the beginning of life outside it is ideally one of close physical and emotional contact with her. The experience of that Garden of Eden type of relationship of perfect unity with nature (initially in the form of our mother) remains deeply embedded in our unconscious memory. The details of the original experience of unity are unavailable to conscious verbal recall, but still manifest in the emotional flavour underlying the nostalgic longing for some state of perfect happiness, perfect intimate closeness with another human being. This desire is a fundamental part of our biological nature, and the closer we get to achieving satisfaction of that desire, the more OK we feel about ourselves, and the deeper the feeling of happiness and peace we experience. The closer we get to achieving that goal, the more we experience a wonderful feeling of contentment, that we have 'arrived', that this is what we have been seeking all our life, that this is the way life is meant to be.

This book has been written in the belief that the ethical principles taught by the charismatic Jewish spiritual teacher Jesus of Nazareth are one powerfully effective guide as to how to live a life that will bring us close to this deeply desired state of, "I'm OK. I really am an OK person".

Nothing takes us further away from that much desired state of bliss more effectively than guilt. Guilt is a totally useless emotion. Feeling it makes no biological sense. It brings nobody any benefits. A major component of it is feelings of anger, even hatred directed at ourselves for something (or a series of things) that we have done or failed to do. But hatred of oneself is not a primary emotion. It is incompatible with those fundamental aspects of our total being, the Will to Live and the Will to Love. If enough of us felt guilty enough for enough of the time, the human race would die out within a very short space of time, our collective will to live having been overcome by self-destructive thoughts, feelings and behaviours.

Manipulating feelings of guilt is the number one weapon those in the authoritarian church use when trying to coerce others into unquestioning acceptance of the beliefs that they themselves hold. Three basic aspects of what St. Paul would call our "carnal mind", in other words of our human nature, have been the particular target of much Christian preaching: thoughts and feelings of anger, of sexual arousal, and the making of mistakes (often described as 'sin' and attributed to the work of the Devil). There is nothing either right or wrong about feeling angry, nor with thinking about those feelings. There is nothing either right or wrong about feeling sexually aroused, nor with thinking about those feelings. In some situations those feelings just spontaneously arise, just as in other situations we feel too cold and in others too hot, and sometimes find ourselves thinking about those feelings. In fact in the course of our lives we probably all feel once or twice or many, many times just about every emotion it is possible to feel. There is nothing morally wrong with feeling any of them, and it is not appropriate to label any feelings we have as good or bad. They just are.

What it is appropriate to regard as either good or bad is how we behave when we have certain thoughts or feelings. It is neither right nor wrong to feel angry or sexually aroused, but how we behave when we do have any such feelings is something which can very appropriately be labelled as right or wrong. Some constructive ways of behaving when we are angry help to make the world a better place. Most of the improvements in the lot of humans and animals have come about because someone was angry about what was happening to some living creatures. Other ways of behaving when angry have just brought destructive misery to the minds and/or bodies of others, and sometimes of ourselves.

Similarly at some times and in some situations acting to satisfy any sexual arousal we feel can lead to much pleasure for one or more people. At other times and in other places it can have just the opposite effect.

As for the making of mistakes discussed earlier in this chapter, such events can be either a tragedy or an indispensable part of our learning experiences. Making a mistake, doing something wrong, is a necessary part of the trial-and-error learning process, the most important mechanism whereby we learn to survive, and flourish as adults in the world. It is what we do when we have made a mistake which is the crucial thing, and can lead us to appropriately describe it as having been either a 'good' or a 'bad' thing that we made whatever mistake we did make. As someone once said, "The only thing wrong with making a mistake is not learning from it." This is delightfully illustrated in a story about Tom Watson Senior, founder of IBM. He reputedly once had a top junior executive who took a business initiative which lost the company $12,000,000. Watson asked him to come to see him, and he went, carrying the letter of resignation he had written in advance. "I'm sure you want my resignation," he said to Watson. "Here it is." "I don't want your resignation," said Watson. "I've just spent $12,000,000 educating you. Now go and get to work, and apply what you've learnt."

The superficial truth about guilt is that in it we are feeling anger with ourselves. The deeper truth is that that anger with ourselves is fundamentally anger felt towards others for their real or imagined condemnation and rejection of us for some perceived wrongdoing on our part which we have retroflected onto (or turned back against) ourselves. It is one of the great benefits that some approaches to psychotherapy have brought to humanity that they are able to help the individual to free themselves from the tyranny of retroflected anger, and identify who in the external world is the real target of their anger. No really life-changing psychological work can be done until clarity on that point has been achieved. The more guilty anyone feels, the more elusive will be the experience of that deep inner peace which we all seek.

It is one of the blessings the humanistic face of Christianity has brought to humanity that it provides a philosophy of life with a profound ethical component which can work hand in hand with those psychological approaches aimed at releasing people from the fears that undermine their natural state of happiness. It is one of the saddest aspects of the history of religion that the corruption of those humanistic principles to be found in the authoritarian face of Christianity has caused so much avoidable suffering and misery to so many people.

11. The Relationship between Psychology and Religion

In the course of writing this book I have been struck afresh by just how much energy some of those in the Christian Church have expended (and continue to expend) on the extremely damaging task of encouraging people to think badly of themselves. They have devoted a great deal of time to encour-aging the faithful to wallow in how bad they are, what miserable sinners they are, and, ludicrously, to beg God to forgive them for the fact that they as a human being, were created (through no wish of their own) with the potential for wrongdoing. In respect of the conflicting aims of psychologists – to make people feel better about themselves, to strengthen their feelings of self-worth – and those of many leaders within the Christian Church – to make people believe they are deeply flawed morally – psychology and much traditional Christianity are diametrically opposed to each other.

But is the work of psychologists *necessarily* in conflict with that of those who are devoted to the preservation and extension of the influence of religion? In regard to Christianity, it is very clear to me that so far as the relationship between psychology and the humanistic face of that religion is concerned, the relationship can be, and often is, one of indispensable mutual benefit. For me at least, insofar as psychology ignores the spiritual depths of life it is failing to reach its full potential, and failing to be as helpful to all humanity as it could be. Equally if Christianity cuts itself off from, or sees itself in opposition to psychology, it is losing a valuable ally in its attempts to remain vividly aware of the truths of the religion. Those truths all too easily become obscured by concepts underlying the less exalted ideas of those well-meaning but all-too-human individuals whose proselytising enthusiasm is often driven by psychopathological forces.

The overall thrust of psychology, insofar as it is concerned with enhancing the welfare and happiness of human beings, must inevitably be one of conflict with the authoritarian face of Christianity. Authoritarian Christianity presupposes an adversarial relationship between human beings and God: humanistic Christianity and humanistic religions in general emphasise the essential unity of God and human beings. Authoritarian Christianity is obsessed with what it sees as the essential weakness and sinfulness of humankind. This state of being 'a miserable sinner' seems to be regarded as persisting throughout life, even after, as proclaimed by the Doctrine of the Atonement, our 'sins have been forgiven'. According to this view, we are fated to constantly sin, and to constantly be forgiven every time we have jumped through whatever hoops are prescribed by the particular branch of Christianity we are part of.

To the psychologist, this emphasis on our propensity to do 'bad' things, to project all our good qualities out of ourselves onto an external God, leaving only all that is undesirable and morally unacceptable as what constitutes 'the real me', is one of the most destructive things we can possibly do to ourselves. However far individual psychologists dealing with the problems people present may fall short of this ideal, the received wisdom in the profession is that building up people's self-esteem, their sense of themselves as a good person, is a fundamentally important part of helping individuals to a state of psychological health. In this respect psychology and authoritarian Christianity are pulling in absolutely opposite directions. Humanistic Christianity and psychology, by contrast, have the potential to enjoy a most beneficial and mutually enriching relationship.

This chapter is just a brief, and to some extent over-simplified account of some of the more important factors affecting the functioning and life-experience of human beings. Those interested in learning more about the subject of psychology will find some information about it in any introductory psychology textbook, and there are many other more specialised books in the fields of both academic and pop psychology which throw further light on this fascinating topic. For a succinct and intentionally very readable account of it for those who want to explore the subject in a little greater depth without getting lost in too much complexity, see my book *Achieving Our Full Potential: Towards More Effective Living,* published in 2009 by New Voices in Cape Town.

Chapter 3

A Very Brief History of the Christian Church

Those who have not learned the lessons of history are doomed to repeat them. – Anon

One of the most important things that needs to be borne in mind by modern Christians in trying to come to a full understanding of their religion is that Jesus himself was never a member of the Christian Church. No such institution existed while he was alive that he could possibly have been a member of. Jesus never broke away from the Jewish religion into which he had been born. He, like most of his compatriots, lived his life expecting the imminent arrival of the Kingdom of God on earth. After his death, his disciples and concerned others drew together in Jerusalem to comfort each other and to try to make sense of what had happened. This group of people initially never saw themselves as being outside the Jewish religion of which they continued to be a part as they waited eagerly for the triumphal return of Jesus to inaugurate a new era.

As the weeks and months of fruitless waiting turned into years, they began to see a new role for themselves which gradually evolved into the idea of forming an independent church. This church at first consisted almost entirely of people who had had some contact with Jesus during his earthly life, and had heard at least some of his preaching. They were Jews by birth, upbringing, outlook, and belief, practising members of the Jewish religion, and regarded themselves as bound by the Law of Moses. They were probably reasonably united with each other at first, although there is some evidence that from quite early on there was a certain amount of rivalry in respect of the leadership of the group. James, the brother of Jesus, would obviously have been a strong candidate for that position and does indeed seem to have been originally viewed in that light. At some point however, that role appears to have been taken over by Peter.

The first major crisis for the unity of the group came with the appearance of Paul on the scene. Paul, a non-Palestinian Jew who had never met Jesus, had before his Damascus Road conversion been a major persecutor of the fledgling Christian Church. In that conversion process he came to believe that Jesus had been the Messianic Saviour-God through whom the demonic powers had been conquered and the Messianic era inaugurated.

Whatever Paul's motivation may have been (and we shall discuss some possibilities in Chapter 7) it became his passionate life's work to bring the Christian gospel to the Gentiles. In this he experienced considerable success, building up communities of gentile Christians in various cities of the Mediterranean world over which he strove to maintain a powerful influence.

One of Paul's profound religious insights was that the circumcision of male gentile converts to the new religion served no spiritual purpose whatsoever, and he refused to require this of those who converted to Christianity under his tutelage. This rejection of a major feature of the Law of Moses brought him into direct conflict with many in the Jerusalem church, some of whom were scandalised by Paul's attitude.

Although Paul's work was eventually given the blessing of at least the leaders in the Jerusalem branch of the Christian church, as his proselytising work began to bear richer and richer fruit, and the non-Jerusalem church grew stronger and stronger, a definite split began to emerge between these two factions. Paul's arrest in 57 CE[16] was a setback for the gentile branch, which led to the views of its Jerusalem church prevailing more strongly over those of the gentile branch. However, in 70 CE the brutal response of the Romans to the Jewish revolt against their Roman overlords led to the destruction of Jerusalem and its temple. The resultant scattering of members of the Jerusalem Christian Church put an end to this dominance. In the post 70 CE attempted fusion of Paul's idea of Jesus as the Saviour-God with the devotion of Jewish Christians to the historical person Jesus, Paul's views became increasingly dominant. This process reached its apogee with the Emperor Constantine's Council of Nicaea, as discussed a little later in this chapter. The almost unchallenged dominance of the Pauline view since that event is also attested to by the fact that the authorship of more than half of the 27 books of the New Testament are (or have been in some parts of the church) attributed to Paul.

The Christian Church has never been one big, happy family. From its earliest days theological differences have abounded and a large number of different groupings, each with their own unique set of beliefs, and in some cases religious practices, have been constantly developing. One of the best known of these groups today was the **Gnostics**. There were a number of sub-types of this category which had in common the teaching that the realisation of Gnosis (esoteric or intuitive knowledge) is the way to the salvation of the soul from the material world. Jesus is identified by some Gnostic sects as an embodiment of the Supreme Being who became incarnate to bring *gnōsis* to the earth. Others adamantly denied that the Supreme Being came in the flesh, claiming Jesus to have been merely a human who attained divinity through gnosis, and taught his disciples to do the same.

Marcionism originated in the teachings of Marcion of Sinope who was active in Rome around the year 144 CE. Marcion believed Jesus Christ was the saviour sent by God, and Paul was his chief apostle, but he rejected the Hebrew Bible and rejected the concept of the Hebrew God it contained as being that of a tyrant. For Marcion, the New Testament consisted of eleven books: a gospel consisting of ten sections from the Gospel of Luke edited by Marcion, and ten of Paul's epistles. All other epistles and gospels of the modern Christian New Testament were rejected. All Marcion's own writings are lost, though they were widely read at the time of their writing and numerous manuscripts must have existed.

The **Ebionites** were a group of Jewish Christians living in different regions of the Mediterranean from at least the second to the fourth centuries CE. Completely different from the Marcionites, they were unique among the many different Christian groups that were around at the time in that they tried to combine Jewish views, ritual piety and lifestyles with the belief that Jesus was the Messiah. They were very strongly monotheistic and denied the divinity of Jesus, believing that he was the natural son of Joseph and Mary, rather than the outcome of a miraculous conception. At the same time they differed from non-Christian Jews in asserting that Jesus' death took place as a sacrifice for the sins of the world and that all other sacrifices had, therefore, become meaningless. According to them, as a sign of his acceptance of Jesus' sacrifice, God then raised Jesus from the dead and exalted him to heaven.

Montanism originated about 156 CE and was named after its founder Montanus. He claimed to have received a number of direct revelations from the Holy Spirit, and to be the incarnation of the Paraclete mentioned in John 14:16. Montanus was accompanied on his missionary journeys by two women, Prisca and Maximilla, who also claimed to be the embodiments of the Holy Spirit. 'The Three' as they were called, spoke in ecstatic visions and in the first person as being themselves the Father or the Paraclete. They urged their followers to fast and pray, placed considerable emphasis on the avoidance of sin and on church discipline, emphasized the importance of chastity and forbade remarriage. Prisca claimed that Christ had appeared to her in female form. When she was excommunicated, she exclaimed, "I am driven away like the wolf from the sheep. I am no wolf: I am the word and spirit and power." The prophets of Montanism did not speak as messengers of God: "Thus saith the Lord," but rather described themselves as possessed by God, and spoke in his person, "I am the Father, the Word, and the Paraclete," said Montanus. Both Montanus and Maximilla reportedly ended their lives by hanging themselves in a frenzy of religious ecstasy.

Initially the **Donatists** differed from the more traditional early churches only over the issue of whether 'lapsed clergy' (those who in times of persecution had abandoned their allegiance to Christianity) should be readmitted to the priesthood once they had repented and done penance. A few decades into the controversy, though, some liturgical and ritual differences emerged. For example, the Donatists' services were strongly charismatic in nature (not dissimilar to those of the Montanists, although there was no elevation of women to the status of 'prophets' in Donatism). Perhaps the most striking difference between Donatism and the more mainstream Christianity of the time was that among Donatists, confession was a public rite, in which the penitent confessed his/her sins before the entire congregation.

The name of the **Docetists** derives from the Greek *dokesis*, 'appearance' or 'semblance', because they taught that Christ only 'appeared' or 'seemed' to be a man, to have been born, to have lived and suffered. Some denied the reality of Jesus' human nature altogether, some only the reality of his human body or of his birth or death. Ian Wilson, in his book *Jesus: the evidence* records that Bishop Clement of Alexandria had written in the second century,

> It would be ridiculous to imagine that the body of the Redeemer, in order to exist had the usual needs of man. He only took food and ate it in order that we should not teach about him in a Docetic fashion.[17]

Manichaeism thrived between the third and seventh centuries, and at its height was one of the most widespread religions in the world. Manichaean churches and scriptures existed as far east as

China and as far west as the Roman Empire. Most of the original writings of the founding father of the religion, Mani (c. 216–276 CE) have been lost, but numerous translations and fragmentary texts have survived. For Manicheans life was a constant struggle between a good, spiritual world of light, and an evil, material world of darkness in which light is gradually removed from the world of matter and returned to the world of light from which it came. The Christian elements of this religion contained a heavy admixture of ideas from Buddhism and the popular Persian religion of Zoroastrianism.

A much fuller account of the often conflicting theological ideas which abounded in the early Christian Church is to be found in Geza Vermes' *Christian Beginnings: From Nazareth to Nicaea AD 30 – 325.*

Political Developments

Meanwhile, on the secular front there was a constant jostling for power amongst those who sought to rule the Roman Empire. So far as the future of Christianity is concerned the most important of these conflicts concerns *Flavius Valerius Aurelius Constantinus Augustus,* (272 – 337 CE), better known to English speakers as Constantine the Great. After the death of his father, the Roman Emperor Constantius in 306 CE, Constantine had to fight many rivals and antagonists before eventually establishing himself as the undisputed ruler of the Roman Empire. By 312 CE Constantine, who proved himself to be a brilliant general, had emerged victorious from all these military clashes and only one man, Maxentius stood in the way of his acquiring supreme power as undisputed ruler of the whole Roman Empire. The decisive battle between them took place at the Milvian Bridge over the river Tiber on 28 October, 312 CE.

Tradition has it that the night before that battle between the army of Constantine and the superior forces of Maxentius, Constantine had a prophetic dream in which he was shown a sign, accompanied by the Latin words: *Hoc signo victor eris* (By this sign you shall be the victor).

> The sign consisted of the Greek letters Chi-Rho, the first two letters of the name Christ, in a monogram form that had recently been adopted by the still persecuted group called Christians, of whom, as Constantine was well aware, there were a considerable number among the ordinary citizens of Rome. That the original Christ preached a form of pacifism would almost certainly never have occurred to Constantine. For him the Chi-Rho seemed an inspired sign to fight by, and at dawn he gave orders for it to be painted on every soldier's shield.[18].

The battle of Milvian Bridge was a triumph for Constantine: the forces of Maxentius were routed and Maxentius himself died in the battle. His dead body was recovered from the downstream riverbank, and:

> he was swiftly decapitated, and with this gruesome trophy dripping from a lance Constantine made his triumphal entry into Rome later that day, the Christian monogram still emblazoned on his soldiers' shields. In a fashion its founder could scarcely have anticipated, the religion of Jesus of Nazareth, or at least a semblance of it, had captured Rome.[19]

The next year, in 313 CE, the new Emperor issued the Edict of Milan, proclaiming a new era of religious tolerance, and after years of sometimes brutal persecution, legalizing Christian worship. Constantine became a great patron of the Church, and set a precedent for the position of the Roman Emperor within it. This alliance of Church and State was consolidated in 380 CE when Christianity was proclaimed the state religion of the Roman Empire.

The early years of Constantine's patronage were, however, not happy ones. In-fighting between different factions within the Christian Church was pretty constant, and this disappointed and angered Constantine. Eventually as the radical disagreement between Arius and Athanasius (discussed below) began to spread beyond a disagreement within the Alexandrian diocese and to draw in church leaders from further afield, Constantine became positively alarmed at the potential of this initially purely theological disagreement to spread more widely through his empire and possibly cause civil unrest.

> Constantine, who had just won the eastern half of the Empire, thereby at last achieving his cherished goal of unity, suddenly found himself in the midst of the seething dispute between two rival groups of Christians, with epithets such as 'maniacs,' 'eels,' 'cuttlefish,' 'atheists' and 'wolves' being hurled between one faction and the other.[20]

It must have been a matter of deep regret to Constantine that no sooner had he achieved his dream of ruling over the whole single, and undivided Roman Empire, in the uniting of which Christianity with its Chi-Rho symbol seemed to have played a highly significant part, than that self-same religion with its fractious and heated disputes about theological matters seemed to be becoming a potentially dangerous source of division and disunity within the Empire.

The proper date for the celebration of Easter was one prominent source of disagreement between some of the factions, but the most deeply significant fault lines showed up in the differing views held by different groups of Christians about the 'divinity' of Jesus. Again, in Ian Wilson's words, the great Lucian of Antioch,

> reflecting Christianity's origins in Jewish monotheism, had

stressed the essential oneness of God, the simple humanity of Jesus, and the importance of the way of life Jesus taught, which those obsessed with theology too easily overlooked.[17]

Such a view is totally compatible with that of those who make up the humanistic face of Christianity today, particularly in respect of the importance placed on living the way of life that Jesus taught.

The Alexandrians, led by their bishop Alexander (and later by Athanasius), held a different view, that Jesus was first and foremost God and had existed as a spirit before time began, coequal and co-eternal with God the father, who at some point in history manifested himself as a human being. The conflict was sharpened by the fact that Arius, who had been taught by Lucian and shared his theological views, ended up working in the Alexandrian diocese where he inevitably got into theological conflict with his bishop, the supreme ecclesiastical authority for the Egyptian and Libyan region.

The conflict became extreme. Arius was excommunicated, but refused to simply accept this church ruling and recruited support from other church leaders whom he knew to be sympathetic to his views and those of his teacher Lucian of Antioch. The spreading conflict became a matter of grave concern to Constantine. His first response to the deteriorating situation was to write an identical and uncharacteristically pleading letter to both Alexander and Arius, begging them to show 'equal forbearance' and to work towards reconciliation with each other.

Constantine the Victor, Supreme Augustus, to Alexander and Arius... how deep a wound has not only my ears but my heart received from the report that divisions exist among yourselves... having enquired carefully into the origin and foundation of these differences, I find their cause to be of a truly insignificant nature, quite unworthy of such bitter contention... Restore my quiet days and untroubled nights to me, so that joy of undimmed light, delight in a tranquil life, may once again be mine.[20]

Sadly, Constantine's deep desire for his life to return to one of "quiet days and untroubled nights" was not fulfilled. Frustrated, Constantine decided to use the sort of strong-arm tactics which had served him well in his political career. He decided to personally summon all major Christian leaders to the first-ever *World Council of Christianity* in order to settle the most pressing of the various theological and administrative disputes which were destroying the unity of the Christian Church. The appointed date was the early summer of 325 CE, and the venue to which the delegates were invited was the lakeside town of Nicaea in what is today north-western Turkey, where Constantine had a suitably roomy palace. Constantine told the delegates that they would enjoy the climate, and ominously, lest they were in any doubt about the seriousness of his resolve to achieve consensus on the controversial issues to be debated, that he intended to "be present as a spectator and participator in those things which will be done".

Some scholars believe that Constantine actually presided over the proceedings of the Council. Certainly it was he who proposed (albeit very probably on the advice of his ecclesiastical adviser, the Spanish priest Hosius (or Ossius) of Cordova) the most significant phrase describing Jesus' nature as being "of one substance" with the Father which was included in the agreed statement of belief which emerged from the Council's deliberations, known as the *Nicene Creed*.[21]

It is worth remarking that this statement of faith, which is repeated every Sunday by thousands of Christians all over the world, is actually there in the creed at the behest of a man, who was far from being any sort of saint (despite the according of that title to him by the Eastern Orthodox and Catholic churches).

Amongst other things Constantine had his son killed and his no-longer-wanted wife got rid of by being boiled in her bath. Such is the psychological parentage of the authoritarian face of Christianity.

The debate in the Council veered back and forth between those who believed that Jesus was God and those who believed that he was divinely inspired but entirely human. Eventually it was down to Constantine to decide which argument was to prevail in the final statement of belief. Ian Wilson makes the extremely perceptive comment that,

> For the judgement of Solomon on the issue, the only appro-priate recourse was to Constantine, almost certainly theologi-cally illiterate, but politically a superb man manager. Exactly what swayed Constantine in that crucial moment we shall probably never know. There can be little doubt but that for him the deification of a man was nothing particularly special. He had had his father Constantius deified, would be accorded the same honour after his own death, and would surely have expected Jesus to be a superior entity in the divine hierarchy. He might well also have taken into account Alexandria's strategic and commercial advantages. Whatever his motives Constantine ruled in favour of the Alexandrians.[22]

An additional reason that could have swayed Constantine in favour of the Alexandrian position might have been that he felt that the Christian Church which he was relying on to act as a unifying structure for the Roman Empire would command greater respect and have greater power to impress and generate authoritarian submission to its dictates if it had a God-Man as its figurehead, rather than just yet another power-seeking human being. Be that as it may, Constantine urged all Council delegates to sign a Statement of Faith which expressed the Alexandrian view that Jesus was both God and a man, on which all Christians should in future agree.

Ian Wilson continues,

> For all those who signed, there was an inducement of an
> invitation to stay on at Nicaea as Constantine's guests for his
> twentieth anniversary celebrations. For those who refused
> there was immediate banishment.[23]

Not surprisingly only two of the 318 delegates believed to have
been present failed to sign as requested, and as Ian Wilson
perceptively comments,

> Among all concerned, it appears to have gone entirely
> unnoticed that the formula they were about to impose on all
> Christians contained not one jot of the ethical teachings that
> the human Jesus had once preached.[24]

Constantine's relief at the success of his strategy must, however,
have been quite short-lived. At least some of the delegates who
had signed the Nicaean declaration of faith were unhappy with
the way they had caved in under Constantine's strong-arm
tactics. On his return home Eusebius of Nicomedia for one wrote
to Constantine expressing his unhappiness with his own
behaviour at the Nicaean Council, saying, "We committed an
impious act, O Prince, by subscribing to a blasphemy from fear
of you".

Despite Constantine's 'victory' at Nicaea the question of the
divine status of Jesus just would not lie down, leading Basil of
Caesarea (St Basil the Great, 330 – 379, Bishop of Caesarea in
Cappadocia in Asia Minor) to lament that,

> It was like a naval battle fought at night in a storm, with crews
> and soldiers fighting among themselves, often in purely selfish
> power struggles, heedless of orders from above and fighting for

mastery even while their ship foundered.[25]

Constantine's Christian heritage

What Constantine's Council of Nicaea achieved was not the unification of Christianity, despite its production of a formula which millions of Christians have (often mindlessly) repeated over the past 1600 years. What the bullying of a despotic Roman ruler did achieve was the co-option of the Christian Church into the power structures of the Roman Empire, whose underlying ethics deviated drastically from the ethics of the Kingdom of God proclaimed by Jesus.

It is no accident that the religion which ostensibly is founded on the teachings and insights of a Jewish religious genius from the humble town of Nazareth in northern Israel was shifted, centuries ago, to the very predominantly gentile city of Rome, at a time when that city was the centre of the most powerful political organisation in the world. At the height of its power, the Roman Empire ruled over probably three-quarters of the population of the then-known western world. What Constantine bequeathed to Christianity was more than a cobbled-together 'statement of faith' to which the splintered factions of the early church were coerced into paying at least lip service. He bequeathed a model of the successful imposition of unity through a display of naked power in pursuit of a political objective. The intermingling of spiritual and political issues has marked the history of Christianity ever since, and an adherence to rigid authoritarian structures has similarly been a striking characteristic of much of the Christian Church's history.

The temporary, and more apparent than real 'unification' which Constantine imposed on Christianity was not brought about through any reverence for the superior moral qualities and spiritual sensitivities of that Roman emperor, and like all authoritarianly-imposed solutions, success was only skin deep, and beneath the surface of apparent unity, conflict and division constantly fermented. This ferment erupted at times in major politico-religious conflict (such as that which occurred at the time of the Reformation).

Numerically, Christianity can be seen as having been a highly successful religion. But even more striking than its overall worldwide growth is the Christian Church's consistent history of schism and splintering into ever more and more denominations and sects. According to the second edition of the *World Christian Encyclopedia*[26] published in 2002 there were no fewer than 33 820 of these at that time, more than half of them extremely small independent churches claiming exclusive possession of 'Christian Truth'.

Why? Authoritarianly imposed patterns always sooner or later breed rebellion (such is the healthy psychological strength of a significant number of human beings). The tendency of authoritarian structures to be underpinned by simplistic dogmatic statements of 'truth' forms part of a vicious circle encouraging such splintering: the authoritarian structure demands rigid dogma, which rigid dogma then becomes unable to accommodate intellectual differences. If the dissonance between the individual's beliefs and orthodox dogma, and the rebellious attitudes bred by coercive authoritarian structures is not too great, the intellectual dissenters capitulate and either conform to the demands of organisational authority or at least agree to quietly differ without making an issue of the point in contention. If the intellectual differences become too great, however, they become a peg on which to hang justification for separation from the mainstream, a plan whose psychological roots sometimes lie more strongly in the desire for self-aggran-disement and/or anti-establishment rebelliousness than in the intellectual content and spiritual aims of the purported reason for the split.

If the Christian Church is ever to achieve its full potential as a force for good and to be united in its efforts to make the world

a dramatically better place for all, it will have to shed its authoritarian attitudes and religious structures and return to its roots in
the powerful humanistic ethics of Jesus of Nazareth.

Chapter 4

The Christian Scriptures

The inspiration of religion lies in the history of religion, ... in the primary expressions of the intuitions of the finest types of religious lives. The sources of religious belief are always growing, although some supreme expressions may lie in the past. Records of these sources are not formulae. They elicit in us an intuitive response which pierces beyond dogma.[27]

– Alfred North Whitehead. *Religion in the Making*

Although different branches of the Christian Church place varying emphasis on the importance of the Bible, it is a book that plays a central role in the life of most parts of the Christian Church. Translated into more than 2000 languages, and with over six billion copies sold in the last two hundred years it is something of a publishing phenomenon in its own right. It is the most widely distributed book in the world. Despite economic recession, evangelical publishers alone sold an estimated twenty million copies in 2009. What is this book into the publishing of which such massive effort has been put?

In the first place, 'the Bible' is not a single unified text written to tell a continuous story, but consists of a collection of a number of shorter books each written at a different period in history, for a time-and-place-specific purpose, with varying time periods between their composition, and written by at least forty different authors (all male). Determining the precise dates of composition of ancient manuscripts is all but impossible, but scholars estimate that the writing of the 39 books of the Old Testament took place over a period of approximately 1100 years from somewhere around 1500 to 400 BCE and the 27 books of the New

Testament over a period of probably less than 100 years from about 40 CE to somewhere around the middle of the second century.

Secondly, so far as the four Gospels of the New Testament (the primary source material on which the argument of this book is based) is concerned, it is to be noted that the language of Jesus and his Galilean disciples was Aramaic, a Semitic language akin to Hebrew, spoken by most Palestinian Jews at that time. It was in Aramaic that Jesus taught and argued with friends and foes, but we have no written record in his 'home language' of anything that Jesus said or did. If there ever existed a written Aramaic gospel, it did not survive for long; and we certainly no longer have it.

The oldest manuscripts we do have, and upon which ultimately all versions of the Christian Bible are based, were all written in Greek, with just an occasional Aramaic word included from time to time. This fact is a result of the success of the primitive church in the Greek-speaking gentile world. Geza Vermes points out the highly significant fact that,

This Greek New Testament is a 'translation' of the expressed thoughts and ideas of the Aramaic-thinking-and-speaking Jesus and of his immediate disciples, a translation not just into a totally different language but also a transplantation of the ideology of the Gospels into the completely alien cultural and religious environment of the pagan Graeco-Roman world.[28]

Thirdly, none of the early bibles and none of the documents on which they were based were printed documents. The production of just one copy of the Bible, hand-written by a team of copyists, was an extremely expensive operation because of the labour-intensive nature of the work involved. There were consequently a very limited number of them in existence for many hundreds of years. The invention of the printing press, and the use of movable metal type in that press by a German blacksmith, goldsmith, publisher, printer, and inventor, Johannes Gutenberg in the fifteenth century changed that situation radically.[29] For the first time in Europe it was now possible to produce multiple identical copies of textual material and so make copies of books available to a mass market at a reasonable price. The first bible printed by this method, was produced in 1450 by Gutenberg.

Before this development, producing even one bible was a Herculean task, and no matter how careful and committed to their task each copyist might be, mistakes inevitably crept in from time to time. Not only were mistakes inevitably made in the copying of the complete bibles, but the documents comprising the various books (Genesis, Matthew, etc.) were themselves often multiply copied, translated, and copied again and again with varying degrees of accuracy by fallible human beings. Most, if not all the originals of those documents have been lost, but despite those losses there are in existence today no fewer than 5650 ancient documents containing parts of what have ended up as the 27 books of the New Testament of the modern Christian Bible of Western Europe. It is clear that the probability that many mistakes have been made in the transfer of text from the original documents of nearly two thousand years ago into the modern Christian bible is very high indeed.

In fact scholars who have studied this matter in careful detail have sometimes found huge variation between different manuscript versions of the same biblical books of the modern Christian bible. Seven major critical editions of the New Testament in its original Greek have been produced. Careful scholarly comparison of different manuscript versions of the same New Testament text in them shows that in nearly 40% of the verses there are differences between different versions of the same text. One particularly striking example of this is the verses to be found in Mark 16:9-20 which according to a note in the New International Version of the English Bible do not appear in, "The most reliable early manuscripts and other witnesses".[30] This is only one of a number of similar instances of more than just a copyist making a mistake, but of someone deliberately modifying the wording of an earlier manuscript because they felt that they could improve on the original.

The evolution of the Christian bible

There is no one bible accepted as 'the true bible' by all Christians. There are at least four major Christian bibles which differ to some extent from each other in the books that they contain. These are the Roman Catholic bible, the Protestant bible, and the bibles of some of the branches of the Eastern Orthodox Church. In addition some smaller Christian sects have their own bibles containing their own selection of biblical books. More than that, some important individuals have created what they believed was a purer canon of biblical truth.

Martin Luther provided a translation of the Bible into German, published in 1534 which, although not the first such translation, was by far the most influential. Luther had strong personal doubts about the suitability of the books of Esther, Hebrews, James, Jude and Revelation for inclusion in the biblical canon. He called the Epistle of James, "an Epistle of straw", and said of the book of Revelation that he could "in no way detect that the Holy Spirit produced it". In his New Testament, Luther placed Hebrews, James, Jude, and Revelation at the end of the Bible and made it clear that he regarded these books as having a less secure claim to be included in the Bible at all than the rest of the Canon, which he considered to be, "the true and certain chief books of the New Testament". His text introduced them with the words, "The four which follow have from ancient times had a different reputation".

Luther further chose to place the Apocrypha, (the Old Testament books whose place in the Christian canon has been strongly disputed over the years, and have been omitted from the

Protestant bible) between the Old and New Testaments, but did not list the books in it in the table of contents of his 1532 translation of the Old Testament. In his 1534 version of the complete Bible they were given the title: "Apocrypha: These Books Are Not Held Equal to the Scriptures, but Are Useful and Good to Read".

Despite his pre-eminence in the Protestant movement, not all of Luther's ideas about the value of various biblical books were shared by those Protestants who shaped the final form of the Protestant bible. The modern 66-book Protestant bible contains the books of Esther, Hebrews, James, Jude, and Revelation and does not contain the Apocrypha.

Thanks to Gutenberg's revolution of the printing process, Luther's bible found its way into almost every German home of his day. One German printer alone, Hans Lufft in Wittenberg printed over one hundred thousand copies between 1534 and 1574 which went on to be read by millions of German speakers. Not everyone whose exclusive preserve the serious discussion of religious matters had been, was delighted by the fulfilment of Luther's dream of the scriptures being available to be read by everyone of his fellow countrymen and women. The German humanist Johann Cochlaeus doubtless spoke for many scholars of the day when he complained that,

> Luther's New Testament was so much multiplied and spread by printers that even tailors and shoemakers, yea, even women and ignorant persons who had accepted this new Lutheran gospel, and could read a little German, studied it with the greatest avidity as the fountain of all truth. Some committed it to memory, and carried it about in their bosom. In a few months such people deemed themselves so learned that they were not ashamed to dispute about faith and the gospel not only with Catholic laymen, but even with priests and monks and doctors of divinity.

Even more radical in conception and implementation than anything Luther envisaged, was the so-called Jefferson bible. This was the work of Thomas Jefferson, the third President of the United States (1801-1809), the principal author of the *Declaration of Independence* of 1776 and the *Statute of Virginia for Religious Freedom* of 1777. He was also the founder of the University of Virginia. He regarded the ethical teachings of Jesus as, "the most sublime and benevolent code of morals which has ever been offered to man," and set himself to produce a bible in which the central elements of that code were not obscured by what he called, "the nonsense ... of the artificial vestments in which they have been muffled by priests, who have travestied them into various forms, as instruments of riches and power to themselves".

Jefferson set to work with a razor and a printed copy of the Bible, explaining that, "I have performed this operation for my own use, by cutting verse by verse out of the printed book, and arranging the matter which is evidently his, and which is as easily distinguishable as diamonds in a dunghill". The result of this process was the production of a slim book of forty-six pages, of "pure and unsophisticated doctrines", entitled *The Life and Morals of Jesus of Nazareth*, which could be seen as the Bible of Humanistic Christianity if such an independent religion existed. Completed in 1820, the book was shown to friends, who dubbed it *The Jefferson Bible*, a name which has stuck to it ever since. Because of what he had omitted some conservative Christians challenged his right to call himself a Christian at all. In response Jefferson boldly declared that on the contrary, what he had produced "is a document in proof that I am a REAL CHRISTIAN".

For some strange reason Jefferson never published his 'purified' bible in his lifetime, but for a time after his death it acquired considerable fame at least in the United States. The most complete form of the book Jefferson produced was inherited by his grandson, Thomas Jefferson Randoph, and was published in 1895 by the National Museum in Washington. The book was later published as a lithographic reproduction by an act of the United States Congress in 1904, and for many years copies were regularly given to new members of Congress.

The content of the Bible

The Christian bible today consists, in all its forms, of two distinct parts, the so-called Old and New Testaments. The position with the Old Testament (originally written in Hebrew except for a very limited amount of use of Aramaic) is fairly straightforward. To a large extent the Christian bible has just taken over the Hebrew Bible as its Old Testament, although the church has not been without dissenters who have objected to that situation. Their voices have, however, not prevailed, and the Hebrew bible has remained an important part of all the reasonably widely accepted sub-types of the Christian bible, although there are some minor differences between the two – the ordering of the books is somewhat different in the two cases, and additionally, books that Protestant Christians divide into two parts (Kings, Chronicles, Samuel, and Ezra-Nehemiah) are each only one book in the Hebrew Bible.

The position with the New Testament is more complicated, however. For more than 300 years after the death of Jesus nothing like our modern New Testament existed, although all the books that were later to constitute that collection of Christian documents had been written by the middle of the second century CE. Distribution of the relatively few copies of Christian writings that were available was very patchy. Copies of the early, one-day-to-be-biblical books on papyrus rolls or parchment *codices*, were difficult to come by and would have been highly valued by those who owned them. Many communities were isolated so that some texts may never have travelled beyond their source. No Christians at this time would have had access to all the texts which were finally included in the New Testament Canon. John, writing in the nineties at the earliest, shows no knowledge of any of Paul's letters. Ignatius, Bishop of Antioch, in the early second century, does not seem to have read the gospels of either Mark or John. Even at the end of the second century, one eminent commentator, Irenaeus, noted that congregations relied on only one gospel: Matthew was chosen by the Ebionites, a group of Jewish Christians, Luke by followers of Marcion, Mark by the Docetists and John by the Gnostics. There were also in existence and circulating in some parts of the early Christian Church many more gospels describing the life and teachings of Jesus than the four which eventually made their way into the biblical canon.

In his Easter letter of 367, Athanasius, Bishop of Alexandria, identified a set of Christian writings that he regarded as authoritative. He described his action as "kanonizomena", canonising, meaning that in his ruling these texts held the core of Christian belief. There were twenty-seven of them. As Charles Freeman points out in his, *A New History of Early Christianity*[31], "This was the earliest reference to the complete New Testament, as we know it today, although less complete lists are known from the end of the second century onwards". Athanasius' final list was not universally accepted, but in 382 the Council of Rome under the authority of Pope Damasus I (366-384) issued an identical canon, and that Pope's decision to commission (c.383) the Latin Vulgate edition of the Bible as an official church resource, was instrumental in the fixing of the canon in the West.

Although at least the main outlines of what constitutes the final agreed canon of the various branches of the modern Christian Church can be discerned in these and other rulings of various Synods and Councils from as early as the fourth century, the final definitive statements on what constitutes the modern Christian bible (which is not hugely, but quite significantly different for Roman Catholics, Protestants, and the Eastern Orthodox churches) were only made in the sixteenth and seventeenth centuries. In other words, within Christianity as a whole there is not, and never has been, any universally agreed clearly demarcated collection of infallibly true biblical books which speak with the 'voice of God'. Each Christian's judgement as to exactly which books, if any, achieve that status is very much dependent on which branch of the church they claim allegiance to. This fact alone should give fundamentalists pause to think before committing themselves to any dogmatic belief in the absolute literal truth of any biblical verse.

The use of the Bible in this book

I make extensive use of biblical quotations in this book, particularly in the central four chapters, five to eight. In looking for the best wording of these quotations, I have primarily used the New Revised Standard Version (NRSV), and the so-called King James Version (KJV), the translation which has dominated Christianity in the English-speaking world for the past 400 years. Although not the first translation of the Bible into English (which was the work of a team led by John Wycliffe[32], a prominent fourteenth-century Oxford theologian) it has probably been the single most influential one.

The KJV was first published in 1611. In the preface to the NRSV, the translators write of the KJV that, "With good reason it has been termed 'the noblest monument of English prose,' and it has entered, as no other book has, into the making of the personal character and the public institutions of the English-speaking peoples. We owe to it an incalculable debt." However, as the translators point out, since the KJV's first publication, biblical scholarship has advanced considerably, and original manuscripts of some of the books of the Bible older than those used by the translators of the KJV have been found. Additionally, the ways in which some English words are used, and their precise meaning, has changed over the years, and in some cases we also have a better understanding of the original meaning of the Ancient Greek and Hebrew words used in the original manuscripts[33]. This obviously calls for a revision of the text of the KJV in some cases. Starting in 1870, numerous revisions of 'the English Bible' have been undertaken, over 200 having been produced and published since 1900[34]. In addition more than twenty-five new translations of the New Testament alone have been produced.

It must be remembered that all the words in any English bible are the result of translation work by dedicated but fallible human scholars. No matter how skilfully a translation is done, it rarely if ever conveys all the subtleties of meaning contained in the original writing. We should be making a serious mistake if we believed that the more modern the translation, the more accurately it reflects the meaning the original writer intended. Whether what is gained by replacing the emotionally-rich phrase "swaddling clothes", by "strips of cloth", or "sounding brass" in Paul's famous paean to love in I Corinthians 13, by the ugly image of "noisy gongs" is substantial enough to compensate for what is lost is highly debatable. As an article in the Guardian of 26th November, 2011 points out, "Sometimes modernised translations can be ludicrous. The New English Bible, for example, replaces "wolves in sheep's clothing" with something more appropriate to Monty Python: 'men dressed up as sheep'", and Rowan Williams, the former Archbishop of Canterbury, in a sermon delivered as part of a special service to commemorate the 400th anniversary of the publication of the 1611 KJV, noted that whilst it is appropriate for those working on a modern translation of the bible to "look for strategies that make the text more accessible", there is also some role for complexity, and sometimes an obscure text in the KJV may "surprise us into seriousness". He noted with approval that the 1611 translators regarded the task of translation as being to let in the light and remove "the cover of the well, that we may come by the water".

The choice of the English words used in any specific translation is governed by much more than just "what the dictionary says", as I discussed to some extent towards the end of Chapter 2. Additionally the philosophical outlook, specific religious beliefs, and general personality of each member of the translating team, as well as the prevailing religious climate in the subculture from which the translators were drawn, all play their part in each individual's deciding exactly how best to capture the meaning biblical writers had in mind when 2000 years or so ago they wrote down what we read in the bible today. As a result different members of every translating team have often been at loggerheads with each other as to the precise meaning of some parts of the original they were translating. The different ways in which four of those well-respected teams translated verses three and four of the seventh chapter of Paul's first Epistle to the Corinthians, as discussed in Chapter 7 of this book, is instructive in this regard. To believe that every word in the Bible is the word of an English-speaking God, is to worship an idol of all-too-human creation.

Although the oldest of the five English translations used in this book, the magnificent language of the KJV often adds significantly to the depth of meaning which lies in the quoted words, and wherever possible I have used this version of the English Bible. Where the meaning of a particular quotation from the KJV might not be entirely clear to modern readers (as is certainly sometimes the case), I have consulted various modern translations, most notably the NRSV (New Revised Standard Version), the NIV (New International Version), NEB (New English Bible) and one of the most readable of modern translations, J. B. Phillips' *The Gospels in Modern English* (GME). The NRSV is the version of the English bible favoured by most scholars today, and so I have as far as possible restricted myself to the use of the KJV and the NRSV, but have not hesitated to use the words of the NIV, NEB and GME where they seem to convey what I believe to be the essence of a quote in a more helpful way.

The second thing to be said about the biblical quotes which provide the backbone of my argument is that those relating to Jesus' thinking come almost exclusively from the first three gospels in the New Testament – the so-called Synoptic Gospels of Matthew, Mark, and Luke. Those relating to Paul's thinking come almost entirely from the seven epistles in the New Testament attributed to Paul, which most modern scholars believe are authentic. These are Romans, I and II Corinthians, Galatians, Philippians, I Thessalonians and Philemon. The weight of modern scholarly opinion is that the remaining six epistles attributed to Paul and the Epistle to the Hebrews (which is sometimes attributed to Paul, and sometimes not) were probably not written by Paul himself.

What are the Synoptic Gospels? All the biblical Gospels were written some years after Jesus' death. They were not written by eyewitnesses seeking to record 'the words of the master' for distant posterity, but for a specific educational purpose in various parts of the early Christian Church of their time.[35] Their composition was spread over a period of 30 years or more. The earliest of these Gospels, that of Mark, was probably written about 70 CE, and Matthew's and Luke's somewhere between 80 and 100 CE. These three gospels, have been named the Synoptic Gospels because they all reflect more or less the same view of Jesus' life and teaching.[36] However, not only were all three of them written about 40 years or more after Jesus' death, but the earliest surviving sources we have for them (in the form of papyrus fragments), date from about 125 CE at the earliest. The fourth gospel, that of John, (probably written around 110 CE, i.e. about 80 years after the death of Jesus) was clearly not intended so much as a historical document as a theological reflection on the significance of Jesus' life.

It is thus the Synoptic gospels which provide the most reliable evidence we have as to what Jesus said and did, but the content of even these needs to be very carefully sifted (as Geza Vermes[14] and Stephen Mitchell[37] amongst others have done), in order to determine how much of what we find there is a reasonably accurate record of what Jesus said and did, and what was added by later writers and editors in the early church to strengthen their own theological and socio-political positions. Geza Vermes, Professor Emeritus of Jewish Studies at the University of Oxford, in his book *The Authentic Gospel of Jesus*, has taken every utterance attributed to Jesus in the Synoptics (together with those in John's gospel which he believes to be of significance), and assessed the probability that something very much like what we find there was in fact said by Jesus, or whether it was probably interpolated into an earlier text by some one or more people in the early Christian Church to achieve a specific objective. He writes,

> But with the exception of his account of the last days of Jesus, John's account is more fiction than history when it is compared with the Synoptics. It is enough to look at his invented lengthy speeches, which are totally incompatible with the style and content of the preaching of Jesus preserved in the first three Gospels.[38]

In order to get as close as possible to a true understanding of Jesus' life, I have very largely restricted myself to the Synoptic Gospels as source material for finding out what Jesus did, said, and thought.

Chapter 5

The Humanistic Face of Christianity

In the course of my studies, I have discovered that the religious quest is not about discovering 'the truth' or 'the meaning of life,' but about living as intensely as possible here and now. The idea is not to latch onto some super-human personality or to 'get to heaven' but to discover how to be fully human.[39]
– Karen Armstrong. *The Spiral Staircase*

Although there are many happy exceptions, in recent years the Christian Church as a whole seems to have become more and more obsessed with the death of Jesus, revelling in the gory details of that death, and sometimes in the gory details of the fate from which that death has 'saved' us. In the process less and less attention has been paid in many parts of the church to the ethical principles embedded in the heart of what we know of Jesus' teachings.

Ethics and Morality

Religions try to guide (sometimes to coerce, using varying degrees of emotional blackmail) our thoughts and attitudes into patterns of behaviour which the leaders of a particular religion believe will bring adherents into the most intimate contact with spiritual reality as they conceive that to be. Christian Ethics are all about the frame of mind, the way of thinking, which the Christian Church believes puts the individual into the closest contact with God, i.e. brings them closest to entering 'The Kingdom of Heaven', the Kingdom of Heaven being seen as an ideal state of being in which everything exists in a state of peace and perfect happiness flowing from being in perfect harmony with God.

Ethics are the general, abstract principles exemplified in what the individual conceives to be 'right behaviour'. Morality is all about specific rules, about identifying some behaviours as right and others as wrong, and the embodiment of those beliefs in a series of injunctions as to what people MUST DO, or MUST NOT DO. The difference between ethics and morality is rather like the difference between the 'carrot' and the 'stick' approach to changing behaviour: ethical principles offer the carrot of general guidelines as to how to be a 'good person' (*"Let your behaviour be guided by the general principle that ..."*) whereas morality offers detailed specific instructions about what anyone aspiring to be a 'good person' must or must not do – the 'stick' of *"Obey these rules, or else ..."*. All moral codes are justified by one or more ethical principles, and all owe whatever validity they may have to being informed by some more profound abstract ethical principle.

Christian ethics are by no means a coherent, consistent set of principles which guide the behaviour of all those who call themselves Christians. Apart from the fact that no two individuals ever hold identical views about anything, there are wide variations among those of us calling ourselves Christians in the importance attached to various ideas and beliefs which are to be found within the wide range of ideas commonly denominated as 'Christian'. The Christian attitude to war is but one example of this. Some Christians, and some groups of Christians, hold to a pacifist position (of varying degrees of absoluteness); others, in situations of political conflict, pray for God's support for their military adventures in raining down death and destruction on their enemies. People in the latter category seem untroubled by the rather odd fact that in asking for God's help with the destruction of their enemies they are not only disregarding Jesus' urging of us to, "Love your enemies" (Matthew 5:44), but are actually asking God to help them to break his own commandment, "Thou shalt not kill" (Exodus 20:13 and Deuteronomy 5:17).

The thinking of that inspired Jewish religious genius, Jesus of Nazareth, and many of his first-century Jewish compatriots was dominated by the expectation of the imminent arrival of the Kingdom of God[40]. In that Kingdom the quality of human relationships would be transformed by the embodying of certain ethical principles in the way human beings relate to each other. The core of the term 'Christian Ethics' refers to those principles embodied in the life and teachings of Jesus. While some of those principles have remained of central importance in defining 'Christianity', some have (as we shall discuss throughout the rest of this book), been corrupted by the psychopathologies inherent in authoritarian attitudes and thinking. Others have been all but completely ignored. From time to time some prominent Christian leader makes a pronouncement which is clearly informed by some principle which is no part of the ethics of Jesus.

One particularly glaring example of that kind of thing is the extraordinary statement of Pope John Paul II that, "Suffering, particularly in the later years of life, is part of God's saving plan for humanity".[41] A more un-Jesus-like, cruel and heartless statement would be hard to imagine. Moreover, the statement is dishonest, because if the papacy really believed this pronouncement of one of its 'infallible' incumbents, they would campaign against medical care for the elderly with the same misguided energy that they campaign against contraception, abortion, and euthanasia. Given the average age at which Cardinals become Popes, the chances of the Catholic Church taking the implications of that statement seriously, and actually condemning (as attempts to undermine the 'saving plan' God has for humanity) the work of medical staff who try to make the last days on earth of the elderly as comfortable as possible, are vanishingly unlikely.

The more one thinks about it, the more obvious it becomes

that if the Catholic Church as a whole really believed its own claim as to the infallibility of papal pronouncements, it would be actively campaigning for the closure of all hospitals and medical practices and condemning the healing work of Jesus as having been 'a grave sin' because it got in the way of 'God's plan' of salvation through pain and suffering. Of course, although logic requires such an implication of the Pope's pronouncement about the value of suffering to be admitted, logical rationality never played much part in papal 'infallible' thinking in this or any other matter where either suffering or sexuality was an issue. The reason for making the blasphemous claim that, "Suffering is part of God's saving plan for humanity", was presumably just to bolster the Church's position in regard to euthanasia, by purporting to know the 'mind of God' in a way which would bully all but the bravest spirits into submission to the Church's views.

One of the influences on the early development of the Christian Church which has had the most devastating effect in shifting the compassionate ethics of Jesus from centre stage, stems from the fact that in the latter part of the fourth century, as discussed in Chapter 3, the Christian Church allowed itself to be co-opted by the Roman Emperor Constantine as the favoured state religion of the Roman Empire. The major result of this event was the indelible stamping of some of the ideas of Roman law on the Christian spirit – so a legalistic, judgemental, rule-following way of being became a major part of the ethics of the Christian Church, in complete contradiction of some of the ethical principles which Jesus proclaimed. It is the principles demon-strated, taught, and lived out by Jesus of Nazareth more than 2000 years ago (before the Christian Church got to work on them) that constitute the humanistic face of Christianity, and which we shall discuss in some detail in the rest of this chapter.

The basic structure of that part of Christian Ethics to be found in the teachings of Jesus

What are the ethical principles taught by Jesus? What are the characteristics of our thinking and behaviour when we have become part of what Jesus believed to be 'The Kingdom of God'?

Love

The most profound, over-arching concept is that of love. It is highly significant that when asked (as reported in Matthew 22:36), "Which is the great commandment in the law?", Jesus did not turn to the so-called 'Ten Commandments' recorded in Exodus 20:2-17, (and more or less exactly repeated in Deuteronomy 5:6-21), 80% of which are prohibitions of the "Thou shalt not ..." type, but rather to verses elsewhere in the Hebrew Bible which have a very different flavour. His answer to the question he was asked about which the greatest commandment was,

> Thou shalt love the Lord thy God with all thy heart, and with all thy soul and with all thy mind. This is the first and great commandment. And the second is like unto it, Thou shalt love thy neighbour as thyself. On these two commandments hang all the law and the prophets.[42]

In elevating the importance of these two great biblical commandments (whose urgings for us to love contain no messages about 'striving against evil', no prohibitions, no finger-wagging injunctions about disallowed behaviours), above all the hundreds of other biblical commandments which are of that type, Jesus indicated very clearly the humanistic thrust of his understanding of what constitutes the Kingdom of God. Those times when we know we are loved by another person (or other living creature), or God, or perhaps most importantly, by ourselves, are the moments in our lives of the deepest happiness and satisfaction.

The fundamental motivation for almost all human behaviour is to expand the number of people whose interaction with us leads us to feel that beautiful emotion of being loved and appreciated. Since the more loving behaviours we show towards others, the more we are likely to get back from them, Jesus' emphasis on the two commandments to love is clearly aligned with all kindly attempts to make the experience of life a more joyful one for us all. They are not just lofty ethical ideals, but two statements of a fundamentally important psychological truth about how to experience happiness.

Jesus' emphasis on the greater importance of love than of prohibitions, his emphasis on the Power of the Positive, is not only in complete harmony with modern psychological wisdom about the most effective way to influence behaviour, but also with the simple folk wisdom contained in those age-old proverbs, "Correction does much, but encouragement does more", "More people are flattered into virtue than are bullied out of vice", and "It is better to light one small candle than to curse the darkness". In so far as Christianity really is founded on the life and teachings of Jesus, this principle, which lies at the heart of the ideas which he proclaimed, will be central to Christian Ethics. It would not have been unreasonable to have expected Jesus to have replied, when asked which was the most important commandment, "Thou shalt not kill". But to feel love, real caring compassion for others, even when they have done wrong and perhaps hurt us, is a far more powerful state of goodness than simply to refrain from killing or trying to injure them.

What determines the choice we make between offering negative feedback in a constructive or a destructive way when we encounter what we believe to be wrongdoing on someone's part is whether or not we feel ourselves to be in an adversarial relationship with them. As we shall discuss in the next chapter, the existence of an attitude of adversarialness lies at the heart of all authoritarian thinking. Its presence in the thinking of many Christians is a major factor in undermining the importance they place on Jesus' identification of love; love for God and love for our neighbour, as being the most important characteristic of those who have entered 'The Kingdom of God'. I shall discuss this in more detail in the next chapter.

Of course it is not just Christians who subscribe to the views of Jesus about the fundamental ethical status of love. Many of those who stand outside the Christian tradition, or indeed outside any religious tradition share the same feelings. Even the eminent philosopher, mathematician, and militant atheist of the mid-twentieth century, Bertrand Russell (whose *Why I am not a Christian* caused something of a scandal when it was first published in 1927) could write,

> There are certain things that our age needs, and certain things it should avoid. It needs compassion, and a desire that mankind be happy: it needs the desire for knowledge and the determination to eschew pleasant myths; it needs above all courageous hope and the impulse to creativeness. ... The root of the matter is a very simple and old-fashioned thing, a thing so simple that I am almost ashamed to mention it for fear of the derisive smile with which wise cynics will greet my words. The thing I mean – please forgive me for mentioning it – is love, Christian love, or compassion. If you feel this, you have a motive for existence, a guide in action, a reason for courage, an imperative necessity for intellectual honesty.

And the twentieth-century author and pioneer in the study of philosophies and techniques to develop human potential, Aldous Huxley, could write, "It is a little embarrassing that, after forty-five years of research and study, the best advice that I can give to people is to be a little kinder to each other". Unlike many of the pronouncements coming from those who are the active agents in the authoritarian face of Christianity, this fundamental principle of Jesus' ethics is something which provides a common bond uniting all people of goodwill, whatever their gender, race, culture, and religious or philosophical background.

But what does it mean to love our neighbour? The idea of loving all living things as a prerequisite to living a deeply satisfying and happy life is a very general statement, easy to assent to as an abstract principle, but less easy to implement in the world of flesh and blood reality. As the American humourist Ogden Nash once admitted, "I love humanity. It's people I can't stand." What do the teachings of Jesus tell us about the specific behaviours, habits, and attitudes of mind which manifest the presence of the love of God and love for our neighbour within us? What are the more detailed ethical principles, acting upon which give the concept of loving God and our neighbour specific content?

In what follows in this chapter I shall deal with seven particularly important aspects of this concept. It is to be noted that some of these principles embodied in the life and teachings of Jesus, are reinforced by some (but not all) of the teachings of St Paul, particularly exemplified in his magnificent paean to love in the thirteenth chapter of his First Epistle to the Corinthians, and in his listing in Chapter 6 of his Epistle to the Galatians, verses 22-23, of the nine "fruits of the spirit": Love, Joy, Peace, Longsuffering, Gentleness, Goodness, Faith, Meekness, and Temperance.

The concepts I shall discuss here are: Compassion, Meekness and Humility; Putting People before Principles; Non-judgementalness; Mutuality/Reciprocity; the Inversion of the Power Hierarchy, and Authenticity. Authenticity refers to a way of being in which what we show of ourselves to the world (our Persona, as Jung termed it), is fully in harmony with all the thoughts and feelings that lie within us, but some of which (our Shadow) we sometimes try to hide from the world. To the extent that our lives are touched by persons whose behaviour manifests the principles of the ethics of Jesus, (the desire to make things better for all), the pain of our sufferings (physical and psychological) is reduced, and our resources to cope with future adversity increased.

1. Compassion

In essence every instance of compassionate behaviour is just a particular instance of the over-arching general principle of behaving in love towards others. The various specific ethical principles discussed later in this chapter are all intimately connected with each other through the connection of each of them with the general principle of compassionate love for all.

The three aspects of compassion discussed in this section all have a common theme of disinterested[43] generosity of spirit, a core attribute of love.

1.1 Compassion for those in need, for all those who suffer in any way

The prototypical story which encapsulates Jesus' attitude of compassionate love for others, not least for social outcasts, and to the healing and caring for the sick characteristic of his piety, is that of the Good Samaritan (Luke 10: 30-35).[44]

And Jesus answering said, A certain man went down from Jerusalem to Jericho, and fell among thieves, which stripped him of his raiment, and wounded him, and departed, leaving him half dead. And by chance there came down a certain priest that way: and when he saw him he passed by on the other side. And likewise a Levite, when he was at the place, came and looked on him, and passed by on the other side. But a certain Samaritan, as he journeyed, came where he was: and when he saw him, he had compassion on him. And went to him, and bound up his wounds, pouring in oil and wine, and set him on his own beast, and brought him to an inn, and took care of him. And on the morrow when he departed, he took out two pence, and gave them to the host, and said unto him, Take care of him, and whatsoever thou spendest more, when I come again I will repay thee.

This parable presents an interesting challenge to the reader. The message Jesus was trying to put across was clearly a positive one towards the kind Samaritan, with a sub-text that social outcasts may well sometimes show greater virtuous behaviour than some pillars of the community. Most of us, on hearing the story (again), will probably find that our positive feelings towards the Samaritan are accompanied by feelings of a degree of harsh judgementalness towards the priest and the Levite who "passed by on the other side", with perhaps a self-justificatory, "Of course I wouldn't behave like that. I would be like the Good Samaritan". Should such a feeling of self-righteousness arise within us it might, of course, be accompanied by a twinge of guilt as we remember another of Jesus' ethical principles, the importance of a compassionate, forgiving attitude towards wrongdoing, rather than a moralistic and judgemental one. The tendency to want to remove a speck of dust from our neighbour's eye when we have an even larger object interfering with the vision in our own (Matthew 7:3-5), and the tendency to harshly blame ourselves for such ethical lapses, can cause much avoidable distress.

1.2 For those caught up in conflict

One special form of psychological and often physical distress of which Jesus as a Jew living in Palestine two thousand years ago must have been all too vividly aware, was that to be found in warfare. After many foreign occupations and brief respites from them, Palestine was occupied by invading Roman forces in 64 BCE, and in 6 BCE was annexed into the Roman Empire, in effect marking the end of Palestine as an independent Jewish state, a situation which lasted nearly 2000 years until the establishment of the modern state of Israel in 1948. Annexure of Jewish Palestine into the Roman Empire did not bring peace to the country and from time to time popular uprisings occurred in the attempt to throw off the Roman yoke. These were brutally suppressed by the Roman overlords, crucifixion being the favoured, gruesome, and very public method of execution of those suspected of instigating rebellions against the occupying power. Jesus thus grew up in a society which had firsthand experience of the horrors of many years of intermittent warfare.

But it was probably not just politically-motivated warfare which formed a constant background to Jesus' thoughts about the distressing effects of conflict, and the near-universal human longing for peaceableness. Although we know next to nothing of the details of Jesus' family life, there are clear indications in the gospel record that there was recurrent tension between him and at least some members of his family. In the incident described in all three of the Synoptic gospels (Matthew 12: 46-50, Mark 3: 31-35, and Luke 8: 19-21) where, "There came then his brethren and his mother, and standing without, sent unto him, calling him" (Mark 3:31), his family does not seem to have received a very gracious response from Jesus, suggestive of his feeling something like, "Who do these people think they are? They mean no more to me than any of you people listening to me here. … 'Whosoever shall do the will of God, the same is my brother, my sister, and my mother'". (Mark 3:35).

If it really happened like that, quite a slap in the face for his closest family. One wonders if when Jesus lamented that, "A prophet is not without honour save in his own country" (Matthew 13:57), he may not have thought of adding under his breath, "and especially in his own family". Even well before he reached adulthood, the incident reported in Luke 2:40-52 of the twelve-year-old Jesus having left his family caravan (when they were returning home after their annual Passover visit to the temple in Jerusalem) to return to the temple and engage in what must have seemed to be very precocious disputation with the religious leaders there, must have raised anxieties about problems to come in the future with this headstrong young man.

At least some of the tension in Jesus' family was probably around the role Jesus saw for himself in inaugurating the Kingdom of God on earth. His family probably understood hardly anything about how fundamentally different the campaign Jesus was conducting was from those of the militaristic Zealots who for the most part had quickly perished in their attempts to institute a new political dispensation for Jews in their homeland. It would be surprising if his family's anxiety for Jesus' safety as he pursued his chosen path did not spill over into some (perhaps quite serious) family conflict. If so his belief, expressed in one of the Beatitudes, that, "Blessed are the peacemakers: for they shall be called the children of God" (Matthew 5:9), must have had a particularly poignant meaning for him.

Jesus' compassionate concern for those caught up in conflict of one sort or another, and his belief that peacemakers have a special virtue, is important in its own right, but is also part of a wider predominantly pacifist philosophy which lies at the heart of his ethics, as discussed below.

1.3 For the well-being of all people whatever their personal circumstances

An important underlying assumption of all the ethical guidelines which Jesus believed those who were part of the Kingdom of God operated under, was that, "It is more blessed to give than to receive".[45] In holding such a view Jesus would not have been implying that it is not blessed, that it is not a source of joy and happiness to be on the receiving end of the generosity of others. Being a puritanical killjoy is no part of what Jesus suggested is the way of being which takes us into the Kingdom of God. It would be manifestly absurd if he believed that in scoring

Brownie points for ourselves by giving to others, we are inflicting a curse on them – obtaining the benefit which accrues to us through our giving at the expense of condemning the person to whom we give to a state of 'unblessedness'. And of course the world cannot be full only of givers; generally speaking, to give implies there is someone who receives.

There has, however, been a strong streak of puritanical thinking within Christianity which preaches just such a travesty of the very psychologically astute observation that pleasant though it is to receive, in the act of giving we encounter a very special extra pleasure. I shall discuss this important matter further a little later in this chapter and also in Chapter 7 below. Self-denial is not a Christian virtue, but rather a psychological abnormality. It is in no way a necessary part of generously choosing to do something to add to the well-being and happiness of another, through which, as Jesus perceptively pointed out, we experience an increase in our own sense of well-being and happiness.

All the instances of compassion demonstrated in Jesus' life and teaching can perhaps best be summed up in his statement of what has come to be called *The Golden Rule*, "As ye would that men should do to you, do ye also to them likewise." (Luke 6:31, and Matthew 7:12). In saying this, Jesus was reflecting the spirit of that saying from the Talmud, "What is hateful to you, do not to your fellow men. That is the entire Law; all the rest is commentary".[46] It is interesting to note the shift in emphasis from the Talmudic formulation in terms of what we should not do, to Jesus' emphasis, consistent with his continual stress on the positive, on what we should do. In favour of the Talmudic wording is the fact that it recognises (consciously or unconsciously) that what one person would like done to them is not necessarily what another person would like to experience. Doing something to or for someone else that we think is the right thing to do just because we would like others to treat us that way, is not necessarily doing them a kindness. Being so passionately focussed on what we want to give to others without sensitivity as to whether the recipient actually wants what we are trying to give them, is the negative, 'do-goodism', shadow side of charity and philanthropy.[47]

The downside of the Talmudic formulation is that making the world a better place through compassionate concern for the well-being of others involves more than just refraining from doing things that make people unhappy. It requires the proactive initiation of loving, appreciative behaviours. As Antoine de Saint-Exupéry, the author of *The Little Prince* put it, "What value has compassion that does not take its object in its arms?"

For some people happiness may mean just the absence of unhappiness, but joy is what we seek in life, not just a neutral, non-negative emotional state. It is to feel filled with the overflowing sense of well-being which feeling loved produces, that we all hanker after. Jesus' modification of the Talmudic original sustains the idea of not doing things to cause distress to others of the original wording, but adds an emphasis on taking proactive positive steps to make people feel good about themselves. Many of these are very simple things like smiling at people, enquiring after their health and happiness, and (particularly importantly) listening attentively to what they are saying when they speak, whatever level of the social hierarchy they occupy – street sweepers, supermarket checkout persons, and those involved in the collection of taxes, no less than doctors, the politically powerful, and mega-rich celebrities.

But Jesus' urging of us to do unto others as we would be done by, goes further than just treating others as important human beings in order to boost their feelings of self-worth. Taking up a theme to be found in Deuteronomy 15:7-8[48] and Proverbs 21:26[49] we are encouraged to, "Give to him that asketh thee, and from him that would borrow of thee turn thou not away" (Matthew 5:42), and told that in respect of those occasions on which we have compassionately fed the hungry, given something to drink to the thirsty, provided comfort to a stranger in need, clothed the naked, or visited the sick or those in prison, "inasmuch as ye have done it unto one of the least of these my brethren, ye have done it unto me" (Matthew 25:40).

But Jesus' concept of what it means to show compassion does not stop even there, and the further implications of this principle are closely tied to the inversion of the power hierarchy, which is an integral part of the ethics that Jesus promoted. But more of that anon.

Implementing the Golden Rule in our lives is one specific recommendation that flows from Jesus' urging of us to, "Love thy neighbour as thyself". Generally overlooked, but implicit in that commandment, is the need to love not just God, and our neighbour, but ourselves as well. If we do not love ourselves then loving our neighbour "as ourselves" will be more of a curse on them than the blessing Jesus obviously had in mind. The abusive way some guilt-ridden Christians treat themselves would cause an outcry if they treated their neighbour in such a way. Exerting strenuous efforts to make people feel bad about themselves (dealt with at some length in the next chapter) is one of the particularly vicious ways in which those actively promoting the authoritarian face of Christianity have subverted the ethical teachings of the God-Man they claim to worship.

If we are to follow not just the letter, but also the spirit of Jesus' urging of us to love our neighbour, we need, first and foremost, to love ourselves: our whole being, body and mind as well as soul. With (as always) some honourable exceptions, the Christian Church does not exactly have a good track record in encouraging human beings to love either their minds or their bodies. The denigration of the body ("a temple of the Holy Spirit" according to St Paul in I Corinthians 6:19) and of our sexuality (which is an integral part of it) by many within the Christian Church is as illogical as it is damaging to the human spirit.

Not quite so universally appreciated is the tendency of some Christians to regard the human mind, and the intelligence which is part of its very nature, as somehow an obstacle to the achievement of ever deeper spiritual experience. The frequently repeated nonsensical riposte to anyone exposing any contradictions or errors they think they have spotted within Christianity that, "These things are beyond human understanding" (or even more damagingly, "Who are you to question God?")[50], has a stultifying effect on the development of the individual's intelligence as well as of their spirituality. Had science adopted an equivalent belief that whatever puzzles and perplexes anyone about any aspect of the physical world does so because the issue is "beyond human understanding", we should all have been dead before we reached the age of 40, after a life of unremitting toil and frequent pain and sometimes bitter hardship. Fortunately more widespread education has brought about a situation where more and more people are able and eager to challenge current orthodoxies in the field not only of science but also of religion. As the nineteenth-century German philosopher Immanuel Kant reminded us,

> Religion on the ground of its sanctity, and law on the ground of its majesty, often resist the sifting of their claims by critical thought. But in so doing they inevitably awake a not-unjustified suspicion that their claims are ill-founded and they cease to command the unfeigned homage which is paid by Reason to that which has shown itself able to stand the test of free enquiry.

Such 'free enquiry' is the hallmark of liberal religion, in which category the humanistic face of Christianity finds a congenial home.

The first requirement for anyone to increase their understanding of anything, is that they throw out whatever restrictive injunctions they may have absorbed, particularly from any misguided religious zealot, NOT TO THINK. All the progress humankind has made in understanding the nature of the spiritual world and its relation to the material one has come about through human thinking, and the only way we shall make further, much-needed progress is through yet more human thinking of a yet more fearless and profound type – honest independent thinking as opposed to mindless, intimidated acceptance of the sort of clichéd, pre-packaged formulas which have too often in the past passed for thinking in many of the faithful adherents of their particular branch of the Christian Church.

The world is in desperate need of more people to behave with more compassion towards all living creatures and indeed towards our planet itself. The more we love God, our neighbour, and ourselves, body, mind and spirit, the more caring, compassionate behaviour will flow from us into the world, and the more St Paul's wish for us will achieve fulfilment, "Let this mind be in you that was also in Christ Jesus" (Philippians 2:5).

2. Meekness and Humility

Fundamental to the state of mind in which we feel love, and a compassionate concern for our fellow-creatures, is an attitude of meekness and humility (Galatians 5:23), in which we are modest and unpretentious, the very opposite of proud and demanding (I Corinthians 13:4 and 5). It is the human qualities of people that we value – not their status and the titles and any other labels attached to them which might appear important to some. In this state we are gentle, courteous and kind (Galatians 5:22 and I Corinthians 13:4), merciful (Matthew 5:7 and Luke 6:36) and indulgent, not strict or severe (I Corinthians 13:4), but prepared to sometimes turn a blind eye to the faults and failings of those who are struggling to live up to the best of which they are capable (Galatians 5:22 and I Corinthians 13:5 and 7). We are very conscious that, "There but for the grace of God go I",[51] and such an attitude of mind is strengthened when we remember Jesus' discomforting instruction to the self-righteous crowd baying for the death by stoning of the woman "taken in adultery", "Let anyone among you who is without sin be the first to throw a stone at her" (John 8:7).

The modest and unpretentious lifestyle and behaviour of the humble and meek is marked by a lack of arrogance, bombast and grandiosity, and any aggressive assertion of their own importance in the world – the question, "How can I serve you?", is constantly at the back of their mind in their interactions with others. In this way of being, without putting ourselves down or denying our good qualities, we do not feel any haughty pride that as a human being we are better than others, of more worth than they (which arrogance, when it occurs, always has a deep, often unconscious feeling of inferiority and inadequacy at its root). Each of us has some good quality or ability which is more fully developed in ourselves than in others, but that does not make us a superior human being to anyone with a different pattern of strengths and weaknesses. Humility is not about denying the good in ourselves, but it is about acknowledging our limitations and shortcomings. A balanced awareness of both our strengths and our weaknesses keeps us from any self-righteous condemnation of others, but equally from any self-loathing rejection of ourselves.

In the parable of the Pharisee[52] and the publican recounted in Luke 18:9-14, Jesus' approval of the behaviour of the repentant publican who prayed for forgiveness for his sins, (as compared with his disapproval of that of the self-righteous, holier-than-thou Pharisee, whose prayer consisted of a self-congratulatory thanking of God for the fact that he was not a sinner like the rest of his fellows), was a pointed illustration of his belief that "every one that exalteth himself shall be abased, and he that humbleth himself shall be exalted" (Luke 18:14).[53] This view is reminiscent of the words reportedly uttered by the pregnant Mary, the mother of Jesus, in conversation with her cousin Elizabeth, recorded in Luke 1:46-55,

> My soul doth magnify the Lord, and my spirit hath rejoiced in God my Saviour. ... He hath shewed strength with his arm; he hath scattered the proud in the imagination of their hearts. He hath put down the mighty from their seats, and exalted them of low degree.

or, in the slightly different wording of the Magnificat in the original version of the Anglican Book of Common Prayer, "He hath put down the mighty from their seat: and hath exalted the humble and meek."

The whole way in which Jesus lived his life demonstrated his commitment to the ethical principle of humility. The fact that he was not a social climber, trying to ingratiate himself with the powerful members of his society but rather the champion of the underdog, spending time with social outcasts and the emotionally needy, led him to be viewed in some quarters of the religious establishment as "a man gluttonous, and a wine bibber, a friend of publicans and sinners" (Matthew 11:19, and Luke 7:34). But a constant theme running through all Jesus' teaching and all the ethical principles he emphasised, is his compassionate concern for the well-being of people, particularly those who are not 'making it' in the society in which they live, the social outcasts, the dregs of society. Taken to task for this by the scribes and Pharisees (as reported in Mark 2:16), his reply was, "They that are whole have no need of the physician, but they that are sick".[54] The picture of Jesus which emerges from the gospel record is of a man who sought primarily to give what he could to others, rather than to accrue benefits for himself from his contact with them.

The vein of distaste for arrogant, moralistic self-righteousness which runs throughout Jesus' life and work is made very clear in his statement of the beatitudes with which his 'Sermon on the Mount' opens, particularly in the first and third of them: "Blessed are the poor in spirit: for theirs is the kingdom of heaven" (Matthew 5:3), and "Blessed are the meek: for they shall inherit the earth"[55] (Matthew 5:5). The meaning of these two statements is perhaps better brought out in the more modern J. B. Phillips *The Gospels in Modern English* translation of them as, "How happy are the humble-minded, for the Kingdom of Heaven is theirs", and, "Happy are those who claim nothing, for the whole earth will belong to them"!

The fact that the ostentatious accumulation of this world's goods, the desire to impress others with our material possessions, is for Jesus no part of behaviour governed by the ethical principles he espoused, does not imply that in his eyes there is anything wrong with taking pleasure in beautiful things or that there is anything wrong in itself with being wealthy. It is the accumulation of wealth at the expense of the health, happiness, and general well-being of ourselves and others, and the ostentatious display of that wealth to raise our status in the eyes of the world, which Jesus asserts to be incompatible with living in the Kingdom of God.

Much the same goes for ostentatious displays of piety, drawing the attention of the world to, "What a virtuous person I am". Such behaviour marks only a very small advance on the attention- and approval-seeking plea of the insecure young child, "What a good boy (or girl) am I". For Jesus, piety was not a matter of public display, but of private meditation, although that state of mind would of course issue in unostentatious good works in the real world from time to time.[56]

One important distinguishing characteristic of the behaviour and way of interacting with others of those who value the qualities of meekness and humility is respect for the uniqueness and autonomy of the individual. When the meek and humble person is in any sort of authority over others, they treat those others with respect, without arrogance, and refrain from imposing anything more than the bare minimum of rules and regulations on them.[57] They see their role as more to lift other people's burdens than to add to them.[58] They see their role as being to guide and influence those whom they have some authority over, rather than to control them.

And this is part of a bigger picture of acknowledgement of the fact that there are forces at work in the universe, both physical and spiritual, on a scale greater than we can as yet fully comprehend, and whilst there is a time to 'make things happen', there is also a time to allow life to unfold in its own way. This bigger picture is hinted at in Shakespeare's belief that, "There's a divinity that shapes our ends, rough-hew them as we will," or in St Paul's words, "All things work together for good to them that love God" (Romans 8:28). It means knowing that in the long-run there is some rightness in the way things are, no matter how wrong they may at certain times seem to be. It means that if we listen carefully to our intuitions we shall know when it is time to 'push the river', and when it is time to just gratefully 'go with the flow' of life. It means that we will find our greatest strength and happiness when from time to time we just relax into the stream of those positive forces which constantly surround us, rather than always trying to impose our intellectual constructions on life, and trying to make it unfold in a way that will give us the greatest short-term gratification.

The humble and meek do not try to arrogantly control other people – "Seek to influence others rather than to control them", is their motto. When we are in this state of mind we see our purpose in life as being to fulfil our potential, to become more and more truly ourselves – not to become a clone of anyone else or they of us, or a mere pawn in any one else's game, and to help others in their own journey to achieve this same objective.

Meekness has had a bad press. It doesn't mean making oneself a doormat. But it does mean not constantly trying to take centre stage in the lives of others. It means not trying to get the energy and attention of others first and foremost directed at ourselves, but rather directing our own energy and attention towards the welfare of others, to enjoying who they are and looking for what we can do to enhance the quality of their lives and experience. I said a couple of sentences ago that meekness does not mean making oneself a doormat, and yet of course some people do labour under the misapprehension that that is exactly what being meek does mean – that it means abandoning the search for the satisfaction of our own needs in favour of allowing others to satisfy their needs, even at our expense.

For the present let us just note that in trying to understand, in any particular situation, exactly where the boundary lies between meekness as a virtue and the psychopathologies of disempowerment and masochism, Jung's dictum that, "Our greatest strengths, taken to excess become our greatest weaknesses," can be most helpful. One of the most difficult things about living a life informed by the ethics of Jesus, is to make intelligent and humane decisions about when any particular ethical principle which Jesus preached should be followed more or less to the letter, and when the overarching guideline of "not sacrificing a person to a principle" requires that it should take a back seat. Joseph Fletcher's writings on 'Situational Ethics', discussed in the next section, are enormously helpful in guiding us to the making of 'Christian decisions' in these matters.

Insofar as any branch of the Christian Church is actively engaged in building up treasure on earth (where not only moth and rust, but human greed and power-seeking corrupt), and encouraging the almost hero-worship of figures powerful in the Christian hierarchy (from the Pope at one end of the spectrum to the Televangelists at the other), it is ignoring, if not actively contradicting, Jesus' views on the blessedness of the state of meekness. Those who worship the hierarchical structure of the organised churches which make up the authoritarian face of Christianity have hardly begun to scratch below the surface of the fact that Jesus placed such emphasis on the desirability of having a humble, non-self-aggrandising attitude, rather than an arrogant, self-righteously opinionated one. In the profound and thought-provoking style of so many of his observations on spiritual matters, Albert Schweitzer ends his short memoir *My Childhood and Youth* with the words, "There is an unmeasured depth of truth in that strange saying of Jesus: 'Blessed are the meek, for they shall inherit the earth.'"

3. People before principles

One of the most powerful truths uttered by Jesus, which puts the stamp of humanism unambiguously on his ethics was, "The Sabbath was made for man, not man for the Sabbath" (Mark 2: 27). Obviously inspired by that concept are those insightful words of Albert Schweitzer, "The essence of true humanitarianess consists in never sacrificing a person to a principle". Although Schweitzer formulated those words as at least a partial definition of humanitarianess, they apply no less aptly to the Christian religion and especially to Christian ethics, which some anonymous deeply spiritual person once perceptively summarised as, "If it comes to a choice between being right and being kind, choose kind".[59]

Jesus' pronouncement about the Sabbath being made for man was made in the context of a discussion of a theme which recurs quite frequently in the gospel record, namely the need for flexibility in applying the Jewish religious law forbidding any work to be done on the Sabbath (Matthew 12: 1-4 and 9-12; Mark 2:23-28 and 3:1-4; and Luke 6: 1-9, 13:10-16, and 14:1-5). From the discussions of this issue in the gospels it is quite clear that Jesus was strongly opposed to any rigid application of the principle of doing no work on the Sabbath. Unfortunately Christians in general have tended to understand the disputes between Jesus and the Pharisees on this matter as representing an 'us versus them', 'Jesus versus the Jews', 'Christianity versus the Jewish religion' situation. Such a view is completely false, not least because Jesus was himself a Jew who never broke with Jewish religion, and because he himself was not a Christian, indeed no Christian Church existed in his lifetime that he could possibly have belonged to. The adversarial 'Jews versus Jesus' idea is also unfortunate in obscuring the fact that adherence to legalistic, fundamentalist views as opposed to those of a more liberal (or "more generously-minded" as Geza Vermes[14] so delightfully calls them) nature on religious matters exists at least as strongly within Christianity as within the Jewish religion[60] (past and present), and probably indeed within all the world's major religions.

The highly relevant illustrations of the ways in which ordinary Jews in a commonsensical way pushed aside the demands of the 'no work on the Sabbath' principle from time to time under pressure of necessity which Jesus uses in making his argument that, "The Sabbath was made for man not man for the Sabbath", are an example of the down-to-earth practicality which runs through so much of his teachings.[61] Jesus may have espoused lofty ethical principles, but he was clearly not so heavenly-minded as to be no earthly use. From time to time he points out the practical advantages of living one's life in harmony with the ethical principles which operate in the Kingdom of God. Indeed it is the fact that Jesus did not try to encourage us to follow his ethical principles because they have such virtuous moral implications but rather because he believed that our following them would lead to a better life for all (not least for ourselves) in the Kingdom of Heaven on earth, that stamp them as humanistic.

Acceptance of the importance of the guideline of 'People first, Principles later,' is one of the things which works together with the principle of meekness and humility to rule out autocratic behaviours of imposing anything more than the barest minimum of rules and regulations on people. When we operate from the position defined by these principles we seek to avoid laying extra burdens on people, and do all we can to compassionately ease the burdens they already carry.

Echoing the German/American theologian Paul Tillich's dictum that, "Love is the ultimate law", William Temple, Archbishop of Canterbury in the mid-twentieth century once wrote, "There is only one ultimate and invariable duty, and its formula is, 'Thou shalt love thy neighbour as thyself'. How to do this is another question, but this is the whole of moral duty".[62] One of the more helpful attempts to clarify exactly which specific behaviours are consistent with loving our neighbour and which are not, while paying due regard to Jesus' urging of us not to sacrifice a person to a principle, was made by Joseph Fletcher, a former Professor of Social Ethics at the Episcopal Theological School, Cambridge, Massachusetts with his concept of Situational Ethics.[63]

Described by the Bishop of Woolwich, John Robinson, in his highly controversial *Honest to God*[64] as profound, but having never quite made it into mainstream Christianity, Situational Ethics has as its most basic principle (as it was for Jesus) that, "There is only one thing that is always good and right, intrinsically good regardless of the context, and that one thing is love". In the case of all other ethical and moral principles their 'rightness' depends on the consequences of applying them in any specific situation. Each ethical principle and moral commandment (for example, "Thou shalt not kill") is neither good nor bad in itself. Its ethical soundness depends on the outcome for human welfare of its application in any particular situation. Fletcher quotes with approval A. N. Whitehead's dictum that, "The simple-minded use of the notion 'right or wrong' is one of the chief obstacles to the progress of understanding".[65]

Situational Ethics requires that decision-making based on ethical or moral principles must flexibly take into account the total situation in which the behaviour occurs, or is going to occur, and the consequences for human well-being that that behaviour has had, or will have. It provides a framework for moral decision-making which is the antithesis of legalistic adherence to rigid moral principles which ignore Jesus' profound truth that the Sabbath, like all ethical and moral principles, exists only to make the world a better place for all. The realities of any particular situation, properly understood, may require disregard of one or more subsidiary ethical and moral principles, if the one inviolable overarching principle of, "There is only one thing that is always good and right, intrinsically good regardless of the context, and that one thing is love," is not to be contravened. The application of any moral principle to any specific case which does not lead to an increase in human happiness is not bringing the Kingdom of God closer to us, no matter how valuable that principle may in general be.

Situational Ethics, being so closely aligned with the ethics of Jesus, is deserving of far more attention than it is appropriate to give it here, but two brief quotes from Fletcher's book will perhaps flesh out the brief summary I have given above of the bare bones of Fletcher's approach.

The first quote relates to a play, *The Rainmaker*, written by Richard Nash in the 1950s which aroused a great deal of media attention. After a lengthy run in the New York Theatre where it was first performed, it was translated into more than 40 languages, and made into a film and a Broadway musical.

But the key to it, ethically, lies in a scene where the morally outraged brother of a lonely, spinsterized girl threatens to shoot the sympathetic but not 'serious' Rainmaker because he makes love to her in the barn at midnight. The Rainmaker's intention is to restore her sense of womanliness and her hopes for marriage and children. Her father, a wise old rancher, grabs the pistol away from his son, saying, 'Noah, you're so full of what's right, you can't see what's good.'[66]

The second quote makes the same point, but even more powerfully.

> The Christian Situation Ethicist agrees with Bertrand Russell and his implied judgment, "To this day Christians think an adulterer more wicked than a politician who takes bribes, although the latter probably does a thousand times as much harm," and he thoroughly rejects Cardinal Newman's view: "The Church holds that it were better for sun and moon to drop from heaven, for the earth to fail, and for all the many millions who are upon it to die of starvation in extremist agony than ... that one soul, I will not say should be lost, but should commit one single venial sin.[67]

To draw this discussion to a close let us remind ourselves that principles, even the profound ethical principles proclaimed by Jesus, are there to improve the quality of human life, not to be obeyed for their own sake. They have no *a priori* validity as a Procrustean bed onto which all human behaviour has to be forced. The criterion for deciding whether or not a particular religious (or any other) principle is a valid one in any particular situation, is whether application of it enhances the quality of human life in this world, never mind about any other.[68] It is profoundly true that, as John de Gruchy put it in his *Being Human: Confessions of a Christian Humanist*, from the perspective of the ethical standpoint which Jesus believed was a core aspect of the Kingdom of God, "People are more important than Religion".[69]

Sadly that is a view shared by very few members of the Christian Church (especially those towards the top end of the hierarchies of its various branches), members who for the most part believe they are part of a religious organisation based on the teachings of Jesus of Nazareth. To believe that the Sabbath, and all the other paraphernalia of Christian ritual and dogma are eternally, universally, and intrinsically true and valuable, and that each of us must put obedience to the dictates of our particular branch of the Christian Church first in our lives, whatever the human cost, is oppressive, anti-life, anti-human-happiness and absolutely contrary to both the spirit and some of the specifics of the ethical principles proclaimed by Jesus.

Insofar as Christianity is indeed based on the teachings of Jesus, any activities on its part which create fear, self-doubt, and seek to impose a rigid legalism on the human psyche, are profoundly unchristian. How far-sighted of Jesus it was to predict that there would be those in the future who in his name would do "many wonderful works", prophesying and casting out devils, and suchlike, to whom he would have to say, "I never knew you: depart from me, ye that work iniquity" (Matthew 7:21-23). 'Calling on the name of the Lord', claiming to be acting on behalf of God or Jesus does not make the activities of anyone acceptable from the standpoint of Christian ethics, whether it be the Pope, George Bush and his ardent evangelical 'Born Again' supporters, the Yorkshire Ripper with his 'God-given' mission to murder prostitutes, or any of the other occupants of mental hospitals who make similar claims of being privileged with a hotline to God. For the Christian who takes seriously the ethical teachings of Jesus, it is the degree of consistency of anyone's actions with the ethical principles that Jesus proclaimed which provides an index of in how far those actions can justifiably be called Christian, and that the motivation for those deeds can be legitimately described as 'divine inspiration'.

4. Non-judgementalness
One of the things which flows from the idea of putting people

before principles is to refrain from publicly condemning and pronouncing moral judgements on any behaviours we see in people we are interacting with which we feel are wrong. Of course we all inevitably form opinions from time to time as to the desirability or otherwise of some of the behaviours we observe in ourselves and others. But it is one thing to hold the belief that any particular behaviour is wrong and that the world would be a better place if that behaviour were desisted from: it is quite another to condemn those who carry out such behaviours as 'bad', or 'wicked' when they do something that we disapprove of.

There are two major reasons why Jesus' principle of non-judgementalness is a helpful one in our quest to become a better and a happier person, to enter more fully into the Kingdom of God, and to help others in their journey along that same path.

The one is a matter of practical psychology. When Jesus said, "Judge not that ye be not judged" (Matthew, 7:1-2), he was not issuing us with a finger-wagging warning of the awful consequences that await us in the next life if we have the temerity to pronounce judgement on other people, things, or situations. He was merely stating the simple psychological fact that whenever we express a judgement we are inevitably putting on display our own standards of judgement, and will in turn be judged as either possessing or lacking praiseworthy standards of good judgement. If I dismiss Rodin's sculpture *The Thinker* as a rather poorly executed attempt to turn a lump of stone into some sort of human likeness, I in no way diminish the value of that profound work of art, but I do expose myself as a philistine in matters of aesthetic sensitivity. If I express admiration of a powerful and ruthless military leader, I expose to the world some of the values that guide my own behaviour. If I enthuse over 'the goodness' of someone who in my opinion has made an important contribution to making the world a better place, I am making public some of the criteria I apply in evaluating anyone's humanitarian efforts, including my own. Anyone who becomes aware of my judgement in such matters will regard me in either a positive or a negative light for having the standards of judgement that I do apply in such matters. It is precisely this truth which Jesus was alluding to when he said, "Judge not that ye be not judged. For with the measure you mete it shall be measured to you again" (Matthew 7:1, Mark 4:24, and Luke 6:37-38).

The other major reason why pronouncing moral judgements on people has no part in the ethical guidelines Jesus believed to operate in the Kingdom of God is the demoralising, demotivating effect being judged as in some way 'bad' has on a person. Telling someone that they are a 'bad' person has effects on that person directly antagonistic to the effects of behaving towards them in the sort of kind, compassionate forgiving way typical of Jesus' way of relating to people. In the more than forty years I have spent as a church organist I have listened to literally hundreds of sermons. The content of most of them has been almost instantly forgettable, but one statement by a deeply spiritual Methodist Minister, Tom Parker, remains vividly etched in my memory. A wonderfully humble man (who started his working life at the age of 15 as a miner in the Durham coalfields in Northern England), he reminded his congregation that, "We never need love more than when we are at our most unlovable." His words echo the thoughts behind those two powerful lines of the hymn, *My Song is Love Unknown*,

Love to the loveless shown,
That they might lovely be.

A corollary to Tom Parker's formulation is of course the equally powerful truth that we never need to hear condemnation of ourselves as morally blameworthy less than when we are at our most unlovable. There is nothing more likely to make it difficult for others to love us, than feeling that we are being persecuted by an inner tyrant who is constantly condemning us for not being good enough in terms of those qualities which our upbringing has taught us to value particularly highly.

When someone seems to have done something wrong, those who try to live their lives in accordance with the ethical principles proclaimed by Jesus seek understanding of what happened, and try to find helpful ways of intervening in the situation. They do not cast stones at the offender, but seek to inspire them to a better life rather than to punish them for their faults. They are quick to see the beam in their own eye before they try to remove the speck of dust from the eye of the wrongdoer (Matthew, 7:2-5). They know all too well that kindness and compassion are not to be reserved just for the good. Jesus was adamant that his message was not primarily directed at 'the good', but rather at "lost sheep" (Matthew 15:24). We all have a right to expect to be treated with kindness, compassion, and respect, not just when we have 'been good', but when we have been anything but good. If Christian love is not to be just a manipulative reward for good behaviour, if it does not flow to both the deserving and the undeserving, it is a sham.

In terms of Christian ethics, love is to be seen, not as a reward for goodness but as something every human being has a right to receive. The birthright of all human beings is to be loved, to be enjoyed, to be found to be a source of pleasure, to be appreciated. We are most truly human when we feel, (and seek to arouse that feeling in others), emotional warmth, and love, kindness and compassion for all human beings, good or bad, whether they have done good to us or wronged us. We may not always like some of them, we may not always want to spend much time with them, but when we see through their unpleasant exterior to the good and beautiful, but often battered and traumatised child within, and pour our love and caring compassion into them, then we are fulfilling our destiny: to become a being through whom the divine light shines – that entity of which Ralph Waldo Emerson wrote,

Within man is the soul of the whole; the wise silence; the universal beauty, to which every part and particle is equally related; the eternal One. When it breaks through his intellect, it is genius; when it breathes through his will, it is virtue; when it flows through his affections, it is love.

It is sad that so many in the Christian Church see not doing wrong as the goal of existence, rather than achieving happiness for ourselves and everyone else, for such is the transforming power which lies at the heart of Christian Ethics that this is an achievable goal.

5. Mutuality/Reciprocity

Forgiveness is the answer to the child's dream of a miracle by which what is broken is made whole again, what is soiled is again made clean. That dream explains why we need to be forgiven and why we must forgive. In the presence of God, nothing stands between Him and us – we *are* forgiven. But we cannot *feel* his presence if anything is allowed to stand between others and ourselves. – Dag Hammarskjöld. *Markings*

If there is one area where humanistic Christianity differs most strongly from authoritarian Christianity it is in the ideas which constitute the conception of the forgiveness of sins. In the next chapter I shall discuss at some length the ideas on this subject to be found among those whose beliefs make up the authoritarian face of Christianity. The conception of what the forgiveness of sins is all about in the ethical teachings of Jesus which make up the humanistic face of the religion is radically different from what is to be found in its authoritarian face.

Forgiveness for our 'manifold sins and wickedness' is not something bestowed (or withheld) by a supreme ruler of the universe, and has nothing whatsoever to do with the suffering and death of Jesus, but flows effortlessly and naturally from the cause and effect way the universe functions. The necessary and sufficient condition for forgiveness of ourselves to take place, for us to be once more restored to harmony with God within us and the universe as a whole, is an attitude on our part of forgiveness towards others – "It is in forgiving others that we ourselves are forgiven", as the last line of that inspired Prayer attributed to St. Francis of Assisi puts it, echoing the reciprocity between the giving and receiving of forgiveness which is implied in Jesus' formulation of those words of the Lord's Prayer, "Forgive us our trespasses as we forgive those that trespass against us."

St Francis' prayer also beautifully and succinctly expresses the more general form of the principle of reciprocity or mutuality ("It is in giving that we receive"), of which the way in which our forgiving of others brings us forgiveness for ourselves is one special case. Well known as it is, it is worth quoting that prayer of St Francis in full because not only does it provide a masterly statement of the ethical principle of Reciprocity/Mutuality which is so central to Jesus' conception of the way the world works, but by preceding those superb last two lines with twelve statements of compassionate intention, it integrates the ethical principles of loving and having compassionate concern for our neighbour with the psychological principles of the Power of the Positive, and the virtues of empowered proactive behaviour into a unified whole.

Lord, make me an instrument of thy peace.
Where there is hate, let me sow love,
Where there is wrong, forgiveness,
Where there is discord, harmony,
Where there is error, truth,
Where there is doubt, belief,
Where there is despair, hope,
Where there is darkness, light,
Where there is sorrow, joy.

Let me strive more to comfort others
Than to be comforted,
To understand others than to be understood,
To love others more than to be loved.
For it is in giving that we receive;
It is in forgiving others that we are forgiven.

It is to be noted that the person praying this prayer is not asking for help in becoming more self-sacrificing. Our first duty in trying to make the world a better place is to look after our own needs. Any puritanical refusal to do that robs our attempts to "Love our neighbour as our self" of much of its potential to provide a blessing for the object of our love. Selfishness, like meekness, has had a bad press, but unless we look after our own welfare first and foremost we have little hope of being all the good that we could be for others. The very structure of our body demonstrates the importance of this principle. The first place to which the heart pumps freshly oxygenated blood is not the brain (as we might expect, because of the control that organ exerts over all aspects of bodily functioning), but to itself. If keeping itself functioning at peak efficiency were not the primary goal of the functioning of the heart, its ability to supply the rest of the body with what it needs would rapidly decline.[70] The virtue of seeking the satisfaction to at least some extent of our own needs ahead of those of others, which we might appropriately describe as 'self-concern', only becomes the vice of what is commonly described pejoratively as 'selfishness' when we forget (or fail to act on whatever memory we have of the principle), that doing good to others can be a very deeply satisfying pleasure to ourselves, and that we can never know lasting peace and joy unless doing good to others plays at least some role in our lives.

Equally though, we need to remember that one may live a life devoted to the service of others without sacrificing one's own happiness. It is all a matter of balance. Sometimes it will be for the greatest good of the greatest number if for a time we sacrifice the short-term meeting of some need or other of our own in order to meet the needs of others, but sometimes it will be for the best for all concerned if for a while we sacrifice the meeting of the needs of others for the meeting of our own. Charity begins at home – literally, and specifically with our own selves.

It would be hard to overemphasize the importance Jesus attached to this principle that a good done to others becomes a good for ourselves, and it is clear that for Jesus, Love, Compassion, and Forgiveness are all closely intertwined with each other. Part of this truth is captured in the beatitude, "Blessed are the merciful for they shall obtain mercy". (Matthew 5:7). It is also illustrated (amongst other places) in his attitude to the prostitute to whom he said, "Thy sins are forgiven". (Luke 7:48). Explaining his attitude to the woman's wrongdoing the punchline is, "Wherefore I say unto thee, Her sins which are many, are forgiven; for she loved much" (Luke 7:47).

The two processes of giving and receiving form a virtuous circle of mutual influence and causation. The more we forgive others the more we shall experience the peace of knowing that our own sins are forgiven, and the more we experience that, the more we shall find it easy and natural to forgive other people for their wrongdoing.

But how do we get the process started? It is sometimes very hard, if not seemingly impossible, to bring ourselves to forgive those who have wronged us or those who are close to us. How can we help ourselves in this difficult task? First and foremost by forgiving ourselves for our own faults and failings (including the difficulty we sometimes have in forgiving others). The more we can come to terms with our Shadow (as described in Chapter 2), and accept that we have the potential to behave in some situations in ways that we dislike and of which we disapprove, the more we are in touch with reality. This is the exact opposite of the situation where we deny and repress parts of ourselves, which causes us to be 'a house divided against itself'.

The more we adopt an attitude of gentle acceptance towards those parts of ourselves that we dislike and want to disown, the easier we shall find it to love ourselves. This does not mean approving of what we do when some aspects of our Shadow are asserting themselves. It just means that we accept that we have certain human failings, and do not condemn ourselves as being 'bad' because of possessing them. In a beautiful paradox, this makes it easier not to actualise the potential we all carry for behaving towards others in unforgiving ways. The more we love ourselves, the more love we shall have overflowing in our hearts to give to others, and the easier and more natural we shall find it to forgive others for their imperfections. Disarming our enemy by loving him or her is a powerful principle which applies as much to any internal enemy we carry within ourselves as to any external one. The more we are able to forgive others for their sins,[71] the deeper will be our own experience of self-acceptance, compassionate love for all, and that "Peace of God which passeth all understanding" (Philippians 4:7).

6. Inversion of the power hierarchy

In the Kingdom of God, power relations are very different from, and often the very opposite of what they are in the everyday world. The theme of, "The last shall be first and the first shall be last", is a recurrent one in the gospels: "But many that are first shall be last; and the last shall be first" (Matthew 19:30), "So the last shall be first, and the first last" (Matthew 20:16), "But many that are first shall be last; and the last first" (Mark 10: 31), and, "Behold, there are last which shall be first, and there are first which shall be last" (Luke 13: 30). There are several different aspects to this theme which is so strongly emphasised in the gospels.

6.1 Gentleness stronger than violence – not resisting evil.

We have already discussed Jesus' belief, expressed in one of the Beatitudes, that, "Blessed are the peacemakers: for they shall be called the children of God", indicative of his compassion for those caught up in conflict of one sort or another. However, his compassion went well beyond merely alleviating the sufferings of those damaged physically or mentally by conflict. It is hard to know whether his reported statements, "Resist not evil" (Matthew 5:39), and, "All they that take the sword shall perish with the sword" (Matthew 26:52), together with the commandment, "Thou shalt not kill", (an important part of the Old Testament law which Jesus said he came to fulfil, not to destroy) (Matthew 5:17), are indicative of his holding an absolute pacifist position, or whether in reality he differentiated between situations in which any violent act should be eschewed at all costs and those in which it must be seen as the lesser of two evils. This part of Christian ethics is one which has caused deep-thinking Christians much soul-searching. Is Jesus really saying that we should refrain from taking violent action under any circumstances whatsoever? If shooting to kill is the only way to stop a would-be murderer from achieving his objective (and that is a big 'If'), should we really refrain from taking such action?

The problem with understanding Jesus' position on 'Resisting not evil' is that what we have recorded in the gospels as Jesus' pronouncements on the subject are virtually certainly not all he had to say on the topic. Just how far even those disciples who were closest to him were from grasping the full depth of his ethics is vividly illustrated by the fact that right at the end of his teaching career, when the "band of men and officers from the chief priests and Pharisees ... (came) ... with lanterns and torches and weapons" (John 18:3) to take Jesus captive "Simon Peter having a sword drew it, and smote the high priest's servant, and cut off his right ear" (John 18:10, Mark 14:47 and Matthew 26:51).

In doing so he earned the rebuke from Jesus, "Put up thy sword again into his place: for all they that take the sword shall perish with the sword" (Matthew 26:52, and John 18:11). The disciples, and even more so those gospel writers who had never met Jesus, were in no position to give us a succinct and accurate summary of exactly what Jesus meant when he said, "Resist not Evil", and he certainly must have said a good deal more on that subject than we have any record of.

What we do know is that Jesus pretty certainly did say something to the effect of, "The Sabbath was made for man, not man for the Sabbath," and insisted on carrying out acts of healing on the Sabbath, reflecting a belief, as Albert Schweitzer summarised it, in "Never sacrificing a person to a principle". To take no action to stop a criminal from wounding and killing others because to do that would involve violating Jesus' ethical principle of not resisting evil is to disregard his other more all-embracing principle of never sacrificing a person to a principle, "The Sabbath was made for man, not man for the Sabbath". The issue of how absolute a pacifist position is most in harmony with Jesus' thinking is a difficult one which needs to be given much more attention than it generally gets. Schweitzer's profound ethical principle of *Reverence for Life* (briefly summarised in Appendix 3) marks one significant step forward in clarifying this matter.

Going one step further

But Jesus' attitude to dealing with wrongdoing goes one daring, revolutionary step beyond mere passive, non-aggressive acceptance of the fact that wrongdoing exists, and refraining from meeting violence with violence. He urges us to be proactive in bringing the principle of loving our neighbour into all conflict situations where in our opinion our neighbour has done something wrong. The core of his teaching in this respect is to be found at Matthew 5:38-48 (and also in Luke 6:27-36).

Ye have heard that it hath been said, An eye for an eye, and a tooth for a tooth: But I say unto you, That ye resist not evil: But whosoever shall smite thee on thy right cheek, turn to him the other also. And if any man will sue thee at the law, and take away thy coat, let him have thy cloke also. And whosoever should compel thee to go a mile, go with him twain. Give to him that asketh thee, and from him that would borrow of thee turn not thou away. Ye have heard that it hath been said, Thou shalt love thy neighbour, and hate thine enemy. But I say unto you, Love your enemies, bless them that curse you, do good to them that hate you, and pray for them which despitefully use you, and persecute you; That ye may be the children of your Father which is in Heaven: for he maketh his sun to rise on the evil and on the good, and sendeth rain on the just and on the unjust. For if ye love them which love you, what reward have ye? do not even the publicans the same? And if ye salute your brethren only, what do ye more than others? do not even the publicans so? Be ye therefore perfect, even as your Father which is in Heaven is perfect.

The recommendation to, "Love your enemies", and to, "Pray for those who despitefully use you" (Matthew. 5:44), is a complete inversion of the attitudes typically found in the world. Although few members of the Christian Church have probably ever given the matter any conscious thought, there is good reason to suspect that many of them either do not take Jesus' urging of us to love our enemies seriously, or regard that as a bridge too far, one that ordinary Christians cannot be expected to cross. Perhaps some who feel that way justify the limits they place on their compassion by saying to themselves, "I do love my neighbour, but my enemy is not my neighbour. He or she has forfeited their right to be regarded as such by making themselves my enemy".

Although of course there are many honourable exceptions to this generalisation, Christians, as a group, are no less prone to demonising their enemies, so as to place them outside the protection of humanitarian law and so (some would feel) outside the limits of applicability of Christian Ethics as are non-Christians. But Christian Ethics are applicable to everyone, friend and foe alike, and to act as though they are not, leads at times to the most appalling abuses of human rights, and to a culture of escalating violence. That the horrendous cruelties practised on suspected Muslim terrorists in the aftermath of 9/11 and the Iraq war were at the very least condoned by some professing Christians is an acutely painful and worrying fact for those of us who are committed to living our lives according to the ethical principles espoused by Jesus. Even more horrifying in some respects is the way in which the pre-1994 South African government subverted the rule of law to create a police state in order to carry out its oppressive cruelties towards the black disenfranchised majority – all in the name of preserving Christian values against the onslaught of 'Godless Communism'.

When someone is behaving in ways of which we approve and that give us pleasure, the more we express our delight in what they are doing, the more we are acting in accordance with that aspect of compassionate love for all, which seeks to fill the lives of others with joy. Many of us are far too slow to express our enthusiasm for the good things we see in other people's behaviour which delight us, and do not make use of the many opportunities life offers us to enrich the lives of others with positive energy. When we do seize such opportunities, we make it more likely that those individuals will continue to behave in ways which we believe to be virtuous.

When someone is behaving in ways which we believe to be wrong, and not in the best interests of themselves and/or others, the principle of compassionate, caring love for all behoves us to communicate that fact to them. How we communicate that disapproval is the crucial factor which determines whether or not in doing so we are acting in accordance with the ethical principles Jesus proclaimed. Even without using any physical violence, trying to hurt someone whom we see as 'our enemy' by telling them that they are morally defective, have a dreadful personality, or some other insulting and judgemental words to that effect is completely unhelpful in bringing about positive change in their behaviour, and completely contrary to the profound ethical core at the heart of Jesus' teaching.

Whether we see someone as our enemy because of some infractions of an ethical or moral principle we hold dear, or because they are engaged in life- or happiness-threatening behaviour towards ourselves or others, what we need to do is to express our feelings to the individual concerned about that behaviour. They need to know that we believe that the way in which they are behaving is not ultimately in their own or anybody else's best interests.

Sometimes of course the person we are communicating with in that way will just ignore what we say to them, but it is often enough to change someone's behaviour to just let them know in a non-aggressive and non-condemning way that we find what they are doing distressing. Nowhere is this more true than in emotionally intimate and family relationships, but we nearly always need to do this whenever we encounter cases of what we believe to be wrongdoing. Sometimes however the situation is of such a nature that it feels to us to be a matter of urgency to put a stop to the behaviour which is angering us, and feel the need to intervene angrily and physically to bring this about as quickly as possible.

Jesus' behaviour in the *Cleansing of the Temple* incident, if it was reported reasonably accurately in the gospels, was probably of this type. In verses 12 and 13 of the twenty-first chapter of the gospel of Matthew[72] we read,

And Jesus went into the temple of God, and cast out all them that sold and bought in the temple, and overthrew the tables of the money-changers, and the seats of them that sold doves, and said unto them, It is written, My house shall be called the house of prayer; but ye have made it a den of thieves.

Two things are important to note about this incident. In the first place it was clearly first and foremost Jesus' intention to put a stop to the commercial transactions taking place in what he obviously strongly believed should be a place of prayer and meditation. He took action to stop what he believed was wrong-doing detrimental to the spiritual growth of those coming to the Temple. He did not just abusively harangue the wrongdoers in the hope of shaming them into seeing the error of their ways, but first and foremost took action to stop what he saw as wrongful behaviour.

Secondly we shall never know exactly how much of what Jesus is reported in the gospels to have said and done during that incident he actually did say and do[73], and how much was an imaginative reconstruction by the gospel writers of the event which tells us more about how they would have behaved in that situation than about what Jesus did actually say and do. It is of course also possible that Jesus was so carried away by his anger towards those who were turning a religiously-inspired temple into a market place for commercial transactions, that he temporarily forgot one of the tenets of his own ethical approach to wrongdoing. If there is any truth in that speculation, reflecting on it should help us to be gentler with ourselves when our behaviour falls short of the ideals we passionately hold as to what constitutes right behaviour.

Whatever the truth of the matter, this incident does usefully remind us of the fact that whilst we shall be able to deal with many of the situations of wrongdoing we encounter in life with an attitude of loving concern for the re-education of the wrongdoer, from time to time we shall encounter examples of what we believe to be wrong behaviour which fill us with anger, and where our urgent priority may well be to stop that behaviour as quickly as possible. If we are committed to the principle of non-violence, as the physiological imperative for vigorous action subsides, we will be able to move into a calmer mode of re-education of the offender. If we are not committed to Jesus' principle of non-violence, we shall probably seek to punish and crush the wrongdoer for their bad behaviour, and add to the sum total of the world's misery by leaving behind a mass of unresolved guilt, anger and resentment.

In trying as far as possible to meet violence not with violence, but with education we are acting in accordance with the principle of loving our enemies. This idea is also expressed in the old adage that, 'Two wrongs don't make a right' that was the basis of the political principle of passive resistance espoused by the powerfully effective Civil Rights activist Martin Luther King in the United States, and before that by Mahatma Gandhi in his eventually successful struggle to win independence for India from Britain.

Implementing a non-violent approach to political conflict requires considerable courage and a willingness to take responsibility for one's own behaviour in creating and maintaining conflict situations, something which is so much more difficult to do than to demonise the enemy and in an adrenaline-fuelled rage seek to annihilate him or her with a display of shock and awe tactics. Apart from the hormonal pressures for vigorous action which build up when we feel threatened, two other factors which militate against the widespread adoption of passive resistance policies of a 'love your enemies' type are, firstly the fact that such approaches often take time to show results, and in our disappointment with the lack of immediate signs of progress in winning over the enemy, we are too easily tempted to believe that the method just doesn't work.

Secondly, persisting in our non-violent attempts to overcome our enemy's antagonism towards us invariably requires us to look with brutal honesty at what contribution our own faults are making to the existence of the problem. Albert Schweitzer, in his *Memories of Childhood and Youth*, has pertinently reminded those of us who try to counter violence with love (one of the most difficult tasks facing those of us who align ourselves with the ethics of Jesus) that,

> All acts and facts are a product of spiritual power, the successful ones of power which is strong enough; the unsuccessful ones of power that is too weak. Does my behaviour in respect of love effect nothing? That is because there is not enough love in me. Am I powerless against the untruthfulness and the lies which have their being all around me? The reason is that I myself am not truthful enough. Have I to watch dislike and ill-will carrying on their sad game? That means that I myself have not yet completely laid aside small-mindedness and envy. Is my love of peace misunderstood and scorned? That means that I am not yet sufficiently peace-loving.[74]

Elsewhere Schweitzer makes a similar point when he says, "Example is not the main thing in influencing others. It is the only thing."

Using gentleness to overcome violence has the potential to create a WIN-WIN outcome of conflict. This is well described by Harold Loukes in his brief summary of one of the reasons why the Quaker movement so wholeheartedly embraces Jesus' belief that gentleness is ultimately stronger than violence. He writes:

> Seek not to crush tyrants but to awaken men's minds to the loving spirit in which they will desire to put by the fruits of tyranny. Counter falsehood with truth, ignorance with knowledge, hardness of heart with a tenderness that seeks the victims of wrong. So shall you save the victim from his tyrant

and the tyrant from his tyranny.[75]

Similar thinking to this underlies the dramatic success of Nelson Mandela's reconciliatory rather than retaliatory stance on his release from 27 years of imprisonment at the hands of the South African apartheid government. Had the country's first black leader at that critical transition period been bent on revenge and the punishment of former oppressors, the country could well have gone up in flames. Describing his feelings at the time of his release from prison, Mandela wrote, "As I walked out the door toward the gate that would lead to my freedom, I knew if I didn't leave my bitterness and hatred behind, I'd still be in prison".

The implication of what we know of the thinking of Jesus in regard to conflict resolution is that it is first and foremost a feeling of compassion towards others which should determine our response to all people, regardless of their behaviour. This of course does not mean turning a blind eye to wrongdoing. Putting a stop to any behaviour which we believe is harmful to anyone is a responsibility we all have, but it needs to be done in the most constructive way possible. Intervening to stop something from happening can be done out of concern for both the injured party and the person inflicting the injuries (physical or mental). Applying moralistic judgements about how sinful or stupid someone is being, is not a loving behaviour. Crucially, people react this way because it relieves their own feelings of frustrated, impotent rage. It may intimidate the other person into stopping what they are doing for a while, but it leaves a trail of hurt, anger and rebelliousness in its wake. For Jesus, being kind is not something we bestow on others as a reward for their good behaviour or withhold from them as a punishment for their bad behaviour, but something which ought to be our default position in our interactions with all nature, human, animal and environmental.

Does it work?

It is often no easy task to decide exactly what response to wrong-doing is most consistent with Christian Ethics, quite aside from the difficulty we inevitably sometimes have in implementing our ideas about how to deal with any particular situation. In trying to gain some clarity on this issue, readers may find it helpful to reflect on two very different responses to wrongdoing, the first of which reflects a view diametrically opposite to that encouraged by Jesus, and the other which is a heartwarming instance of the power of taking literally Jesus' urging of us to do good to those who have harmed us.

The first is the recent American-led and British-supported war in Iraq to topple Saddam Hussein's regime. There was widespread acknowledgement of the brutality of that regime, but the effects of tackling it by unleashing massive 'shock and awe' military destruction on the country has in many ways created an even more horrendous situation in terms of human suffering than existed before the 'liberation' of the country by the forces of 'democracy'. That this way of dealing with the problem of Iraq, in which 'devout Christians' played such important leadership roles runs counter to just about every tenet of the ethics of Jesus, must inevitably be a source of deep concern to those who see their spiritual home as lying within the human-istic face of Christianity.

The other totally different, Jesus-like approach to dealing with wrongdoing is exemplified in a story about Albert Schweitzer and his mission hospital in Lambarene in tropical Africa. The story comes from a Methodist church magazine of a few years ago.

People who think the Sermon on the Mount is not possible in action should hear a little story of Schweitzer. A man stole his canoe but did not get the paddle. Hearing of the theft, Schweitzer went to see the man, who stoutly denied it. 'O, yes,' said Schweitzer, 'you did take it, but as it won't be much use to you without the paddle, I have brought you that.' He laid down the paddle and went away. It is not surprising that the next morning both canoe and paddle were found outside his house! A clear case of the cloak and the coat also.

There is, I believe, a great deal more to the related principles of forgiveness, loving our enemies, and "doing good to those who despitefully use us" that Jesus recommended, than most of us have yet understood. If Christians were to spend more time reflecting on and discussing the practical implications and difficulties of applying these ideas, and less on wallowing in the blood of the Lamb, the world would be a much gentler, kinder, and more beautiful place than it is today. One example of the sort of thinking about this subject which I have found helpful in my own life is contained in a parable written by the late Catholic priest Father Anthony de Mello, S.J.,

A grocer came to the Master in great distress to say that across the way from his shop they had opened a large chain store that would drive him out of business. His family had owned his shop for a century, and to lose it now would be his undoing, for there was nothing else he was skilled at.

Said the Master, "If you fear the owner of the chain store, you will hate him. And hatred will be your undoing."

"What shall I do?" said the distraught grocer.

"Each morning walk out of your shop onto the sidewalk and bless your shop, wishing it prosperity. Then turn to face the chain store and bless it too."

"What? Bless my competitor and destroyer?"

"Any blessing you give him will rebound to your good. Any evil you wish him will destroy you."

After six months the grocer returned to report that he had had to close down his shop as he had feared, but he was now in charge of the chain store and his affairs were in better shape than ever before.

Common sense and the ethic of non-violence

One of the reasons for the wide appeal of the ethics which Jesus proclaimed is that although they touch profound spiritual depths, many of them have sound commonsensical validity. For example there is more to recommend following Jesus' advice to, "Agree with thine adversary quickly, whiles thou art in the way with him," than just chalking up ethical Brownie Points. As Jesus goes on to explain, "lest at any time the adversary deliver thee to the judge, and the judge deliver thee to the officer, and thou be cast into prison" (Matthew 5:25). Fighting with people in the hope of forcing them to accept the rightness of our own position more often than not just elicits the determination on their part to impose a WIN-LOSE outcome of the dispute on us, and as often as not they are successful in that attempt. This adds force to Jesus' recommendation not to try to counter violence with violence as one of the practical guidelines which flows from his belief that gentleness is stronger than violence. His thinking in this respect is very much in line with that of the writer of Proverbs who wrote, "A soft answer turneth away wrath: but grievous words stir up anger" (Proverbs 15:1).

The psychological fact that antagonism produces an adversarial attitude is a powerful reason why responding to wrongdoing with a forgiving generosity of spirit instead of retaliation is not just ethically praiseworthy, but sound common sense practical advice.[76] This philosophy is delightfully illustrated in an old fable about a contest between the sun and the wind as to which of the two was most powerful.

The North Wind and the Sun once fell into a dispute as to which was stronger of the two. They related their most famous exploits and each ended as he began, by thinking he had the greater power.

Just then a traveller came in sight, and they agreed to test the matter by trying to see which of them could soonest make the traveller remove his cloak.

The boastful North Wind was the first to try, the Sun meanwhile watching behind a grey cloud. He blew a furious blast and nearly tore the cloak from its fastening; but the Man only held his cloak more closely and Old Boreas spent his strength in vain.

Mortified by his failure to do so simple a thing, the Wind withdrew at last in despair. 'I don't believe you can do it, either,' he said.

Then out came the kindly Sun in all his splendour, dispelling the clouds that had gathered and sending his warmest rays down upon the traveller's head.

The Man, looked up gratefully, but growing faint with sudden heat, he quickly flung aside his cloak, and hastened for comfort to the nearest shade.

It is also powerfully expressed in some words of Albert Schweitzer written near the end of his life towards the end of his book *My Childhood and Youth*.

As one who tries to remain youthful in his thinking and feeling, I have struggled against facts and experience on behalf of belief in the good and the true. At the present time when violence, clothed in life, dominates the world more cruelly than it ever has before, I still remain convinced that truth, love, peaceableness, meekness, and kindness are the power which can master all violence.[77]

6.2 Spiritual greatness does not come from one's positional power and status in the world

In the Kingdom of Heaven greatness is not measured by how much earthly power one wields, but rather by how much one does for others. "Whomsoever would be greatest among you, let him be your servant." (Luke 22:24-26), "But he that is greatest among you shall be your servant." (Matthew 23:11), and, "Whosoever of you will be the chiefest, shall be servant of all". (See also Mark 9:33-34; Matt 18:1; and Luke 9:46).

In living in accordance with the ethical principles Jesus propounded, "How can I serve you?", rather than, "What use can you be to me?", is the dominant unspoken thought which pervades much of our interaction with others. It is who one is as a person, as a human being, not one's place in society that is really important. Being in the Kingdom of God means being in a state of mind in which (among other things) one responds to people for who they are, rather than because of the power and influence they wield in the material world.

The inversion of the power hierarchy in Christian Ethics is further illustrated in Jesus' polemic against the scribes recorded in Mark 12:38-40 and in Luke 20:46-47:

Beware of the scribes, which love to go in long clothing, and love salutations in the market places, And the chief seats in the synagogues, and the uppermost rooms at feasts: Which devour widows' houses, and for a pretence make long prayers.

In Matthew 23: 5-7, similar criticism is launched against both the scribes and the Pharisees:

All their works they do for to be seen of men; they make broad their phylacteries, and enlarge the borders of their garments And love the uppermost rooms at feasts and the chief seats in the synagogues, And greetings in the market, and to be called of men, Rabbi, Rabbi.

After which, at verses 11 and 12, he reminds his disciples that:

But he that is greatest among you shall be your servant. And whosoever shall exalt himself shall be abased; and he that shall humble himself shall be exalted.

In discussing these words of Jesus, Geza Vermes in his invaluable *The Authentic Gospel of Jesus* writes, "Note that in Mark's warning against the behaviour of the scribes there is no hint at false teaching on their part; neither are they blamed for preventing ordinary Jews from serving God. It is for their misguided zeal, self-importance and exhibitionism that they are criticized".[78] This is obviously closely connected with the ethical principle of meekness and humility which we looked at earlier in this chapter.

But the most dramatic illustration of Jesus' rejection of the unattractive spiritual poverty which he believed lay behind the ostentatious display of worldly power and wealth was his choice of the style of his triumphal entry into Jerusalem in what he knew was going to be the grand finale of his mission on earth. Instead of entering the city on a richly decorated, powerful and intimidating warhorse, he chose to enter it riding on a simple donkey, the ultimate symbol of non-self-aggrandising humility. And instead of being accompanied by a band of armed supporters ready to attack, it was the palms waved by the enthusiastically welcoming crowd which were in evidence. Although that triumphal entry ended in disaster in the eyes of the world at the time, Jesus' teachings live on to exert a powerful humanising effect on a huge number of people, more than were ever influenced by them during his lifetime. In his death Jesus has exerted an even more powerful effect than he did in his life. Even that seems to give some powerful support to the validity of his belief in the value of inverting the traditional power hierarchy.

6.3 Becoming as little children

One of the most striking differences between the path to spiritual perfection as outlined by Jesus in the ethical principles which he taught, and what we find in so many religions (including Christianity), is in attitudes towards our biological nature. For so many leaders in the field of religious thinking there is a fundamental dichotomy between the physical and the spiritual, and the desire to satisfy our longings in each of those realms are (in their opinion) in constant conflict with each other. In this way of looking at things, 'the world, the flesh and the devil', our 'carnal mind', 'the old Adam', is a snare and a delusion, tempting us into the paths of error and sin away from our 'real destiny' as children of God. Jesus' very different thinking in this respect is absolutely consistent with, indeed even a necessary consequence of his total commitment to the ethical principle of love of God, of our neighbour, and of ourselves. Nowhere does Jesus suggest that physical pleasure is something which takes us away from the experience of oneness with God. Geza Vermes writes,

> In sharp contrast to his (early) mentor John the Baptist who lived on a diet of locusts and wild honey, Jesus did not dislike a good meal. He sat at the table of wealthy publicans. In the famous parable of the prodigal son the father, symbolising God, welcomes the return of his wayward child with a lavish party.[79]

He clearly enjoyed the sensual pleasure of having his feet massaged with ointment by the woman "who was a sinner" (i.e. most probably a prostitute) as reported in Luke 7:37-38. As to healing those suffering and in pain, if Jesus had believed anything even remotely like Pope John Paul II's nonsense about suffering being part of God's saving plan for humanity he would never have spent as much time and energy as he did in healing the sick and suffering. In this respect St Paul, despite the valuable work he did in the early church and the beautiful spiritual insights he was sometimes capable of (as expressed for example in I Corinthians 13, and Galatians 6:22-23) got it wrong.

Paul's thinking expressed in such statements as, "To be carnally minded is death; but to be spiritually minded is life and peace" (Romans 8:6), "The carnal mind is enmity against God" (Romans 8:7), and, "If ye live after the flesh, ye shall die: but if ye through the Spirit do mortify the deeds of the body, ye shall live" (Romans 8:13), is a thousand miles away from anything that we know of Jesus' thinking about the biological realities of our human nature. We shall look at this issue in some detail in Chapter 7.

Whilst so many approaches to deepening spiritual experience involve a life of abstinence from any sort of physical pleasure, of going through rituals and obeying rules and regulations to control and suppress our normal human nature, to take us further and further away from the uninhibited physicality of the childhood state to adult spiritual bliss, Jesus preached exactly the opposite. In the context of answering the question his disciples asked him, "Who is the greatest in the kingdom of heaven?" (Matt. 18:1), Jesus asserted, "Unless you change and become like little children, you will never enter the kingdom of heaven. Therefore whoever humbles himself like this child is the greatest in the kingdom of heaven" (Matthew 18:3-4), and a little later, "Jesus called them unto him, and said, suffer little children to come unto me, and forbid them not: for of such is the kingdom of God". This subject is one on which all three of the synoptic gospels show particularly strong agreement.

For Jesus, childhood is not a state of spiritual immaturity but rather one of spiritual richness from which most of us become increasingly alienated as we grow older.

What insight did Jesus have about little children that led him to say that, "of such is the kingdom of heaven"? Simply that as very young children our body, mind and spirit are in complete harmony with each other. The young baby does not agonise over whether it is right or wrong to feel hungry, or thirsty, or lazy, or energetic, or wakeful or sleepy, or too cold or too hot. If it feels any of these things it issues a cry for help, for someone to create a happier, pleasanter situation than it can do for itself without outside help. In this state the physical world and the spiritual world are in complete harmony with each other. The nineteenth-century English poet William Wordsworth glimpsed something of this when he wrote in his poem *Intimations of Immortality*:

Not in entire forgetfulness,
And not in utter nakedness,
But trailing clouds of glory do we come
From God, who is our home:
Heaven lies about us in our infancy!
Shades of the prison house begin to close
Upon the growing boy.

It is only once we begin to learn that certain behaviours are 'not allowed', are 'wrong', that the two come into conflict – the conflict between what our mind tells us is morally 'wrong' and not in our best interests, and the demands and urgings of our biological needs. It is the Garden-of-Eden-like harmony between the physical and spiritual worlds in which we start life, which all our religious questing is an attempt to regain. The (usually unconscious) desire to regain this state is what Hammarskjöld was referring to when he wrote those words about the child's dream quoted at the beginning of the section of this chapter dealing with forgiveness. It is also what underlies probably all experiences of nostalgia – the desire to regain that sense of total harmony between all that is (including God), and all parts of ourselves, a state which under all the pressures of teenage and adult life for many people seems to become a more and more distant reality. Thomas Hood's much-loved poem of childhood memories, "I remember, I remember," is a reminder of this. It ends with the moving verse,

I remember, I remember,

The fir trees dark and high;
I used to think their slender tops
Were close against the sky:
It was a childish ignorance,
But now 'tis little joy
To know I'm farther off from heav'n
Than when I was a boy.

Many people have a sense that in our adult life we are living in a state of 'Paradise Lost,' that heaven did somehow lie more closely about us in our infancy than it does now, that at some point in our growing up, "shades of the prison house" did begin to close in upon us, and that we are indeed now further off from heaven than when we were a very young child. Jesus' belief that unless we become once again something of what we were then, we shall not experience being in the Kingdom of Heaven, resonates with that part of ourselves that seeks to enjoy the experience of 'Paradise Regained'.

It is widely acknowledged that the predominantly positive or negative nature of the mental state we daily live with can have a significant effect on our physical health. An article entitled, "The Heart that Failed," published in the Guardian newspaper a few years ago contains some thought-provoking suggestions that as an adult, becoming in some respects 'as a little child' may have physical health benefits as well as spiritual ones. The author, the American writer Clancy Sigal, grew up on Chicago's West Side around the time of the great depression of the late 1920s and early 1930s. In the article, written while he was recovering from heart surgery, he muses on the effects of some of his growing up experiences on his physical health in later years. He writes (in part),

I'm not sorry I missed being a teenager. However, I deeply regret having lost sight of the golden city, a place of the individual imagination beyond the first fears of childhood. When that special landscape of a child's heart misted over, when I grew tough and "realistic", I'm sure I began the process that landed me in intensive care.

The case is unprovable. I'm still doing the conventional expected things; I diet, exercise properly and listen to my friends' and doctors' advice. But, behind their backs as it were, sometimes at night when the light is out, I snap open my imaginary telescope and scan the turreted battlements of a far-gone time which, if I don't relocate it fairly exactly, surely will finish me off as efficiently as a fat-clogged artery.

We leave behind too much in the scramble to sit at the adults' table. By wiping themselves out with "cardiac events" in such massive numbers, men may be voting with their hearts to get out of the trap at whatever cost. If untended, the child within us becomes a terrible and terribly powerful enemy.

A longer extract from this article is given in Appendix 2.

Being born again

It is a return to the spiritual state of childhood that Jesus is referring to in talking about being born again (John 3:3) as a necessary pre-condition for entry into the kingdom of God, not the emotional release of authoritarian submission beloved of many who make up the authoritarian face of Christianity. Being reborn, becoming as a little child again (Matthew 18:3), is a return to childish innocence, but without the ignorance which is associated with it in our earliest years on this planet. It is a situation to which T. S. Eliot's words about "returning to the place where we started, and knowing it for the first time" apply.[80]

As a newborn, on the negative side we are very largely ignorant about the realities of life beyond the protective shield of our mother's womb. On the positive side, however, we are born in a state of innocent enjoyment of complete unity with God and the spiritual world. In losing our ignorance through our education in the school of life, the school of hard knocks (of which formal educational institutions are sometimes a particularly vicious part), we all too often lose something of our innocence: we become disillusioned, hard, cold and cynical. We lose a lot of our spontaneity, our sensitivity, our idealism. When we are 'born again' we retain the intellectual knowledge about 'how life works' which gradually replaced our childish ignorance as we grew older, but we regain that childish innocence and purity of heart which flowed from the experience of oneness with the fountain of all life, love and beauty with which we were originally born into the world. As Wordsworth put it in his poem *Intimations of Immortality* quoted above, we come into this world "trailing clouds of glory, from God, who is our home".

Jesus' valuing of the state of childhood is entirely consistent with his emphasis on the desirability of the qualities of meekness and humility. One of the endearing qualities of early childhood is the simplicity of understanding exhibited by young children. The limitations of their intellectual equipment means that they respond to life's situations in a much simpler, more gut-feel way than adults generally do. Intellectual game-playing to create a facade of defence mechanisms to hide the truth about our emotional state is a trick which is learnt in later childhood. The simplicity and emotional honesty of very young children is part and parcel of the sort of authentic living which is the last aspect of Jesus' ethics, to which we now turn our attention.

7. The need for authenticity

In Chapter 2 I discussed the fact that we all have two sides to our personality, our Persona and our Shadow.

Our Persona is the face we present to the world (and there may be many of these faces, which one we adopt in a particular situation being determined by which we feel will generate the most approval of ourselves from the audience we have at that particular time).

Our Shadow consists of those parts of ourselves of which we disapprove and try to disown. But the parts of our psyches which we try to deny the reality of, and banish to our Shadow, *are* parts of ourselves, and sometimes very important parts (like our sexuality and our anger, for instance, which some people have sadly been taught, through an unfortunate upbringing, to believe are 'bad').[81] The more we try to disown parts of ourselves, the more split our personalities become – the more we become "a house divided against itself" (Matthew 12:25), and the more hypocritical and troubled in spirit we become. One of the major aims of much psychotherapy is to help the client to heal those splits in their psyche, so that there is no longer a lack of consistency between what they really believe deep down inside, what they say they believe, and how they act. The therapist tries to help their client to lose the fears that make it difficult for them to live with authenticity – in other words in a way that what they say and what one sees of their behaviour, is a genuine reflection of what they believe – that 'What you see is what you get'.

It is the desirability of living our lives in a fully authentic way, in other words with emotional honesty, and purity of intention, which Jesus captures in those two beatitudes, "Blessed are the pure in heart, for they shall see God," and, "Blessed are they that hunger and thirst after righteousness, for they shall be filled" (Matthew 5:6 and 8). It is also concern for such values that underlie Jesus' criticism of the Scribes and the Pharisees to be found in Chapter 23 of Matthew's gospel, and Chapter 11 of Luke's. These passages contain a catalogue of colourful images of characteristics of the scribes and Pharisees which illustrate the lack of authenticity which Jesus accused them of in many aspects of their behaviour. They are accused (amongst other things) of not practising what they preach ("For they say, and do not"

(Matthew 23:3)), of being "like whitewashed tombs, which outwardly appear beautiful, but within they are full of dead men's bones, and all uncleanness," (Matthew 23:27), and of being more concerned with outward appearances than with inner reality, spending their time cleansing the outside of eating utensils and ignoring the inside, whose cleanliness is of much greater importance.

> Woe unto you, scribes and Pharisees, hypocrites! For ye make clean the outside of the cup and of the platter, but within they are full of extortion and excess. Thou blind Pharisee, cleanse first that which is within the cup and platter, that the outside of them may be clean also.[82]

Relatedly the scribes' and Pharisees' obsession with ritual observances and the defiling effect of failure to observe any of these requirements comes in for devastating critical comment. The Pharisees' criticism of the fact that on one occasion Jesus' disciples did not wash their hands before eating ("Why do thy disciples transgress the tradition of the elders? For they wash not their hands when they eat bread" (Matthew 15:2)), is responded to by Jesus with, "Not that which goeth into the mouth defileth a man; but that which cometh out of the mouth, this defileth a man" (Matthew 15:11). A little later in response to Peter's request for further explanation Jesus reportedly replied, "Those things which proceed out of the mouth come forth from the heart; and they defile the man. For out of the heart proceed evil thoughts, murders, adulteries, fornications, thefts, false witness, blasphemies: These are the things which defile a man: but to eat with unwashen hands defileth not a man"[83] (Matthew 15:18-20). (See also Mark 7:15 and 18-23).

Insofar as we know and act on the belief that what lies within us is more important than the façade that we present to the outside world there will be congruence between our feelings and our actions. We shall be practising what we preach, and not be among those to whom Isaiah refers when he says, "This people honours me with their lips but their heart is far from me" (Isaiah 29:13). What we say will be a true statement as to the actual state of affairs within us, genuine, not pretended. These qualities are the opposite of hypocrisy.

Did Jesus really speak about the Scribes and the Pharisees in the harsh terms reported in the Gospels?

The gospel records of Jesus' teachings are certainly not a verbatim account of what he did actually say on any particular occasion. Some significant statements he is reported to have made clash with the whole spirit of his ethical principles, and have undoubtedly been inserted by the early church before the detailed text of the various gospels had been standardised and widely distributed. One particularly clear example of this is to be found in Matthew's gospel (Chapter 26, verse 28), where Jesus is reported to have said, "This is my blood of the New Testament," many years before the New Testament was created.

Surveying all the statements attributed to Jesus in the synoptic gospels as a whole, Geza Vermes, widely regarded as "the foremost Jesus scholar of the twentieth century," concludes that:

> If there is one certain conclusion which no serious reader endowed with insight and logic the size of a mustard seed can escape, it is that these hundreds of sayings have not been produced by one and the same teacher. They patently represent irreconcilable variations; indeed again and again they display flat contradictions.[84]

We shall never know for certain exactly what Jesus did say to his disciples about the scribes and the Pharisees, but it almost certainly was not as venomous as the account we have in the gospels of his attack on them. In particular it is about as certain as anything can be that Jesus did not consign the Pharisees to Hell (Matthew 23:14, 15, and 33).

There are two reasons for thinking this. The one is that the idea of the very existence of Hell and the idea of God 'sending' anyone there, is in total contradiction of the concept of God Jesus seems to have held, and everything he had to say about the forgiveness of sins. Either Jesus was, like Paul, a split personality, or what he said has been misreported. The other reason for being suspicious as to how accurate the gospel record is in reporting the details of Jesus' diatribe against the Scribes and the Pharisees is that it has more than a hint of an anti-Semitic attitude about it – a point to which I shall return a little later in this book.

Nevertheless, however far the Gospel account of the language Jesus used in his polemic against the Scribes and the Pharisees may depart from what he actually said, it is likely that the amount of space devoted to this matter in the gospels is a reflection of the importance Jesus did place on the need for authenticity, for non-hypocritical honesty, particularly in religious leaders. Dishonestly claiming, for the sake of appearances, to believe anything which we do not really believe, and does not match our behaviour; caring more about outward appearances and legalistic rule-following than about meeting human needs and what lies in the hearts of people, is for Jesus no part of the behaviour of those who are living in the Kingdom of God.

Flowing from the much greater importance Jesus attached to our inner state of mind than to our outward behaviour (not that what people see of our outward behaviour is unimportant), is his intense dislike of ostentatiousness, a quality he saw as frequently exhibited by the Pharisees and to which he took particularly strong exception. Seeking the chief seats in the synagogues, and the uppermost rooms at feasts (Mark 12:39; Matthew 23:6; and Luke 20:46) are behaviours which have no place in the Kingdom of God, for "all their works they do for to be seen of men"

(Matthew 23:5). This public display of superior social status is bad enough in itself, but it is doubly unacceptable when it is accompanied by a self-righteous, holier-than-thou, 'What a good boy am I' attitude, whose main purpose is to impress onlookers with the superiority of the speaker over ordinary mortals in matters of religious piety. Making long prayers "for a pretence" (Mark 12:40), and under the misapprehension "that they shall be heard for their much speaking" (Matthew 7:7), and boasting about one's moral superiority over others (Luke 18:11-14), are incompatible with an attitude of meekness and humility and authentic living, and for Jesus, they are no part of the behaviours that belong in the Kingdom of God.

Part of the reason why ostentatious displays of what at least part of us believes is our superiority over others is unacceptable, is that whenever we say, whether in so many words or in more subtle ways, that, "I am better than you," we are unavoidably at the same time saying, "You are inferior to me". Not only do we impoverish ourselves if we cannot appreciate the way in which the diversity of the different talents and qualities we each possess enriches life, but damaging people's self-esteem is unloving, uncompassionate, hurtful behaviour, absolutely contrary to the spirit of the ethical principles Jesus espoused.

Another reason is that the more time we spend trying to boost our image in the eyes of the world (through material possessions, or through more psychological factors like the amount of power and influence we wield), the less time and energy we have available to develop the spiritual side of our being – to build up for ourselves "treasure in heaven" (Matthew 6:19-21, and Luke 12:33-34). In addition we are, of course, not only in danger of losing sight of some of our spiritual values altogether, but of getting into the habit of conveniently pushing them aside from time to time in order to 'make a quick buck,' or to gain some other form of short-term advantage.

The devastating damage the ethically unprincipled pursuit of short-term financial benefits has had recently on the world economy, and the many lives that have been miserably ruined in the process, is a striking illustration of the danger of seeking success in the eyes of the world at the expense of doing what is ultimately right for the welfare of humanity. Fortunately there are brave businessmen around who continue to see the success of their company as serving a higher purpose than just making money. It is, as Jesus said, "Easier for a camel to go through the eye of a needle than for a rich man to enter into the kingdom of God" (Mark 10:25), not because there is anything wrong with being wealthy, far from it, but because it is so easy to lose sight of deeper ethical values when business pressures mount. Authenticity can all too easily be sacrificed to expediency in pursuit of financial advantage.

Although Jesus' fierce attack on the superficial approach of the Scribes and Pharisees to religion was doubtless at least to some extent justified, its significance has unfortunately been misunderstood by some Christians and seen as an attack by Jesus on all aspects of Jewish religion. This false belief has sometimes fuelled a latent anti-Semitism in parts of the Christian Church. Its frequent surfacing has been one of the saddest and most illogical blots on the reputation of a religious organisation which claims to be based on the insights of a deeply spiritual Jewish religious teacher – Jesus of Nazareth.

Jesus himself never rejected Jewish religion. He saw his role as being to reform the religion of his fellow religionists, in a similar, but much more fundamental way to that in which, over the centuries, generations of Jewish reforming prophets had striven to bring their people back to their spiritual roots when they thought these were being lost sight of under the encumbrances of unspiritual ideas and practices. Jesus' attack on the hypocrisy which he saw the scribes and Pharisees of his time as manifesting, contains absolutely no implication that the charge of hypocrisy could be laid at the door of all his compatriots.

However Jesus was well aware of the potential for hypocrisy and a lack of authenticity to manifest itself outside the ranks of the scribes and the Pharisees, for example his warning, "Beware of false prophets, which come to you in sheep's clothing, but inwardly they are ravening wolves" (Matthew 7:15). Insofar as there is an anti-Semitic undertone to anything Jesus is reported to have said about the Scribes and the Pharisees, it almost certainly comes from the thinking of the increasingly gentile early Christian Church rather than from Jesus himself.

7.1 Experiences which militate against the development of Authenticity

One of the many destructive effects of living in an environment in which people sense that their thoughts and behaviour are subject to continuous moralistic scrutiny and judgement, is that they will reveal less and less of the full range of their true selves, that their Persona will become progressively more impoverished, while their unacknowledged Shadow becomes bigger and bigger. In holding out to us a vision of the world as it might become if humanity lived according to that key tenet of Christian ethics – non-judgementalness – Jesus foreshadowed by nearly two thousand years the thinking which has now become central to most forms of psychotherapy.

Unfortunately hypocrisy has manifested itself on a grand scale in the Christian Church itself over the nearly two thousand years of its history. One early example of this is to be seen in St Paul's challenge to Peter, which challenge incidentally throws an interesting light on the internal conflicts and rivalries which have wracked the church almost since its inception. The issue of bringing Gentiles into the church was clearly one which troubled the early (all Jewish) Christian Church leaders greatly. Paul (whose views eventually prevailed), pushed very strongly in favour of this development, while James, the brother of Jesus and apparent leader of the group of disciples in Jerusalem in the earliest days of the church, seems to have been strongly opposed to it at first. Peter, who also had a powerful leadership role in the early church, appears to have wavered on this point. He seems to have mingled freely with the Gentiles, but in an unprincipled way tried to hide this from those in the early church who disapproved of this behaviour on his part. This incensed Paul who apparently took Peter to task publicly for his hypocrisy (Galatians 2:1-14).

Manipulative pressure on church members to 'be good', and to behave in the way the church tells them to, has caused widespread conflict and massive guilt in the minds of many Christians over the years. Many have coped with that conflict by mouthing pious acceptance of official church positions, but behaving in ways which are in conflict with those professed beliefs. The Vatican-controlled Roman Catholic Church is one glaring (but by no means unique) example of the way in which rigidly authoritarian structures foster the development of this type of behaviour. Fortunately there are signs that dissenting voices, which have always been present in the Catholic Church, are becoming more strident in the expression of their discontent with the status quo, and there are signs of a significant popular movement arising, even among the priesthood, to challenge the prevalent oppressive views of the upper echelons of that church on issues such as the celibacy and sexual orientation[85] of the priesthood, contraception and the ordination of women priests.

Voices of protest

One of the few people prominent in the Catholic Church hierarchy who might provide intellectual and spiritual backing for such a movement had he been alive today, is the highly-respected church father Thomas Aquinas, who flourished from 1225 to 1274. Described in *The Oxford Companion to Philosophy*[86] as "the greatest of the medieval philosopher-theologians", he held the view that the core of all moral behaviour, or ethics, is being true to one's own conscience (sense of integrity), even in matters which the Church would call mortal sin, i.e. that it is worse to go against one's sense of integrity out of fear of breaking 'the law' or the commandments than actually breaking them. It is astonishing that this view, so consistent with the ethical principle of authenticity and the avoidance of hypocrisy[87] which Jesus proclaimed, and coming from someone whose works *Chambers Biographical Dictionary*[88] describes as having "exercised enormous intellectual authority throughout the Church", should so far have had so little impact on the underlying autocratic management style of the Vatican-based Catholic Church.

On the contrary, less than three hundred years after Thomas Aquinas, an even more influential voice in the thinking of the Roman Catholic Church expressed a view absolutely contradictory to that discussed above. This was the teaching of Ignatius Loyola (1491-1556), or Saint Ignatius Loyola as he was to become after his death. Ignatius rose to prominence as a Catholic religious leader in the Counter-Reformation, the Roman Catholic Church's response to Martin Luther's Reformation initiative. He founded the Society of Jesus, more usually known today as the Jesuits. The attitude of mind which Ignatius sought to inculcate in his followers towards any conflicts arising between the Church's pronouncements and what their own conscience and intelligence tells them, is one of absolute acceptance of the Church's opinion. In his handbook of instruction, *Rules For Thinking Within The Church*, he wrote, "If the church should have defined anything to be black which to our eyes appears white, we ought in like manner to pronounce it black".

With the exception of a few free spirits, the words of the revered church-father Thomas Aquinas seem to have fallen on deaf ears. The prevailing organizational climate of the Roman Catholic Church is one which is far more strongly influenced by the autocratic dictates of Ignatius Loyola than by the teachings of Thomas Aquinas, despite the fact that requiring unconditional assent to any rigid dogmatic structure is an outright contradiction of Jesus' teaching about putting people before principles.

One courageous exception to the prevailing let's-not-rock-the-boat mentality in the Catholic Church is Kevin Dowling, the Catholic Bishop of Rustenberg in South Africa. His recent remarks to a meeting of Catholic lay leaders in Cape Town[89] followed the almost unbelievable formal announcement by papal representatives at a news conference recently that, "in the eyes of the church, ordaining women was as grave an offence as is priestly paedophilia". Following in the footsteps of Thomas Aquinas, Bishop Dowling protested that, "As Catholics, we need to be trusted enough to make informed decisions about our life, our expressions of faith, and involvement in the world on the basis of a developed consciousness". He went on to remind his audience that the present Pope when, as Josef Ratzinger, he was an expert theological advisor to the Bishops at Vatican II had given as his considered opinion (echoing the beliefs of Thomas Aquinas) that: "Over the Pope, as expression of the binding claim of ecclesiastical authority there stands one's own conscience which must be obeyed before all else, even, if necessary, against the requirement of ecclesiastical authority."

The timing of the July 2010 decision by the Catholic Church to revise its internal laws and to raise the status of the 'crime' of the attempted ordination of women priests from 'more grave' offence to that of DELICTA GRAVIORA, or 'highest crime' (where it joins the ranks of heresy, apostasy, and paedophilia), can only be viewed as a public relations disaster for that church. To make that decision, and to announce it at a time when the revelations about priestly sexual misbehaviour have brought public confidence in the integrity of the Catholic priesthood to its lowest ebb ever, looks like nothing less than behaviour driven by a death wish. Perhaps even further demonising the idea of accepting women into the priesthood was a panic reaction on the part of the Vatican to the realisation that they were losing ground among their own followers in their opposition to the ordination of women. It cannot have been coincidental that in that same year a NYTimes/CBS poll indicated that 59% of American Catholics were in favour of the ordination of women.

As if that DELICTA GRAVIORA faux pas were not enough, a mere four months later the Vatican dropped another bombshell, although this time with what at first sight appears to be a more liberalising intent. This event was the publication of a new book *Light of the World; the Pope, the Church and the Signs of the Times* based on an interview with Pope Benedict XVI, a couple of years before his retirement. "In an exchange with the author of that book about Aids in Africa, Benedict said that for some people – such as male prostitutes – using condoms could be a step in assuming moral responsibility because the intent is to 'reduce the risk of infection'". This has really set the cat among the pigeons in the Vatican with contradictory claims and counter-claims emerging from it about what the Pope really meant by his statement and even about the status of his opinions if they were merely expressed in a published book! The Rev Joseph Fessio speaking on behalf of Ignatius Press, the publishers of the book, apparently maintains that, "nothing new has happened, the Church's teaching hasn't changed". More perceptively perhaps, John Haas, a moral theologian who is president of the National Catholic Bioethics Centre in Philadelphia, says tersely, "It's a mess," while Russell Shaw, a writer for the Catholic publication, *Our Sunday Visitor*, and a former spokesman for the bishops' conference, has expressed a view that few will disagree with: "We're in for a long period of confusion," he said recently.[90] One very important aspect of that confusion, the clearing up of which could have very significant implications for the future of the Vatican-based church, is whether Pope Benedict's hinted at relax-ation of the blanket ban on the use of condoms "for some people, like male prostitutes," would exclude the case of the use of condoms in order to "reduce the risk of infection" in sexual intercourse with a woman, as it has been suggested might be the intention. The thinking in some quarters seems to be that the use of a condom in homosexual intercourse serves one purpose only – to reduce the risks of infection to either of the parties involved. In heterosexual intercourse, the use of a condom serves the same purpose, but additionally serves a contraceptive function. This of course violates one of the most emotively-held beliefs of orthodox Roman Catholicism (or at least of the childless old men who mostly populate the upper ranks of its power hierarchy) – that any interference with the reproductive aim of heterosexual sex is a grievous sin.

So what to do about that? One possibility of course is to sacrifice protection from infection for the woman and ban the use of condoms in heterosexual sex, or permit their use only in heterosexual anal sex[91]. The mind boggles at the possible next pronouncement from the Vatican! Certainly, given a few more examples of the mess created by the Vatican's seeming inability to rise above restrictive rigid legalism in its dictates about good human behaviour, it can only be a matter of time before the Vatican-based Catholic Church collapses under the weight of its own internal contradictions, and the resultant damage to its credibility. As an institution committed to continuing the healing work of its supposed founder, it has suffered a considerable loss of face-validity in hitching its fortunes to St Paul's misogynistic and deeply pathological fear of sexuality. The preservation and creation of life at all costs is a pretty poor substitute for Jesus' humanistically-inspired urging of his followers, and indeed of all of us to, "Never sacrifice a person to a principle".

A silver lining to a dark cloud?

One positive consequence of the situation discussed above has been to draw attention to the fact that there is now an alternative branch of the Catholic Church, the so-called 'Old Catholic Church', which is growing particularly strongly in Europe. This denomination split off from the previously monolithic parent body in the nineteenth century, mostly because of a disagreement over the doctrine of papal infallibility. These churches are now part of the Union of Utrecht, and in full communion with the Anglican Church. Although a few individual churches in that federation do not accept the ordination of women priests, most of them do. Currently there are about a hundred women priests in Old Catholic churches affiliated to the Union of Utrecht in Germany and Switzerland, making up about 10% of their clergy.

Probably following not far behind on the path to schism with the Vatican-controlled Catholic Church is the Austrian Catholic Church. In a so-called *Priests' Initiative,* a group of more than 300 of its priests, under the leadership of a former Vicar-General of Vienna, Mgr Helmut Schüller, have formed an organisation which has openly called for disobedience to the dictates of the Vatican-based church in respect of priestly celibacy and Holy Communion for remarried divorcees and non-Catholics. It also supports women priests, lay preachers, and the use of the term 'Priestless Eucharists'. The organisation also seems to support homosexual unions. In 2010 87 000 people in Austria left the Catholic church, many of them in response to allegations of sexual abuse by priests. Twenty years ago Austria was 85% Catholic. Today less than 50% of the inhabitants of its capital city Vienna are. Various recent surveys put the level of public support for the actions of the *Priests' Initiative* at over 70%, with a similar percentage of Austria's 3500 catholic priests approving of at least parts of their programme of rebellion.

The independent-of-Vatican-control Catholic churches are likely to be the major beneficiaries of any mass disaffection with the Vatican-based Catholic Church. Such mass disaffection seems to be an inevitable development if that church fails to engage in a radical rethink of the relationship between the fundamental ethical principles which it espouses, and those proclaimed by Jesus as operating in the Kingdom of God. The fact that a Google search with the probe 'Austrian Priests' Initiative' yielded 3 750 000 hits, while a similar search with the probe 'Old Catholic Church in Europe' yielded no less than 66 100 000 suggests that these schismatic developments are something more than a storm in a teacup.

A few final thoughts

In living life according to the ethical principles which Jesus expounded, we are manifesting our 'love of God' and are indissolubly joined with him as all the positive forces of the universe flow through us to our neighbours (not excluding the animal kingdom, and indeed the whole of nature). We cannot, 'love God,' without loving our neighbour; and in loving our neighbour, treating others with compassionate respect, giving them loving support and encouragement, we are demonstrating our love of God. Many of the ideas contained in Jesus' ethical principles were not first brought into human consciousness by him. He was a Jew and grew up within the Jewish religious tradition, from which he absorbed, sometimes in embryonic form, and sometimes *in toto*, at least some of the ethical principles which he taught and lived by.

Jesus never rejected his Jewish heritage; he never founded a new religion – it was his disciples who did that, forming what was at first an entirely Jewish organisation that later, largely under the influence of St Paul, became a predominately gentile institution, with at some times and in some places, a distinctly anti-Semitic undertone. Far from starting a new movement, Jesus was at pains to point out his groundedness in the Jewish religion, as witness his frequent reference back to (and sometimes direct quoting from) books in the Hebrew Bible (more or less identical with the Old Testament of the Christian Bible), and his explicit statement that, "Think not that I am come to destroy the law, or the prophets: I am not come to destroy, but to fulfil". (Matthew

5:17).

Jesus stood in the tradition of a long line of inspired prophets (of whom Elijah, Amos, Micah, Hosea, and Isaiah stand out particularly strongly), who sought to reform the religion of their communities from within, rather than to splinter them into a number of warring factions. Christianity has experienced similar passionate attempts (from Luther to John Robinson, the Bishop of Woolwich[92]) to rescue the spiritual essence of their religion from stultifying legalistic formalism and magical thinking. Unfortunately the preferred route for many Christian reformers has not been to reform from within, but rather to try to establish a new power base outside that of the parent religion.

And of course, some of the ethics which Jesus proclaimed are not unique to the Judeo-Christian tradition, and can be found in other religions, and in the thinking of enlightened individuals who have no religious affiliations at all).[93] Exactly which of the ideas of the ethics of Jesus were original to him, it is impossible to say with any certainty, the historical records of the religious thinking of individuals in the past being patchy to say the least. But certainly Jesus brought a uniquely integrated understanding of the sorts of behaviours which both flow from, and lead to, the experience of being in harmony with all the positive forces in the Universe, of being with God in the Kingdom of Heaven. The ideas underlying all that we know (with reasonable certainty) that he taught, demonstrate a profoundly humanistic position, in which the welfare of human beings is paramount. The Kingdom of Heaven is not some place we have to be dragged away to in order to keep God happy that people are behaving themselves properly. "The Kingdom of Heaven is within you" (Luke 17:21), which words of Jesus are echoed in Emerson's bold claim that, "Other world? There is no other world! Here or nowhere is the whole fact".[94] In Jesus' thinking (unlike St. Paul's), entering the Kingdom of God is not something that anyone *has* to do "*or else* …". It is a state of blessedness which anyone who follows the ethical principles that Jesus taught will automatically enter. "The Sabbath was made for man, not man for the Sabbath." Sadly, in most people's experience, this humanistic face of Christianity is not by any means the most prominent aspect of the religion in the world today.

Chapter 6

The Authoritarian Face of Christianity

Religions commit suicide when they find their inspirations in their dogmas.[27]
– Alfred North Whitehead. *Religion in the Making*

In talking about authoritarian attitudes and ideas, it is important to distinguish between *authoritarian* and *authoritative* ways of communicating our thoughts and wishes to other people. Both words derive from the same root word 'authority', and both authoritarian and authoritative convey the fact that the person, or the utterance so described, has a claim to some sort of authority. The two words do, however, have very different meanings. The term 'authoritative' derives its meaning from the third of three alternative meanings that the COED gives for the word 'authority', namely "the power to influence others based on recognized knowledge or expertise". When we say that someone has spoken authoritatively, we mean that we are impressed by the extent of the knowledge and/or insight the person displayed in putting across their message. We regard the person as something of an expert in whatever field of knowledge they were talking about, and therefore feel either an inclination to adopt the point of view they were expressing or that it could be productive to engage in debate with them on any ideas they expressed with which we do not agree.

By contrast, "authoritarian" (defined in the COED as "favouring or enforcing strict obedience to authority at the expense of personal freedom") is a word that derives its meaning from the first of the three alternative meanings that the COED gives for the word 'authority', namely "the power or right to give orders and enforce obedience". An authoritarian statement is one which derives its authority from the status of the person making that statement; they have positional power, in other words power because of the position they hold in some organisational hierarchy, religious, academic, political or financial. The last six words of the dictionary definition of 'authoritarian' quoted above ("at the expense of personal freedom") reinforce the idea implicit in the opening words, "enforcing strict obedience" – the idea that this enforcing leaves no freedom on the part of the person on whom someone else's will is being imposed to do anything other than submit to what is being forced upon them, very often not even any discussion of a different point of view or course of action being allowed.

The essence of an authoritarian organisation is the existence of a power hierarchy in terms of which those lower down the hierarchy have to accept the ideas and dictates of those higher up within it, not on the grounds of their perceived appropriateness, truth or value, but because of the power wielded by the person who is trying to force acceptance of their point of view. But unless and until our will is crushed by destructive forces we encounter in our earlier life, we all have a biologically-determined propensity (of great adaptive value) to fight against any attempts to make us conform to the demands of others, if these are made with a display of naked power, along the lines of, "Just do as you are told (or believe what I say), because I am more powerful than you, and if you don't …".

The implied threat is of course one of punishment. Authoritarian systems by their very nature try from time to time to impose ideas and behaviours on us which conflict with our own understanding of the world and our own natural tendencies and desires. The only way to force us against our will, as opposed to respectfully persuading us to accept those things which do not come naturally, is through the use of punishment and the threat of punishment. The more any system has a power hierarchy within it which requires those lower down the status ladder to respond with complete obedience to the edicts of those higher up it, the more authoritarian it is, and the more it will require punishment of those who rebel against such subservience, if the status quo of the power balance is to be maintained.

Although authoritarian systems are much less common in the Western world today than they were in all aspects of life in the past, they seem to flourish almost as strongly in the field of religion as ever they did. The particular characteristics of authoritarian religions are:

- Centralized power and control.
- Significant uniformity of belief among members. Conformity to rules and uniformity of belief are the hallmarks of those who are part of such a system.
- Reluctance on the part of church members to challenge the prevailing orthodoxies.
- Dogmatic intolerance.

Most Christian Churches have a clear authoritarian power hierarchy, with a minister, a pastor, a priest, a bishop, or an archbishop, in charge of whatever control structures that particular denomination has in place. This Top Dog has positional power and speaks and acts with the authority which that positional power is seen by adherents of the religion to confer upon him or her (but more usually 'him'). Of course from time to time open opposition to that authority arises, sometimes sufficiently strongly for the existing structure to lose some of its members to a newly-formed sect or denomination, in which a new leader claims the position of ultimate authority. Most Christian denominations and sects are organised in this way, and those at the top of the hierarchy in each of them seek with varying degrees of energy to retain the acquiescence of adherents of the religion in their authority.

Different Christian leaders go about this task of trying to

ensure that their authority in religious matters is accepted without challenge by their flock in different ways, but the Roman Catholic Church stands out as the one that has gone to the most extreme lengths in this respect, unashamedly publicly claiming absolute infallibility for the pronouncements of its very human leader – the Pope. It is probably true, however, that many of the leaders of small (or sometimes not-so-small) sects share a similar belief in the absolute correctness of their own views, where these differ from those of the leaders of other denominations or sects claiming to be 'Christian'.[95] The more authoritarian the structure of any organisation, the more rigidly it tries to enforce conformity of belief and practice in line with the wishes of the leaders of the organisation, the greater the probability that rebel groups of like-minded dissident members of the organisation will break away to form their own independent structure, differing to a greater or lesser extent from the beliefs and practices of the parent body. It is a measure of the strength of the authoritarian tendencies within Christianity that the acceptance by that church of the unification of the religion into a single church with uniform belief forced upon it by the Roman Emperor Constantine in 325 CE had, by the start of the third millennium split into more than 30 000 different Christian denominations and sects, some of them quite miniscule, but sometimes having a negative impact on the world out of all proportion to the very small number of adherents they have.

One such is the inappropriately named *Dove World Outreach* in Florida in the United States. In September 2010 it had a membership of only about 50, with an average attendance at its services of about 30. Aggressive threats by its pastor, Terry Jones, to burn copies of the Qur'an provoked an international outcry. On March 20th, 2011 he held a 'Trial of the Qur'an' which he found to be guilty of 'crimes against humanity'. The verdict was followed by a public burning of a copy of that Muslim scripture. Worldwide protests erupted, and in one northern Afghanistan city more than 30 US and UN personnel were killed in the violence provoked by this action of a 'Christian Church'.

Of course despite the strenuous attempts of some individuals to impose uniformity of belief, and sometimes of practice on all adherents of their particular branch of the Christian religion, there is always some degree of diversity in the views of those making up any particular denomination or sect.[96] This makes it particularly inappropriate to try to identify which branches of the Christian Church can be said to represent the humanistic face of Christianity, and which the authoritarian one. What is more helpful is to consider in what ways the authoritarian tendencies in the Christian Church have corrupted the implementation of those very non-authoritarian ethical principles so passionately promoted by Jesus which we discussed in the previous chapter. This is the necessary first step for those of us who wish to do what we can to help free Christianity of some of the psychopathologies which stand in the way of its becoming an increasingly powerful force for the elimination of the brutality and cruelty which has marred, and continues to mar the lives of so many people, some of it[97] with the blessing of, or even at the instigation of the Christian Church itself.

What are the chief characteristics of the authoritarian face of Christianity?

Respect for, and obedience to authority

Not all leaders in the authoritarianly-inclined branches of the Christian Church demand unquestioning obedience from their flock, but the bottom line of the final response to any permitted challenges is generally something along the lines of, "It is not for man to question the inscrutable mind of God". Unfortunately many people are so intimidated in such situations that it rarely occurs to them to make the simple, and entirely justified response to such a discussion-stopping pronouncement, "I'm not questioning the mind of God. I'm questioning your understanding of the mind of God".

The nature of God

The demand for subservience by rank and file church members to the higher authority of their leaders is frequently seen as the embodiment on the purely human level of the relationship believed (by those whose Christianity is of the authoritarian type), to exist between humans and God. The concept of an authoritarian, 'supreme ruler' God, endemic in Authoritarian Christianity is not the only one to be found within Christianity as a whole, but it is probably the most widespread belief as to what constitutes 'God' among those who assert their belief in such an entity, and certainly is what most people think Christians mean when they talk about God. It is also the concept of God which stokes the fires of militant atheism of the Richard Dawkins variety.

What is the definition of this concept of God to be found at the heart of authoritarian Christianity? The COED states that God is the "creator and ruler of the universe; the Supreme Being". To this the Shorter Oxford Dictionary adds, "The one object of supreme adoration". In common Christian parlance this God is regarded as the acme of perfection – Omnipotent, Omniscient, Omnipresent and wholly good, to be worshipped, adored, and, most importantly, to be obeyed. We shall look at this concept in more detail in Chapters 8, 10, 11, and 12, in the context of the very different concept of God which lies at the heart of humanistic Christianity. For present purposes we need just to note that the demand for respect for the authority of church leaders and obedience to their dictates on the part of ordinary church members draws its justification from the similar relationship which some authoritarian Christians seem to believe exists between God and the human being, church leaders standing *in loco Dei*[98] because of their special status in the power hierarchy of the Christian Church.

Preoccupation with wrongdoing: Disobedience and the concept of 'sin'

A major concern of those whose views constitute the authoritarian face of Christianity is with the wrongdoing of humans. From this perspective 'doing wrong' means doing something which the church has decreed people are not allowed to do, or not doing something which the church has proclaimed they ought to do. In theory these edicts of the church are divinely inspired, and church leaders, because of the elevated position they occupy in their church's power hierarchy, are supposed to have a more direct hotline to the mind of God than ordinary mortals do. Failure to obey the church's rulings, to accept the moral codes the churchmen have formulated (and it is almost always churchmen rather than churchwomen) is thus seen as tantamount to disobedience to God himself. This flouting of 'God's will' is what constitutes sin, defined in the COED as "an immoral act considered to be a transgression against divine law", for which atonement[99] must be made. In the time-honoured tradition of all authoritarian systems, that atonement must include punishment as a key component.

That punishment may take many forms that lie on a continuum of severity. At the milder end lie experiencing the disapproval of fellow church members and clergy, sometimes with public denunciation and ostracism. In some ways slightly more severe than that (although in other ways less so because both the sin and its prescribed punishment can remain a private matter between priest and penitent) are the penances prescribed by the presiding priest in the confessional (mostly the generally mindless repetition of prayers). For some devout individuals these mental punishments are not enough and self-inflicted self-denials and 'mortifications of the flesh' are voluntarily undertaken. Perhaps occurring less frequently in the Western world today than they were at times in the past, the psychopathological practices of self-flagellation and other forms of self-harming encouraged in the controversial Roman Catholic Opus Dei[100] society, take us towards the extreme end of the punishment continuum where intense mental and physical pain is inflicted, sometimes culminating in death.

Although punishments of this extreme type are less common now than they were in the heyday of the Inquisition and the crusade against heretics and witches, they are by no means unheard of today, and that most cruel of mental punishments for the devout believer, the practice of excommunication is still employed, and not only by the Roman Catholic Church. As to the pronouncement of the death penalty on backsliding Christians for their sin, the advances of human rights legislation in secular society have probably put an end to this practice. One does wonder, however, what those in the authoritarian Christian camp who believe that everything in the Bible must be accepted as literally true make of the often quoted last verse of Chapter 6 of St Paul's Epistle to the Romans, where it is clearly stated that, "the wages of sin is death", not "the wages of sin *was* death before Jesus' atoning death took place", but, "here and now, despite Jesus' atoning death on the cross, the wages of sin *is* death".

The fundamentally adversarial relationship between God and humankind

Implicit in the idea of God as a supremely powerful controlling being whose behests we must obey, regardless of our own wishes or beliefs, is the idea that there is a fundamentally adversarial relationship between God and humanity. Although created by this omnipotent being, we have a fundamental design flaw, and cause our maker grief because we 'incline towards sin'. Rather like disobedient children, we know our duty, we know how we ought to behave, but constantly rebel against 'being good'. There is a great gulf fixed between God and humankind, between the all-good God and sinful man, and it requires the intervention of the church to bridge that gulf. Amongst other things, the church provides for the faithful the opportunity to participate in endless pleadings, spoken or sung in the form of hymns, for forgiveness of their sins, for their failure to do the will of God.

Sometimes the belief underlying this habit seems to be that prayers for forgiveness for the sins of their flock coming from a pastor or minister or priest are more likely to be answered than those of mere rank and file members of the church. Sometimes it seems to be believed that the church's intervention is needed to maximise the number and intensity, and therefore effectiveness of the petitions for forgiveness reaching God's ears. From the perspective of humanistic Christianity, this is a totally pointless exercise, since Jesus stated (as reported in Matthew 6:12 and 14-15), that all that is required for forgiveness of our sins is that we forgive those who have sinned against us. Even from the perspective of authoritarian Christianity where the Doctrine of the Atonement holds sway, this ceaseless begging for mercy and forgiveness for sins committed is an oddity, since Jesus' death is supposed, in terms of that doctrine, to have 'washed away our sin', as I discuss at some length in the next section. Perhaps the real reason (and often an entirely unconscious one) for all the self-deprecatory breast-beating is to keep the mind of the hapless churchgoer filled with a sense of his or her sin and guilt – a most unworthy goal to have, and which from both a psychological and spiritual perspective is viciously damaging.

Some of the prayers and hymns produced by Christians when in this frame of mind are nauseating in their imagery, for example,

I am coming, Lord,
Coming now to Thee:
Wash me, cleanse me by the blood
That flowed on Calvary.

The idea that we can be 'cleansed' by being washed in blood comes from a dark place deep in our primitive past, that same place from which rituals of human and other animal sacrifice in so many religions have sprung. It is the antithesis of the spiritually enlightened thinking of the ethics Jesus preached. Others betray a profound ignorance of the way the human mind works. The hymn *Heal me, hands of Jesus* is sometimes sung at Anglican Eucharist Services. Its third verse runs:

Know me, mind of Jesus,
And show me all my sin;
Dispel the memories of guilt
And bring me peace within.

Showing people all their faults may be a good way of getting them to buy the salvation package one is peddling. It is not a good way to start the process of helping them to attain inner peace and freedom from guilt, and it is the antithesis of the way Jesus went about healing the damaged human psyche.

Guilt, Punishment, Temptation and the Devil

Let us remind ourselves that, as discussed earlier in this chapter, a key feature of authoritarian organizational systems is control of subordinates by a centralized authority. The flow of power in them is entirely top down. The individual at the top of the hierarchy dictates the rules to which the behaviour of those lower down the hierarchy must conform. The freedom of action and limits of discretionary decision-making of these underlings are tightly circumscribed by the edicts issued by those at the top of the hierarchy. In such systems, obedience is the greatest virtue, and independent thought and action, unless specifically sanctioned, a serious misdemeanour. In the eyes of those church leaders operating as part of the authoritarian face of Christianity, such wrongdoing is labelled sin, which must be punished to discourage its repetition.

Punishment and the threat of it, is a crucial part of the establishment and maintenance of authoritarian systems. That punishment, like all punishment, initially arouses anger on the part of the punished person against the person inflicting it, but the more the individual being punished is carrying a sense of not being a good person, the more quickly they will turn that anger back against themselves. The feeling that, "It is wrong that you should hurt me in this way (physically and/or psychologically)" being converted into, "I am a bad person so I deserve to be treated in this way," and so the anger originally felt towards the punisher is turned back against the self, where it is experienced as guilt. All attempts to make people feel bad about themselves, to, "grovel before the Lord" in sackcloth and ashes, physical or metaphorical, are punishing and therefore, except in the case of those whose healthy confidence in their essential goodness is at a high level, guilt-inducing.

There is however another reason why people in general suffer from high guilt levels. Human beings being by nature independent thinkers ('breaking a child's will' being seen by those of an authoritarian bent as one of the main objectives of child rearing), even quite severe punishments do not generally put an end to our desires to sometimes behave in ways of which the churches, self-appointedly speaking on behalf of God, disapprove. What they very often do, is to cause the individual to put a lid on those illicit impulses. Sometimes the lid fits tightly enough for the person to lose all consciousness of their forbidden desires, although even in this case those desires have a clever way of circumventing the blocks to their natural expression, and may appear as any one of a host of often strange and bizarre behaviours, thereby providing a happy hunting ground for psychotherapists intent on helping people to understand and get rid of their psychological problems.

More frequently our suppressed desires do not completely

disappear from consciousness but from time to time re-enter it quite assertively, demanding satisfaction with some urgency. When this happens we experience 'temptation', temptation to act in ways which we believe, because of some of the teachings of our parents and/or other authority figures (especially in the church) that we have been exposed to, are not in line with the 'Will of God'.

If we are comfortable enough with ourselves, and have a strong enough sense of self-worth, we will be able to admit that the 'temptation' we are experiencing comes from parts of ourselves to which we do not wish to give free rein. If the individual's sense of being an OK person is too fragile, if the implications of admitting that these intrusive troublesome thoughts and feelings were really coming from parts of themselves are too catastrophic for them to contemplate, then what the individual does is to split off a part of their psyche from their conscious self, labelling it 'Not Me'.

The next step is to attribute this disowned part of themselves to an invasion of their mind by a malicious spiritual power (the Devil) to account for their temptations to 'ungodly' behaviour. If they are able to successfully reject the temptations of this devil they feel a virtuous glow and are able to give thanks to God for using his power to save them from committing yet another sin. Unfortunately so much of our normal human nature has been so vigorously proscribed by those making up the authoritarian face of Christianity that all of us inevitably succumb to temptation of one sort or another from time to time, thereby, in the eyes of those who see things from the perspective of authoritarian Christianity, committing a 'sin'.

The absurdity of this way of thinking is amusingly illustrated in something which appeared in *The Gospel Magazine* for 1775. It was in this magazine that one of the all-time favourite hymns of many in the Christian Church, Augustus Montague Toplady's, 'Rock of Ages, cleft for me,' was first published. Strangely, the hymn itself was prefaced by a list of the number of sins which a man might be presumed to commit in the course of a lifetime. The catalogue begins at ten years of age, by which time the unfortunate child is found chargeable with 315,036,000 sins, which number rises to over two and a half billion by the age of 80! It is hard to know which is the funniest aspect of this ludicrous exercise – the final result of the counting process (with its spurious precision, and the very debatable criteria used for the categorisation of any particular behaviour as a sin), the completely pointless uselessness of the finished product, or the picture of someone bending over their desk for the many months, if not years it must have taken to complete this exercise in single-minded devotion to a religious task whose spiritual value must be as close to zero as it is possible to get.

Perhaps though, the fact that this was done does have some value in illustrating the morbid fascination with sinfulness which haunts the lives of probably a larger number of Christians than most of us realise, and for whom the idea of impending punishment for sin hangs like a black cloud over their lives.

Clearly there is a financial incentive to the Christian Church for people's lives to be dominated by belief in its dogmatic formulations about sin, life after death, and its mediating role in sparing us from an eternity of suffering. One can only speculate about how great a role this has played in the Church's development of its dogmas about sin and its forgiveness beloved of those whose Christianity is of the authoritarian variety. But it certainly is the case that traditional Christian beliefs in this area (which have got precious little to do with anything Jesus spoke about) inevitably create and maintain a never-ending cycle of temptation, sin, repentance, confession, penance, and then further temptation, more sin, more repentance, and then more confession and so on *ad infinitum*, which has been a cash cow for much of the Christian Church for centuries.

The more the Church defines basic human needs (like for

example sex, sex without necessarily procreative consequences, freedom from pain, and other aspects of living a happy and fulfilling life) as sin, the more it is entrenching the experience of succumbing to temptation as a common human experience. The more successfully it persuades people of its indispensable role in providing an escape route from the hideous consequences of their sin (in complete contradiction of Jesus' teaching) the more it entrenches itself as a sought-after institution in any society in which empowered thinking for oneself is relatively rare.

The Doctrine of the Atonement

The apex of the development of theological theories about the relationship between God and humankind by those active in the authoritarian face of the Christian Church was reached with the development of the theory (or doctrine, or dogma as religious theories are usually called) of the Atonement, defined in the COED as "the reconciliation of God and mankind through the death of Jesus Christ". This doctrine asserts that:

- Long long ago the omnipotent and all-knowing God of Christian belief created the universe and everything in it which he judged to be 'very good' (Genesis 1:31).
- It later turned out that this creation had at least one design flaw, which this omnipotent, omniscient God seems to have been unaware of until Adam disobeyed his commandment not to eat of the tree of the Knowledge of Good and Evil (Genesis 2:16-17). The flaw was that his human creation didn't always work properly – a pretty serious flaw in any design project!
- When this first breakdown in proper functioning occurred, a previously unknown law of the 'very good' universe that God had created was revealed: Disobedience is a sin and must be punished.
- So because they had disobeyed God's instructions by

eating "of the tree of the knowledge of good and evil",
Adam and Eve were banished from paradise and
condemned to a life of hard labour and a perpetually
adversarial relationship with snakes (Genesis 3:14-19).

- Following hot on the heels of the discovery of that first
design flaw, was the discovery of another even more
serious problem – not only had it turned out that God's
human creations were not the 'very good' creatures he
thought they were when he created them, but their
propensity to sin would be passed on by them to their
children, who in turn would pass that propensity onto
their children, and so on from generation to generation.
The trouble all started with Adam[101] (although of course it
was all Eve's fault – Adam would never have disobeyed
God had Eve not used her feminine wiles on him,
tempting him to disobedience!).

- And so, because Adam and Eve had disobeyed God, the
whole human race became infected with 'original sin' (by
a process which no theologian or biologist has ever been
able to rationally explain),[102] and would inevitably have to
be punished for it. So God either there and then created
Hell as the place of punishment for sin, or perhaps he had
had the foresight to do that while he was creating everything else, although if so, it is strange that this fact was not
mentioned in either of the two Genesis Creation accounts
– Genesis 1:1-31 and Genesis 2:1-25.

- But it seems that at some point God's conscience must have
started to trouble him about the huge and ever-increasing
number of people suffering in Hell, and the more humane
side of his personality began to assert itself. Perhaps he
said to himself something like, "I've begun to feel that this
really isn't quite fair. All these people suffering for all
eternity just because, without realizing it, I created them as
imperfect creatures who would inevitably sin from time to

time. What must people think of me when they learn that I created these creatures "in my own image"? I must restructure things."

- There were obviously a number of options open to God at this point. In fact being an omnipotent being there were probably an infinite number of options open to him. But just four come readily to mind.

  i The most obvious solution is that God could have abolished that law of the universe (which he himself created) that wrongdoing (sin) must be punished.

  ii Alternatively he might have decided to re-programme all human minds, past, present, and future, in such a way that humankind would never do (or have done) any wrong – a difficult task to be sure, but, "with God all things are possible" (Genesis 18:13; Job 42:1; Jeremiah 32:17 and 27; Matthew 19:26; Mark 10:27; Luke 18:27).

  iii A third possibility would have been to pre-empt Jesus' announcement that all that is necessary for us to have our sins forgiven is that we forgive others for their sins. God could have arranged that everyone woke up one morning knowing that provided they forgave others for their sins, their own wrong-doing would in turn be forgiven.

  iv For some strange reason, according to those who developed the theory of the Atonement, God decided against using any of those three humane solutions to his problem. Instead he chose an option whose most striking characteristic is that it is one that preserves the concept that wrongdoing must be punished – there is no such thing as a free pardon; forgiveness cannot take place unless there is some addition to the total amount of pain and suffering in the world.

What was that solution? According to the more vindictive of his self-appointed representatives on earth, God decided that although it is actually the whole human race that should suffer in Hell for all eternity because of Adam and Eve's sin, in his boundless wisdom and mercy, he would, as a loving father to all humanity, allow a whipping-boy to take the punishment which we, the human race, actually deserve for all that we have done wrong, starting with having chosen to be born of sinful parents, and grandparents, and ... and ...

And so it happened, that God arranged for his until-then-not-previously-mentioned son to die a horrible death on the cross. This would then enable this kindly, loving and generous heavenly father of ours to cancel the punishment debt owed collectively by all the members of the human race, who would then have a loving God and his sacrificed son to thank for their escape from an eternity[103] of suffering.

An acceptable theory?

There are a number of serious problems with this theory. It is, of course, absolutely true that in an authoritarian system where there is an overt adversarial relationship between those at the top of the power hierarchy and those lower down it, punishment is essential if the stability of the system is to be maintained. So if the relationship between God and the human race is seen as an authoritarian one, punishment will be seen as a necessary control mechanism. What is not true is that the relationship between God and humankind is *a necessarily* adversarial, authoritarian one. Any human being can think themselves into having such a conflicted relationship with whatever they conceive God to be, but the adversarialness of such a relationship lies in the mind of the person believing that to be the case, not in any external reality. There is much truth in Voltaire's aphorism, "God created Man in his own image, and Man repays the compliment". When our thinking about any aspect of nature seems to suggest a contradiction, that contradiction lies not in nature itself, but in our intellectual understanding of 'the way things are'. The whole thrust of the ethics of Jesus is incompatible with the assumption that an adversarial relationship exists between us and God. "Thou shalt not, or else ..." is certainly not the spirit which breathes through the humanistic face of Christianity.

What are the problems with the Theory of the Atonement?

God's Personality

In the first place acceptance of the truth of this theory requires belief in one of two alternative views about the nature of God's personality, both probably quite unacceptable to most people who are happy to call themselves Christians: Either God is far from all-powerful, or he is a psychopath[104], a hypocritical, bloodthirsty, tyrannical despot who harbours murderous intentions towards his "dearly beloved son," and created the fiction of his own powerlessness to rescind the principle that wrongdoing must be punished, as a smokescreen to deflect attention away from his sadistic cruelty. It is to be further noted that if God is indeed omnipotent, in creating a world order which requires the death of his son, God was breaking his own commandment, "Thou shalt not kill".

Ambiguity in some of the details of the theory

Secondly the doctrine is not as simple as the brief outline of it I have given above would suggest, and it exists in several variant forms in different Christian traditions and in several different books in the bible. A search of the New Testament reveals that for some biblical writers there are no caveats attached to the idea that because Jesus died a horrible death, all our sins have been forgiven, e.g. in John's gospel, Chapter 1, verse 29, "Behold the Lamb of God, which taketh away the sin of the world", in Paul's Epistle to the Romans, Chapter 5, verse 11 ("... through our Lord Jesus Christ, by whom we have now received the atonement"), in the Epistle to the Colossians (which may or may not have been written by Paul himself), Chapter 1, verses 13-14, "... the kingdom of his dear Son: in whom we have redemption through his blood, even the forgiveness of sins", and in the first Epistle of John, Chapter 1 verse 7, "The blood of Jesus Christ his son cleanseth us from all sin".

In none of the above biblical passages is there any suggestion that 'us' or 'we' refers to only a small sub-group of the human race. But there are also explicit statements to be found in the New Testament to the effect that the benefits of Jesus' sacrificial death accrue to everyone without exception. For example in verse 2 of Chapter 2 of the aforementioned Epistle of John quoted above we find, "He is the propitiation for our sins: and not for ours only, but also for the sins of the whole world", and Paul in his second Epistle to the Corinthians, Chapter 5 verse 14 makes the same unambiguous assertion. Referring to the death of Jesus he writes, "We are convinced that one died for all".

However it is also clear that not all biblical writers let the hapless sinner off the hook so easily. For other Christians, some of whose views are to be found in the Bible and others in the pronouncements of non-biblical authors and church leaders and spokespersons, the free pardon for sins committed is not available to all and sundry but only to those who have met one or more of the following requirements:

- They believe in the existence of God, the Divinity of Jesus (Mark 16:16; John 8:24; and Acts 16:30-31) and that he died to save us from our sins. "... the redemption that is in Christ Jesus, whom God put forward as a sacrifice of atonement by his blood, effective through faith" (Romans 3:25).
- They have repented of their sins (Luke 13:3 and 5; and Acts 2:38 and 22:16).
- They have been baptised (Mark 16:16; and Acts 2:38 and

22:16).

- They have had a conversion experience (Mark 4:12; and Acts 3:19 and 26:18) and have been 'born again'. I discuss this widely misunderstood phrase at some length a little further on in this chapter.
- They obey divine injunctions, or rather those injunctions which those at the upper end of the church hierarchy claim to be divine injunctions. Writing of Jesus, the author of the epistle to the Hebrews states: "And being made perfect, he became the author of eternal salvation unto all they that obey him" (Hebrews 5:9).
- They believe with their heart and confess with their mouth. "For one believes with the heart and so is justified, and one confesses with the mouth and so is saved" (Romans 10:9-10).
- Some dispensations have additional requirements that salvation from the consequences in the life after death of sins committed can only be achieved by those who attend church/mass/confession regularly and have received absolution for their sins from the ministrations of a priest just before their death.

The fate of those who died before Jesus did

Thirdly, yet another problem with the doctrine of the atonement is that no serious rational thought seems to have been given by those who believe in the theory, to the question of what has happened to all those people who died before Jesus did. If Jesus' atoning death was all the human race needed to ensure that we all go to heaven then presumably at the moment of his death all the souls who were in Hell (or purgatory) would somehow or other have been instantly translated into heaven – a remarkable event, before the technicalities of which even the brightest human mind must stand flummoxed, perhaps taking comfort from the despairing cry of Dr Johnson, the compiler of the first English

Dictionary, when he said of the plot of Shakespeare's play *Cymbeline*, "It is impossible to criticise unresisting imbecility".

Yet a further problem presents itself if the idea is accepted that the benefits of the atoning death of Jesus are available only to those who meet some of the additional requirements listed above (like "confessing with the mouth", as Paul asserts in Romans 10:9-10). Since the dead cannot meet this or any of the other additional requirements for the forgiveness of their sins, it would seem that they would then have to spend the rest of eternity in Hell for no better reason than that they happened to have died a few years, or minutes or even seconds too early. Perhaps Einstein was wrong and God really does play dice with the universe!

Or perhaps God had a secret plan which we remain in the dark about to this day, and granted a special dispensation to allow those who died before Jesus to be immediately translated into heaven at the moment of his death, while the rest of us who were born even only a fraction of a second afterwards still have to meet one or more of the vaguely-defined additional criteria scattered throughout the New Testament. Whether that would mean granting further immunity to those who at the time of Jesus' death were too young to do anything about meeting those further requirements, and if so until what age that immunity was valid, and whether that same age at which immunity ceased to be available applied to every child regardless of their level of intellectual ability (genius or severely mentally handicapped), or whether each case would be handled on its merits, and whether God would be employing psychologists to assist him with the assessment process, and ... and ... . How beautifully simple Jesus' teaching seems by contrast with that theological minefield of purely human construction – in the words of St Francis of Assisi, "It is in forgiving others that we ourselves are forgiven".

The moral unacceptability of the punishment of an innocent person

Finally, the Theory of the Atonement is unconvincing to many 21st-century Christian minds. The idea that we (all multi-trillions of us) should be punished for all eternity because some extremely remote ancestor of ours ate an apple, is so ludicrous as to be unbelievable to an increasing number of people. Moreover, the idea that we can do a great wrong (by being born of sinful parents, as the doctrine of original sin tells us we were), and get off scot-free for it because of someone else's suffering and death, offends some deep moral instinct of the human mind. On the grounds of this factor alone some would describe the Atonement dogma as a blasphemous slander on God's reputation, imputing to him some of the qualities of human beings at their worst.

Am I one of the 'saved'?

Any uncertainty (about just whose sins have been forgiven) aroused in the minds of 'true believers' by the bible quotes listed above, will be heightened when read in conjunction with the statement attributed to Jesus in verse 28 of Chapter 26 of Matthew's gospel to the effect that, "This is my blood of the new testament, which is shed *for many* for the remission of sins". Although it is pretty certain that Jesus never spoke those words which the Gospel writer has put into his mouth[105], the fact that supposedly the greatest authority (bar God the Father himself) on the subject of just what Jesus' death was to achieve, is reported as saying that the shedding of his blood was "for many", cannot but raise the anxiety levels of many 'true believers' as to who is one of the "many" and thus 'saved', and who is not.

And that is not the end of the matter for those who have the misfortune to stumble on verse 31 of the tenth chapter of the Epistle to the Hebrews (which was most probably not written by Paul, but by someone else in the early Christian Church), and written long after the 'atoning death of Jesus' had taken place. "It is a fearful thing to fall into the hands of the living God" – a chilling thought, reminiscent of the advice of that much revered Roman Catholic former President of the United States, John F. Kennedy, "Forgive your enemies, but remember their names".

Paul himself, although a major figure in the development of the theory of the Atonement, and therefore presumably qualifying for salvation in terms of it, seems to have been by no means totally confident of his own salvation status. He may have written in Romans 10:13, "Everyone who calls on the name of the Lord shall be saved", but he also wrote, in Romans 2:5-9, "On the day of wrath ... he will repay according to each one's deeds. ... There will be anguish and distress for everyone who does evil". Given that Paul believed that, it is hardly surprising to find him writing in II Corinthians 5:11, about "Knowing ... the terror of the Lord" – this in the context of his saying in the preceding verse that "... we must all appear before the judgement seat of Christ; that everyone may receive all things done in his body, according to that he hath done, whether it be good or bad."

This, of course, is totally contradictory of the idea that Jesus' death secured the forgiveness of humanity's sins, whether it be the whole of humanity or just a select sub-group who are thus favoured. It is doubtless the fact that Paul held such contradictory views about the forgiveness (or non-forgiveness) of sins that led him in I Corinthians 9:16, to cry, "Woe to me if I do not proclaim the gospel!", and, referring to the many varying reasons why different people preach it, he expresses his conviction that, "Through your prayers and the help of the Spirit of Jesus Christ this will turn out for my deliverance" (Philippians 1:18-19). Most unreassuringly of all to those relying on Paul's guidance in spiritual matters, in Philippians 2:12 he tells his readers to, "Work out your own salvation with fear and trembling".

Many Christians, despite seemingly believing in the doctrine of the Atonement, are often wracked with guilt over their past sins, and any others they might commit if 'the Tempter's power' becomes too great for them to resist. For many, the complexities and lack of clarity as to the details of the theory of the Atonement (as well as, for some, its almost too good to be true nature), make it no match in their thinking for that simple, punchy concept that, "The wages of sin is death" (Romans 6:23).

A recent development

Just how chaotic the details of the Doctrine of the Atonement still are in the 21st century, is well illustrated by the reaction of the Vatican-based Roman Catholic Church to the pronouncement of its newly-elected (as of March 2013) Pope Francis, that:

> The Lord has redeemed all of us, all of us, with the Blood of Christ: all of us, not just Catholics. Everyone! ... Even the atheists. Everyone!

Despite the still-in-force, though somewhat ambiguous doctrine of papal infallibility, the Vatican spokesman Father Thomas Rosica issued a 'clarification' of what Pope Francis really meant, which effectively contradicted the new Pope's message. He made it clear that the Roman Catholic Church's position remained that merely being 'good' is not enough to avoid going to hell: "They cannot be saved who, knowing the Church as founded by Christ and necessary for salvation, would refuse to enter her or remain in her." A thought-provoking account of the beginnings of the alarm generated by the new Pope's apparently liberalising pronouncement is to be found at http://www.independen t.co.uk/news/world/europe/what-the-hell-vatican-caught-in-two-minds-over-damnation-for-nonbelievers-8635121.html?origin =internalSearch.

Most Christians are probably not particularly interested in the details of the theory of the Atonement, which many theologians have agonised over for many years. For most it may well all boil down to just the belief that, "The wages of sin is death", and that the benefits of Jesus' atoning death are available only to those who have "repented of their sins". It is probably very largely the gnawing anxiety that if God does not realise just how sorry they are for those sins, he will withhold the benefits of the atoning death of his 'dearly beloved son' (despite its being already promised), which fuels the obsessional requests to God built into the structure of nearly all Christian religious services for forgiveness for our sinfulness.

The Didache

Although the broad lines of the arguments I advance in this book have been steadily growing in my mind for as long as I can remember, in the course of the extensive research I have needed to undertake in writing it, from time to time facts have emerged which illuminate with dazzling clarity some aspect of traditional Christian theology which has always troubled me. One such epiphany occurred with my discovery of the existence of an early church manuscript called the *Didache: The Lord's Teaching Through the Twelve Apostles to the Nations,* still relatively unknown to most Christians. Geza Vermes describes this in his book *Christian Beginnings* (on page 135) as, "one of the most significant literary treasures of primitive Christianity". This is a manual of moral instruction and church practice, containing many of the sayings of Jesus, which claims to have been authored by the twelve apostles. It was written in Greek, as were all the earliest New Testament documents we have today, and is dated by scholars as having been originally written somewhere between 50 and 120 CE, though additions and modifications may have taken place well into the third century. There are several references to it in early Christian literature but it was 'lost' for many centuries until it was re-discovered in 1875 in the Jerusalem Monastery of the Holy Sepulchre at Constantinople.

Probably designed as some sort of handbook for new

Christian converts, the book is divided into three sections. The first six chapters consist of Christian lessons, drawing heavily from the teachings of Jesus; the next four give descriptions of the Christian ceremonies, including baptism, fasting and the Eucharist (or communion), while the last six outline aspects of church organization. The work was never officially rejected by the Church, but was excluded from the canon of the New Testament on the dubious grounds of its lack of literary value.

Of striking interest so far as the Doctrine of the Atonement is concerned is the fact that Chapter 9 of this document, dealing with the Eucharist, makes no mention of the supposed sacrificial nature of Jesus' death. Far from quoting the words of "institution of the Lord's Supper" recorded in Matthew (26-28), Mark (14:22-24), and Luke (22:19–20), Chapter 9 of the Didache starts off with the words, "Now concerning the Eucharist, give thanks this way. First, concerning the cup:

We thank thee, our Father, for the holy vine of David Thy servant, which You madest known to us through Jesus Thy Servant; to Thee be the glory for ever.

And concerning the broken bread:

We thank Thee, our Father, for the life and knowledge which You madest known to us through Jesus Thy Servant; to Thee be the glory for ever. Even as this broken bread was scattered over the hills, and was gathered together and became one, so let Thy Church be gathered together from the ends of the earth into Thy kingdom; for Thine is the glory and the power through Jesus Christ for ever.

At no point in the chapter (or indeed in the whole document) is any mention made of Jesus' death, or its supposed atoning signif-icance, nor of any belief that in partaking of the Eucharistic meal,

Christians are eating the body and drinking the blood of Jesus, either literally or metaphorically, nor of a loving God who condemned his son to suffer and die for the sins of humankind.

Intriguingly the "words of institution of the Lord's Supper" in one of the New Testament gospel sources (Luke 22:19–20) were not present in the earliest and most reliable manuscript sources of that gospel.

> Then he took a loaf of bread, and when he had given thanks, he broke it and gave it to them, saying, "This is my body which is given for you. Do this in remembrance of me." And he did the same with the cup after supper, saying, "This cup that is poured out for you is the new covenant in my blood."

It is striking that Paul in I Corinthians 11:23-25 puts into Jesus' mouth almost the identical words that appear in later manuscript versions of Luke's gospel.

> The Lord Jesus on the night when he was betrayed took a loaf of bread, and when he had given thanks, he broke it and said, "This is my body that is for you. Do this in remembrance of me." In the same way he took the cup also, after supper, saying, "This cup is the new covenant in my blood. Do this, as often as you drink it, in remembrance of me."

Paul's reporting of anything from the life of Jesus without modifying and distorting it, is a very rare event. Although other explanations are possible, drawing the conclusion that Luke 22:19-20 is an interpolation into the original manuscripts of that Gospel by the early church (possibly to bolster the credibility of its developing atonement doctrine), is almost irresistible. Paul claims that he "received" his knowledge of what Jesus had said in instituting the sacrament of the Lord's Supper "from the Lord" (I Corinthians 11:23). It seems very likely that if there is any truth at all in that way of looking at things, the Lord had some very human help in imparting that knowledge to Paul. Be that as it may, it is quite clear from the Didache that the doctrine of the Atonement was very far from universally accepted in the early Christian Church.

On the need for a conversion experience and being 'born again'

The word 'conversion' is derived from the Latin word *convertere* which means to turn around, to transform. The Shorter Oxford English Dictionary gives the theological meaning of conversion as, "The turning of sinners to God; a spiritual change from sinfulness to a religious life". Traditionally within orthodox Christianity that process has been seen and experienced as a largely intellectual one – a decision to change from a way of life governed by values of which the church or sect to which the individual is converting disapproves, to a lifestyle governed by values of which they do approve.

Although that process must always have had at least some emotional component to it, in the 20th century, pioneered by the explosively growing and emotionally volatile charismatic and evangelical churches in the United States, South America and Africa, any even mildly sophisticated analysis of what the individual was converting to and from took very much a back seat in favour of the pursuit of powerful emotional release. For many years now the vast majority of Christian conversions have had the doctrine of the Atonement as their point of departure. That doctrine's appeal has always been to those tormented with guilt about their sinfulness and the fear that eternal punishment will be their lot because of all the sins they have committed. Although there are many exceptions to the rule, in general the more guilty anyone feels about their sinfulness, the more relevant the doctrine of the Atonement will inevitably seem to be, and the stronger will become the attractions of embracing the idea of the truth of that belief.

The highly authoritarian charismatic and evangelical churches have mounted a massive public relations campaign to promote their brand of the conversion process. In most of those churches it is believed that in becoming converted, the individual becomes 'born again', and for many people in those churches this is the defining experience of Christianity – without which no one can honestly claim to be a Christian. Not wishing to be left behind in the matter of providing their flock with a more emotionally alive experience of their Christianity, these habits of thought have also spread from time to time to the more mainstream churches.

The now-typical Christian conversion process consists firstly of heightening the individual's sense of guilt about the "manifold sins and wickednesses" they have committed, secondly of heightening their fears that eternal punishment awaits them as a penalty for their wrongdoing, thirdly of convincing them that Jesus' suffering and death was authorised by God as a substitute punishment for all their sins, and finally that all they need to do to have all their sins washed away is to accept Jesus Christ as their 'personal saviour' (or words to that effect). Most individuals who allow themselves to be led as far through the ritual as this last step, will eagerly 'surrender themselves to Christ', meaning in theory that they will no longer follow their own natural (and therefore sinful) instincts, but in practice that they will stop thinking for themselves and will believe whatever the church of their choice tells them they should believe, that church of course speaking on behalf of God/Christ/Jesus, to whose mind the leaders of their chosen branch of Christianity are believed to have uniquely privileged access as to what constitutes 'good', and what constitutes 'bad' behaviour.

Having probably wrestled for years with the problem of which of their natural, spontaneous behaviours are good and will keep them out of trouble in the next life, and which are bad and will ensure them an eternity of painful misery after their death, many people are more than happy (for a while at any rate) to submit themselves to the authority of whatever church is promoting this escape route from a life of high-stakes risks. This process is usually accompanied by a huge flood of emotion, a massive sense of relief at their escape from the hellish idea of suffering an eternity of punishment (at the hands, of course, of a loving God), or even just being unloved and rejected by this heavenly father-substitute.

Unfortunately for those who have gone this route, this highly-emotionally-charged experience has nothing whatsoever to do with the forgiveness of sins, or any other aspect of spirituality. What it has got to do with, indeed what it is, is the experience of authoritarian submission – the convert giving up their right, indeed their desire and their responsibility to think for themselves with all its attendant uncertainties, in favour of absolute obedience to 'the will of God', as interpreted by the converting organisation. It cannot be too often repeated that this has nothing to do with being 'born again' which Jesus spoke about as one of the defining characteristics of entry into the Kingdom of God. The central place which conversion and born again experiences and their associated emotional wallowing have acquired in the evangelical churches is a major reason for their success in attracting a large following among those who have been left cold by the intellectually unconvincing and largely emotionally unsatisfying didactic approach of many of the very Left-brain-oriented mainstream churches. But the 'conversion' and 'being born again' experiences discussed above are not primarily spiritual events and not what Jesus meant when he talked about the need for us to be 'born again'. What he very probably did mean was discussed in the previous chapter.

It is hard to fathom how the experience of authoritarian submission provided by the evangelical churches' version of the conversion process ever came to be associated with the profound insights about the spiritual value of becoming like a little child attributed to Jesus in the gospels. The only obvious link between the states of authoritarian submission and being a young child is that in both these states the individual is more highly suggestible than the average adult. Accepting Jesus (or Christ, or Jesus Christ) as a 'personal saviour' (to use the clichéd language of the 'saved'), and the emotional release which generally accompanies this act, is in other respects nothing like the behaviour and experience of the typical child referred to by Jesus.[106] The typical Christian conversion can only be regarded as a rebirth process in the loose sense in which we describe significant events that happen to us as marking the beginning of a new life.

The words "born again" appear only three times in the Bible (in John 3:3 and 7, and in I Peter 1:23) none of which references throw any light at all on why, "Accepting Jesus as our personal saviour" should have anything to do with being born again. In other words there is no more any scriptural basis than there is any psychological basis for identifying the highly emotional, guilt-based conversion process beloved particularly of the evangelical and charismatic branches of authoritarian Christianity as a necessary condition for entry into the Kingdom of Heaven. Abandoning one's right to think critically about where one's life is going in favour of accepting the autocratic dictates of any institution, religious or otherwise, may be a huge relief to those who have little confidence in their own self-worth, but it has nothing whatsoever to do with the deepening of their spirituality, and specifically does not in itself bring the convert into that way of being which Jesus described as being in the Kingdom of God.

Uniformity of belief and rigid dogma

Many of the characteristics of authoritarian Christianity can be traced to the fact that in accepting the poisoned chalice of

Constantine's 'gift' of immunity from persecution, (and the later co-option of the religion as the state religion of the Roman empire), Christianity became to a considerable extent a political institution, and one which inevitably came to bear the imprint of the legalistic thinking which was one of the factors which had once made Rome great. Whatever the merits of the Roman legal system in the political arena, it was disastrously unsuited to a church which was ostensibly promoting the ethical principles of Jesus of Nazareth. Ideas such as, "Judge not that ye be not judged", "If it comes to a choice between right and being kind, choose kind", and, "Whosoever among you would be greatest, let him be your servant", central to the humanistic face of Christianity, would be anathema to the leaders of the domination-seeking Roman state and were soon consigned to the 'lunatic fringes' of the early church.

A fundamental requirement of legalistic religious thinking is to have a clear, unambiguous statement of what constitutes 'right', and what constitutes punishable 'wrong' behaviour and belief. This being so it is not surprising that, at least since the time of Constantine's enforced unification of the church, the Christian Church as a whole has been preoccupied with dogma. A huge amount of scholarly ecclesiastical effort has been put into arriving at rigid statements as to what constitutes 'right belief' for the Christian, but the more rigid such formulations become, the more they increase the probability that splits will occur in the parent body. A. N. Whitehead's vivid statement with which I started this chapter, "Religions commit suicide when they find their inspirations in their dogmas," is a powerful truth.

Paradoxically the more effort that is put into trying to ensure that individual differences are ironed out at the level of dogma, the more strongly will individual differences appear in the organisational structure of the Christian Church. The human being's biologically-based resistance to imposed conformity is psychologically one of our most valuable possessions. It is what enables us to retain at least a modicum of that biologically-determined diversity of thought and behaviour which is natural to human beings and without which creativity is stifled, novelty cannot emerge, and the whole human enterprise becomes a lifeless, dull, boring, repetition of past habits.

In Appendix 1 is a poem written by an anonymous high school student shortly before she committed suicide, which vividly portrays the effects of dogmatic intolerance in the educational field. Pressure to conform to norms is at least as damaging in matters of religion as it is in the educational field. The subtle (and sometimes not so subtle) pressures that leaders within the authoritarian face of Christianity exert on their flock to give up their natural instincts to question and debate received wisdom in respect of spiritual matters, is damaging to those on the receiving end of such pressure. Unless permission to do so is forcefully denied to us in early life, we naturally love exercising our mind in analysing and trying to understand spiritual things, as much as any other aspects of our human experience, and only in that way can we arrive at an authentic and meaningful understanding of the spiritual world and our relationship to it. To be intolerant of challenges to the sacred cows of traditional religious dogma so common in authoritarian religions, with their mantra of, 'Don't question, just accept,' is one of the most dangerous temptations to which institutional religions can fall prey, and one of the gravest disservices they can do to individuals when they succumb to it.

Fundamentalism

Given the black and white nature of the demand for uniformity of belief so often to be found within authoritarian Christianity it is not surprising to find quite a widespread tendency in that branch of the religion to treat with suspicion any attempts to view the Bible as anything other than a divinely-inspired creation, in which everything that is said there is absolutely and literally true. To admit the possibility that some parts of it should be understood as being a humanly-created historical document, or a symbolic or imaginative way of expressing some almost intangible truths, would be to open a Pandora's box of different and often conflicting interpretations of some of the really puzzling aspects of the Christian religion. Such uncertainty would be anathema to the minds of authoritarian Christians. Adopting a simplistic, fundamentalist belief in the literal truth of the Bible is an easy way out for those who don't want to have to think critically about the complex concepts which are embedded in most sets of religious beliefs, or to take the risk of getting hold of some wrong ideas which might seriously compromise their chances of escaping punishment in the afterlife.

The obsessive belief that every single thing written in the Bible is the unchallengeable 'Word of God' is common among those who make up the authoritarian face of Christianity, but is by no means universal among them. Even among those who devoutly believe that the universe and everything in it came into existence in a matter of six days[107], there must surely be few who can honestly claim to believe that when the Bible records that Paul wrote in I Corinthians 15:31, "I die everyday – I mean that, brothers", this means Paul's heart stops beating every day but that he comes back to life after every one of those 'deaths'. This is so manifestly absurd that Paul's insistence in that sentence that he means what he says has an almost comical effect.

Similarly, even the most diehard fundamentalist is unlikely to take from the verse at II Corinthians 5:1, "Now we know that if the earthly tent we live in is destroyed, we have a building from God, an eternal house in heaven", the idea that God is running a real-estate business in heaven. In fact St Paul (of "Wives submit yourselves to your husbands" fame), eminent religious autocrat though he was, was no slave to the literal truth of verbal expression. With rare penetrating spiritual insight he could assert, "... the letter kills, but the spirit gives life" (II Corinthians

3:6), and the intellectual gymnastics he performs in providing a figurative rather than a literal interpretation of the Genesis story of the origins of Abraham's two sons Ishmael and Isaac is quite remarkable and must be quite a puzzle to strict fundamentalists. Genesis Chapters 16 to 18, and 21 describe how Abraham's eldest son Ishmael was born of Hagar, a slave of Sarah his wife, conceived (with the agreement of all three parties involved) when it was thought Sarah was barren. Some years later, although "Abraham and Sarah were old and well stricken in age", and Sarah was no longer menstruating (Genesis 18:11), Abraham's second son was reportedly born of Sarah. Treating the Genesis account of this 'apparent' bit of history as an extended metaphor, Paul claims (on the flimsiest of evidence) that the Genesis story is in fact an allegory, contrasting the state of those who are "born after the flesh" with that of those who are born "by promise". Paul's tortuous reasoning here is difficult to make much sense of, but perhaps the 1961 New English Bible translation is more helpful than most of the other English translations in that task. It reads,

This is an allegory. The two women stand for two covenants. The one bearing children into slavery is the covenant that comes from Mount Sinai: that is Hagar. Sinai is a mountain in Arabia and it represents the Jerusalem of today, for she and her children are in slavery. But the heavenly Jerusalem is the free woman; she is our mother. For Scripture says, 'Rejoice, O barren woman who never bore child; break into a shout of joy, you who never knew a mother's pangs; for the deserted wife shall have more children than she who lives with the husband.' And you, my brothers, like Isaac, are children of God's promise. But just as in those days the natural-born son persecuted the spiritual son, so it is today. But what does Scripture say? 'Drive out the slave-woman and her son, for the son of the slave shall not share the inheritance with the free woman's sons.' You see, then, my brothers, we are no slave-woman's children; our mother is the free woman. Christ set us free, to be free men. Stand firm, then, and refuse to be tied to the yoke of slavery again" (Galatians 4:24-31, and 5:1).

Given such remarkable interpretative powers, if Paul were alive today he would probably have experienced very little difficulty in developing a metaphorical interpretation of the two Genesis Creation stories which would harmonise the two of them with each other and with at least the main features of the modern scientific view of evolutionary biology.

Chapter 7

Humanistic and Authoritarian Christianity: The ideas of Jesus and Paul compared

No idea is determinate in a vacuum: it has its being as one of a system of ideas.[108]
– Alfred North Whitehead. *Religion in the Making*

Although the writings of Christians and other interested parties over a period of 2000 years are an important source of information about what constitutes the religion of Christianity, the primary source material for the knowledge we have on that subject comes from the New Testament of the Christian Bible. The previous two chapters have given a brief account of what can be gleaned from that source as to what constitute the two very different religions that go under the name of Christianity – the one a humanistic one (in which the religion exists to help make the world a better and happier place for all, in other words to bring about the Kingdom of God on earth), and the other an authoritarian one (in which the 'truths of religion' are seen as having an unassailable claim to absolute validity, to which human beings must accommodate themselves if they are to escape the awful consequences in the afterlife of not having lived their lives according to the dictates of the church).

The ideas expressed by Jesus and the early church as recorded in the New Testament did not just drop out of heaven into the laps of those eagerly waiting in total darkness for such illumination. Some of the ideas that Jesus taught were (so far as we know) new. Some had a long tradition in Jewish thought, and some in the writing and thinking of other religious traditions as well. Some have provided at least the germ of an idea which has grown into a philosophy of life, a way of seeing and being in the world which has both inspired and been added to by people; scientists, psychologists, philosophers and other thinkers, some of whom have no connection (or at least no conscious connection) with Christianity. The ethical ideas urged upon us by Jesus, where and whenever they may have first been expressed, have been immensely influential in developing the thought and behaviour of European civilisation. Many of the ideas contained in the Sermon on the Mount have provided the heaven at work in the growth of compassionate understanding in many human lives which have blessed the world with a significant reduction in the sum total of human misery and suffering.

In this and the following chapter I want to contrast the essential features of the two faces of Christianity as detailed in Chapters 5 and 6, but also to set our understanding of those differences in a wider psychological context.

What are the differences in the understanding of the world: the ethical values, and the vision for the future of humanity which permeate each of the two faces of Christianity, and where have they come from?

The two most influential sources of ideas about spiritual reality and humankind's relationship with it in the New Testament are two Jewish men: Jesus and Paul. Their ideas are by no means always in harmony, and insofar as they differ, probably account for most of the differences between the humanistic and authoritarian faces of Christianity. In trying to understand those differences and how they could have arisen, it is important to remember that Paul and Jesus never met, even though the estimated date of Paul's birth is only about five years after that of Jesus (4 BCE and approximately 2 CE, in terms of our present calendar). When Paul started his work of expanding the influence of the Christian Church among the Gentiles, Jesus had been dead twenty or more years, so all the information Paul had about the personality and teachings of Jesus was at best second-hand. That being so one can hardly be surprised if Paul got hold of the wrong end of the stick at times as to what Jesus' message was all about. One cannot but wonder whether Paul did not at times feel a sense of deep regret that he had never met the man who played such an important role in his life, especially since they were both alive and living in the same country for 80% of Jesus' life.

Paul's divided self

To judge from what Paul wrote in his epistles he was not a happy man, and clearly was to quite a considerable degree a split personality. Most, if not all of us are 'Divided Selves', to quote from the title of an epoch-making book by the 20th-century Scottish Psychiatrist Ronald Laing. We all have some different aspects of ourselves which are incompatible with each other. In certain situations one part of our personality shows itself, in another situation we may exhibit a very different one. We sometimes behave very differently in front of our parents from how we behave in front of our own children, and very differently from how we behave in the presence of a spouse, or a lover, or our boss, or a subordinate, or perhaps a priest, or a policeman or a doctor. If we don't feel guilty about any of these behaviours when carried out in the appropriate context, we are usually aware of what aspect of our personality is coming across in different situations, and how these relate to each other. Some people, however, are completely unaware of just how radically different, indeed sometimes downright contradictory some of the ideas they hold on a particular topic are, particularly if they feel guilty about some of the thoughts they are tempted to harbour. This is particularly the case with those who grew up in a very authoritarian environment in which they were forced to accept beliefs and carry out patterns of behaviour imposed on them by powerful authority figures.

Such a process results in some people's minds being so split up and compartmentalised that although there is no conscious conflict between the contents of some of those compartments, many of the ideas in those compartments are irreconcilable with each other, and the person does not realise just how much they lack a unified, coherent view on certain topics. This situation is exacerbated if the individual feels uncomfortable about any aspect of themselves. The temptation to deny the existence of those parts of themselves can become overwhelming. The unwanted parts of the person's self may become completely split off and banished from consciousness. These shut-away parts do not communicate with each other, and so the person can have very different sets of thoughts, ideas, beliefs, and potentials for behaviour co-existing within themselves. Because there is no communication between them, incompatible ideas can coexist for long periods without open conflict, but sooner or later one of the long-suppressed ones will force its way forward and strange and sometimes bizarre things are said and done.

Depending on the number of splits in their mind, and the strength of the forces maintaining those splits, the person's behaviour and emotional experience may lie anywhere on a continuum from near 'normality' to the severe psychiatric condition of Multiple Personality Disorder.[109]

Where does Paul lie on such a continuum, and what grounds are there for placing him on that continuum at all? His awareness of the fact that there is a split between his Real Self and his Ideal Self, and the distress that fact causes him is a characteristic he shares with just about the whole human race. "For the good that I would I do not: but the evil which I would not, that I do" (Romans 7:19). The translation of the International Standard (2008) version is even more revealing, "I don't understand what I am doing. For I don't practise what I want to do, but instead do what I hate."[110] Although from a Mental Health point of view, a split between one's Real Self and one's Ideal Self has the potential to be an abnormality which can cause significant problems in the individual's life, from a statistical point of view there is nothing unusual about this. This is especially true in Paul's case, since he is aware of his situation, and sometimes able to honestly admit this aspect of who he is.

Less 'normal', and of more direct relevance to an evaluation of the validity of Paul's spiritual 'insights', is the fact that the whole of the seventh chapter of Paul's Epistle to the Romans up to the last verse is an agonised and rather repetitive attempt (which goes nowhere in any way enlightening), to understand the paradox of the unwilling sinner. Verse 19 quoted above is an almost exact copy of verse 15 of the same chapter, and the theme of tortured self-criticism ends, in the penultimate verse, with a cry of despair, "Wretched man that I am! Who will rescue me from this body of death?"

Paul undoubtedly made some very valuable contributions to the early development of Christianity, and was capable of some profound spiritual insights which are of lasting value. One of these is his paean to love in the thirteenth chapter of his first Epistle to the Corinthians, the chapter which begins, "Though I speak with the tongues of men and of angels, and have not love, I am become as sounding brass, or a tinkling cymbal," and ends, "And now abideth faith, hope, love, these three; but the greatest of these is love". His listing of the "Fruits of the Spirit" in Galatians 5:22-23, his insight into that profound truth that, "The letter killeth but the spirit giveth life" (II Corinthians 3:6), and his conviction that, "All things work together for good to those who love God" (Romans 8:28), are further examples of this deep spiritual awareness. Most strikingly his conviction that circumcision is of no spiritual value at all, and his determination not to allow the enforced circumcision of uncircumcised male converts to Christianity (almost all Gentiles) as a criterion for admission to the Christian fold was both spiritually insightful and courageous. Unfortunately, however, not all the views he held are of this type: there are other characteristics of his thought which raise serious concerns about Paul's mental health.

Paul's concepts of God

Paul was well aware of a split between his Real Self and his Ideal Self, but there were other splits in his mind, of some of which he may well never have been aware. One of the most serious of those splits, significant for the negative effects it has had on the people whose religious thinking has been influenced by Paul's teachings, has been that which clearly existed in respect of his concept of God. Close detailed inspection of every verse in the seven Pauline epistles which just about all modern biblical scholars agree were written by Paul himself[111], shows very clearly that Paul had two contradictory beliefs about the nature of God in his head, and sometimes one, and sometimes the other managed to control what he said on that subject. The one, which is in complete harmony with the concept held by Jesus, is of a loving, compassionate being. The other, which is completely incompatible with that view of the nature of God, is of a harsh, unforgiving and vicious entity, very much of the same type as that 'God' whose cruel edicts some of the Old Testament writers reported with relish.[112]

Not only do different parts of Paul's mind obviously believe that each of these incompatible and contradictory descriptions of the nature of God are true but, significantly, he refers to the loving God of Jesus' experience on only a handful of occasions.

I am convinced that neither death, nor life, nor angels, nor rulers, nor things present, nor things to come, nor powers, nor height, nor depth, nor anything else in all creation, will be able to separate us from the love of God (Romans 8:38-39).

The Father of compassion and the God of all comfort, who comforts us in all our troubles so that we can comfort those in any trouble with the comfort we ourselves have received from God (II Corinthians 1:3-4).

By contrast there is a much larger number of references to a very different type of divine being, an angry God who is anything but a comfort in times of trouble. For example in the first chapter of Romans, in verses 29 to 31, Paul lists 22 instances of wrongdoing, and in verse 32 he writes that, "...the judgement of God (is) that they that commit such things are worthy of death". Amusingly two of the listed items of wrongdoing are being "implacable" and "unmerciful"! Two of the others, being "proud" and "boasters" are 'faults' which elsewhere Paul freely admits to (but not as faults), while two others, "debate" and "being disobedient to parents", make quite clear that these sentiments belong unambiguously to the authoritarian face of Christianity. One wonders whether Paul ever read over what he had written in his epistles. Surely even Paul at his most angry did not seriously believe that the "judgement of God" is that those who "debate" issues, or are "disobedient to parents" are worthy of death? And yet this seems to be what he wrote.

The "wrath of God" and the consequences of this for those who misbehave is a constantly recurring theme in Paul's epistles. Had he been challenged about it, Paul would probably have defended the fear that he sought to instil in his flock through the aspects of his preaching contained in the quotes below, as "making holiness perfect in the fear of God" (II Corinthians, 7:1).

Romans 1:18. "For the wrath of God is revealed from heaven against all ungodliness and unrighteousness of men".

Romans 2:5-8. "But by your hard and impenitent heart you are storing up wrath for yourself on the day of wrath, when God's righteous judgement will be revealed. For He will repay according to each one's deeds: to those who by patiently doing good seek for glory and honour and immortality, He will give eternal life; while for those who are self-seeking and who obey not the truth but wickedness, there will be wrath and fury."

Romans 2:9. "Tribulation and anguish, upon every soul of

man that doeth evil."

Romans 12:19 (referring back to Deuteronomy 32:35). "Do not take revenge, my friends, but leave room for God's wrath, for it is written: 'It is mine to avenge; I will repay,' says the Lord."

I Corinthians 3:16-17. "Do you not know that you are God's temple and that God's Spirit dwells in you? If anyone destroys God's temple, God will destroy that person. For God's temple is holy, and you are that temple."

I Thessalonians 1:10. "Jesus, who rescues us from the wrath that is coming".

I Thessalonians 4:6. In respect of men who defraud their brother, "...the Lord is the avenger of all such, as we also have forewarned you and testified".

Inspired by such a concept of God, in respect of a particularly scandalous instance of fornication in the nascent Corinthian church[113], Paul recommends a public denunciation of the man's wrongdoing and really viciously commands the church,

> You are to hand this man over to Satan for the destruction of the flesh, so that his spirit may be saved in the day of the Lord (I Corinthians 5:5).

When a different part of Paul's mind is in control of what he is saying, a very different concept of God emerges as lying behind what he says. In the second chapter of Paul's second Epistle to the Corinthians, the "punishment" Paul recommends for someone who has caused the community pain and distress is,

> You should forgive and console him, so that he may not be overwhelmed by excessive sorrow. So I urge you to reaffirm your love for him. ... Anyone whom you forgive I also forgive 114 (II Corinthians 2:7-8, and 10).

In Galatians 6:1, Paul's advice to the church about how to deal with wrongdoers is again inspired by a concept of God as, "the God of all comfort, who comforts us in all our troubles so that we can comfort those in any trouble" (II Corinthians 1:4). Paul writes, "My friends, if anyone is detected in a transgression, you who have received the Spirit should restore such a one in a spirit of gentleness".

The speed with which Paul can switch from his concept of a harsh and angry God to that of a loving and compassionate one is quite remarkable. In I Corinthians 16:22 he calls down a curse on any one who does not "love ... the Lord Jesus Christ". He writes, "If any man love not the Lord Jesus Christ let him be Anathema Maranatha". Bearing in mind that Anathema means 'accursed', and Maranatha (used only once in the New Testament) means "The Lord is coming," the meaning of this verse is quite clear: "Watch out! The Lord is coming and he will execute his judgement against your accursed self." Given that we are told (in Romans 9:28, quoting Isaiah 10:22-23) that, "The Lord will execute his sentence on the earth quickly and decisively," it seems rather unnecessary to be warned, using the imagery of God breaking off the unprofitable branches of a barren olive tree, to "be afraid," because just as God did not spare the olive branches which did not perform as he wanted them to, "he will not spare you either" (Romans 11:20-22). Nevertheless Paul does tell us these things and their combined effect, together with many other similarly threatening statements sprinkled throughout his epistles, does have the effect of creating in all but the least easily intimidated minds, a concept of God as a harsh and angry being, implacable in his punitive judgements.

The concept of God reflected in the tirade quoted above (I Corinthians 16:22 about the fate of those who do not "love ... the Lord Jesus Christ") is one of a being who most certainly does not believe in the virtue of loving one's enemies and doing good to those who despitefully use us. That entity is radically different from the one, descriptions of whom abound in those words of Jesus that can be regarded as authentic.[14] The character of such a loving God is also reflected in the radically different tone of the two verses that immediately follow that vicious one quoted above: "The grace of the Lord Jesus be with you. My Love be with all of you in Christ Jesus, Amen" (I Corinthians 16:23 -24).

The time-gap between the swing from the concept of a loving God to that of a harsh and cruel one is sometimes so much reduced that the two ideas almost coalesce into a single self-contradictory one: for example, "The God of peace will shortly crush Satan under your feet" (Romans 16:20), and, "The goodness and severity of God" (Romans 11:22).

Being harsh, punitive and vengeful is only part of the picture Paul paints of the personality of his Angry God; that Being has, according to Paul, some even less savoury aspects. For one thing, unlike the God of Jesus, this God of Paul's imagining hates things which are not to his taste. In Romans 9:13, referring back to Malachi 1:2-3, without any criticism of the quality of the idea expressed there, he puts in God's mouth the words, "Jacob I loved but Esau I hated". In Romans 12:9 Paul goes even one step further, instructing Christians to give free rein to an emotion which for Jesus was no part of the Kingdom of God: "Hate what is evil".

But that is nothing compared with the really twisted nature of the God that Paul sometimes presents as the true God of Christianity. This God is again completely unlike the God of Jesus. According to Paul, a major motivator of God's actions is his desire to demonstrate his power: "I have raised you up for the very purpose of showing my power in you, so that my name may be proclaimed in all the earth" (Romans 9:17), and, "To show his wrath and make his power known" (Romans 9:22). The section of Paul's Epistle to the Romans from which these strange statements come (Romans 9:17-23), is instructive. Paul is here clearly projecting onto the being he conceives God to be, some of his own very unadmirable qualities. Paul suggests that God deliberately created two kinds of human beings, the one kind were "prepared for destruction" (Romans 9:22) from the start, the other "prepared beforehand for glory" (Romans 9:23).[115]

Paul apparently regards this as entirely acceptable behaviour on God's part for three reasons. In the first place, Paul seems to believe that God's toleration for so long of the bad behaviour of those whom he had deliberately created with the intention of eventually destroying because of their faults (enduring "with great patience the objects of His wrath" (Romans 9:22)), would earn him great respect in the eyes of the world. The uncomfortable parallel between God's supposed behaviour in this respect and the cruel way in which cats play with small creatures before delivering the *coup de grâce* to them, seems to have troubled Paul no more than the fact that this hypothesized behaviour on God's part is diametrically opposed to just about everything in Jesus' vision of the ethics of the Kingdom of God.

The second reason Paul gives for why God's behaviour in the matter under discussion is perfectly legitimate, is worded as a question, "What if he did this to make the riches of his glory known to the objects of his mercy, whom he prepared in advance for glory?" (Romans 9:23). Although the question remains a rhetorical one and therefore not verbally answered, it is clear that Paul regards the desire to impress humanity with what a wonderful person he is as a worthy intention for God to have. Of course this is precisely one of the attitudes which Jesus declared has no place in the kingdom of God, and for the possession of which he criticized the Pharisees heavily. (Interestingly Saul, the pre-conversion Paul, was a Pharisee, and the son of a Pharisee). In any event, the desire to impress anyone with an ostentatious display of, "What a good boy (or powerful person) am I!" is not a desire which motivates the behaviour of anyone who is secure in the knowledge of all the good within themselves. On the other hand, trying to impress others with our superior qualities is typical behaviour of those all-too-human beings who have low self-esteem. As shown later in this chapter Paul certainly belonged to that latter group. His belief that God is a being who, like himself, seeks to impress the world with "his power and his glory," is a pure projection onto God of one of the less impressive sides of Paul's personality. As an omnipotent, omniscient, and omnipresent perfect being it seems unlikely that God has any self-esteem problems!

The third reason Paul finds God's behaviour in this matter acceptable, is because it demonstrates that he is not answerable to any higher authority – it is his right to do whatever he wants to do for no better reason than that he feels like it, and he cannot be subject to any punitive consequences for whatever he chooses to do – a dream-state for many children, as it probably was for the young Paul. Quoting with approval Exodus 33:19, he asserts that God's position is, "I will have mercy on whom I have mercy, and I will have compassion on whom I have compassion" (Romans 9:14), and using the metaphor of God as a maker of pots asks, "Has the potter no right over the clay, to make out of the same lump one object for special use and another for ordinary use?" (Romans 9:21). For Paul, God is clearly first and foremost the ultimate authority figure, and a pretty irrational one at that.

Two final points to note about this passage are that, firstly, perhaps in tacit acknowledgement of the dubious ethics of the God Paul believes in, he moves quickly to declare off-limits any criticism of God's 'rights and privileges': "Who indeed are you, a human being, to argue with God?" he autocratically demands. "Will what is moulded say to the one who moulds it, 'Why have you made me like this?'" (Romans 9:20). The conversational gambit of demanding to know by what right someone says something, is one beloved of authoritarian people, and all too often puts an end to rational argument, unless the person thus addressed has a really good sense of self-esteem. No one who is an earnest seeker after truth will use that technique, which is nothing more than a bully-boy tactic.

Secondly, Paul's thinking on this topic is not coherent. Two chapters further on in his Epistle he drops the distinction he had made earlier between 'good' and 'bad' people (using the symbolism of God as a potter), in favour of the view that God in fact created everyone with the same fault of disobedience so that he could generously forgive us all for that endemic fault in our personality. "God has imprisoned all in disobedience so that he may be merciful to all" (Romans 11:32). It is hard to discern on what possible grounds Paul can make this unqualified generalisation in view of his predestination-type speculations in the verses preceding this one, and in his similar highly speculative ramblings of two chapters earlier. It would seem that Paul has such blind faith in the truth of what he 'knows' that he feels no need of any logical justification for his religious views. But facts do not just go away when they are ignored or denied, and whether Paul accepts or denies the need for rational argument in support of his opinions is irrelevant to the question of whether such rational argument is necessary for most of us if we are ever to come to share Paul's passionate convictions.

Before moving on to consider where Paul stands on the democratic/authoritarian continuum of personality let us look at what is probably the most extreme example of Paul's deep psychological problems overwhelming his rational self and his spiritual sensitivities – the eruptions of anger which underlay the attitude of cruelty which all too frequently intruded itself into Paul's religious thinking.

In the fifth chapter of his Epistle to the Galatians, in the context of warning the Galatians to ignore the 'agitators' who have, contrary to Paul's teaching, been urging the practice of male circumcision on those of their number who have converted to Christianity, Paul tries to impose his passionately felt, but very autocratically expressed contrary view, saying, "Listen! I Paul am telling you that if you let yourselves be circumcised, Christ will be of no benefit to you" (Galatians 5:1), and proclaims his conviction that, "Whoever it is that is confusing you will pay the penalty" (Galatians 5:10). He does not go on to speculate what penalty God will impose for this misdeed, but in verse 12 gives an astonishing display of unchristian viciousness when he writes, "I wish those who unsettle you would castrate themselves," – a small slip of the knife and circumcision could easily become castration! It is presumably the splits in Paul's mind that are responsible for his displaying in the course of just a few verses his spiritually enlightened belief that, "In Christ Jesus neither circumcision nor uncircumcision counts for anything" (Galatians 5:6), and a completely spiritually-unenlightened wish that someone would castrate themselves. Poor Paul. Had he ever encountered what he wrote in Galatians 5:12 above, side by side with what he wrote in II Corinthians 2:14 – 15, ("Thanks be to God, who in Christ ... through us spreads in every place the fragrance that comes from knowing him. For we are the aroma of Christ to God"), he would perhaps have indulged in another round of despairing breast-beating about the frequency with which he did things that he believed to be wrong and failed to do what he believed to be right.

Before rushing to pronounce unchristian moral judgement on Paul for his viciousness, we might pause and sympathetically consider the pressures Paul was under in trying to hang on to his inspired convictions about the wrongness of requiring male circumcision as a prerequisite to admission to full membership of the Christian community. There was clearly enormous pressure from some of the early Jewish Christians for the church to reject Paul's position. And he did indeed waver at one point fairly early in his career. In Acts 16:1-3 we read:

Paul went on also to Derbe and to Lystra, where there was a disciple named Timothy, the son of a Jewish woman who was a believer; but his father was a Greek. He was also well spoken of by the believers in Lystra and Iconium. Paul wanted Timothy to accompany him; and he took him and had him circumcised because of the Jews who were in those places, for they all knew that his father was a Greek.

In the incident reported in Galatians 2:1-3, Paul managed a very different outcome to the pressures for the circumcision of the convert Titus, whose father was, like Timothy's, "a Greek".

> Then after fourteen years I went up again to Jerusalem with Barnabas, taking Titus along with me. I went up in response to a revelation. Then I laid before them (though only in a private meeting with the acknowledged leaders) the gospel that I proclaim among the Gentiles, in order to make sure that I was not running, or had not run in vain. But even Titus, who was with me, was not compelled to be circumcised, though he was a Greek.

Perhaps Paul had found the experience of having had to succumb to pressure from the pro-circumcision lobby to acquiesce in the circumcision of Timothy humiliating, and this fired up a determination to resist such pressures more strongly in the future. To what extent Paul got his way with Titus because of some such redoubled determination on his part, and to what extent it was because of the more enlightened attitudes of "the leaders" of that time we shall never know. But given his experience with Timothy we can sympathize with Paul in his frustrated anger with those in the early church who were so belligerently insistent on the need for circumcision of gentile converts, albeit he expressed that anger in unacceptable ways.

Be that as it may, few things show up the radical difference between the religions of Jesus and of Paul better than the extra-ordinary castration-wish Paul expressed towards his adversaries. It would be shocking enough if Paul had wished on those with some of whose religious ideas he disagreed, some form of mutilation which did not have any specifically sexual connotations. But to wish on a fellow Christian male evangelist who preached a slightly different message from his own, a form of deliberately inflicted physical injury which strikes at the heart of his manhood throws some light on one part of the can of worms which is Paul's feelings about sexuality, his own and other people's. We shall look at that extremely important subject a little later in this chapter.

The authoritarian nature of some of Paul's pronouncements

Paul's *Angry God* discussed above is a very authoritarian being who requires everyone to submit to his authority. It is quite clear that such a personality characteristic was congenial to Paul, indeed was part of a projection onto God by Paul of some of his own personality characteristics. Paul was certainly not averse to laying down the law in an autocratic way, especially when he felt there might be a challenge to his authority. Indeed the language Paul uses often gives a clear indication of the authoritarian role he sees for himself in respect of his followers – for example in verse 21 of the single chapter of his Epistle to Philemon he writes, "Confident of your obedience, I write to you, knowing that you will do even more than I ask", and in I Thessalonians 4:11 "… as we commanded you". In verse 12 of the next chapter Paul talks about church leaders as being people who, "… have charge of you in the Lord; and admonish you," and in the next verse gives an example of that admonishing when he instructs the Thessalonians in respect of those church leaders who "are over them," to "esteem them very highly". In verse 3 of Chapter 10 of Paul's Epistle to the Romans, he bemoans the fact that the Jews, "going about to establish their own righteousness, have not submitted themselves unto the righteousness of God," and, echoing the words of Isaiah 45:23, quotes with approval God's supposedly saying, "As I live ... every knee shall bow to me" (Romans 14:11).

In Philippians 2:10-11 Paul extends the image of bowing before divine authority. Speaking of Jesus, Paul writes,

> Therefore God also highly exalted him, and gave him the name that is above every name, so that at the name of Jesus every knee should bend, in heaven and on earth and under the earth, and every tongue should confess that Jesus Christ is Lord.

As he does here, Paul was not above claiming to be speaking the mind of God in making some of his pronouncements on religious and spiritual matters, thereby claiming for himself and his assertions an ultimate, unassailable authority. In similar vein, in the penultimate verses of his first Epistle to the Thessalonians, Paul writes, "Greet all the brothers and sisters with a holy kiss. I solemnly command you by the Lord that this letter be read to all of them" (I Thessalonians 5:26-27). Not for Paul any polite request to, "Please try to ensure that this letter is read to all of them". Despite the exemplary behaviour of the Thessalonian brothers and sisters for which Paul lavished praise on them throughout this Epistle, he obviously felt that they still needed to be intimidated by all the force of his authority into doing as they were told.

Paul's authoritarian attitude to those whose religious life he sought to control becomes clear at many points in his epistles. In II Corinthians 10:6 we find the logically-flawed admonition, which in its syntax is as poorly expressed as its content is spiritually unacceptable, "We are ready to punish every disobedience when your obedience is complete". In Philippians 2:12 Paul writes, "Therefore my beloved, just as you have always obeyed me," and his authoritarian edicts extend beyond attempting to control the behaviour of his flock to (outrageously to a psychologist), trying to control their emotions as well. In II Corinthians 6:12-13 he writes, "Our heart is wide open to you. There is no restriction in our affections, but only in yours. In return – I speak as to children – open wide your hearts also". In a similarly emotionally intrusive way, Paul tells the Philippians, "I am glad and rejoice with all of you – and in the same way you must also be glad and rejoice with me" (Philippians 2:17-18).

The pew leaflet of 28th April, 2013 of a leading Cape Town Anglican church contained a request to a fully capitalised "ALMIGHTY AND EVERLASTING GOD" (whose Son, we are told, "commanded us to love") to, "make us love what you command". For those of us making up the humanistic face of Christianity it would be hard to imagine any prayer that would be less likely to deepen the supplicant's spirituality. Sadly, the spirit of St Paul lives on into the twenty-first century, antagonising those for whom authoritarian submission is not a religious virtue, but rather a psychopathological abnormality which presents a very real impediment to spiritual development.

In his Epistle to the Galatians, (in verse 1 of Chapter 4), Paul gives his opinion that, "Heirs, as long as they are minors, are no better than slaves". Apart from the radical difference between this view and Jesus' respectful attitude towards little children, this expressed attitude on Paul's part raises some serious questions about the value of his attempts to shape the thinking of those Christians whose spiritual welfare he regarded as his responsibility. His description (in I Corinthians 4:14) of the recipients of his Epistle as "my beloved children", seems on the face of it to show a warm, loving, nurturing feeling towards them. Sadly, however, for Paul, being a child, and therefore "a minor," clearly means being slavishly obedient to adult commands. For the humanistically-oriented Christian who has made Jesus' ethical principles their own, such a concept of love is a travesty of what Parent-Child relationships at their best can be.

There is another aspect of Paul's description of his adult

Corinthian flock as his "beloved children" in the verse under discussion, which needs to be considered, particularly in the light of the content of the next verse in the Epistle. I Corinthians 4:15 reads, "In Christ Jesus I became your father through the gospel". This sentence, which makes no sense on any literal interpretation, is obviously to be understood metaphorically, and one cannot but wonder whether Paul's choice of the metaphor of fatherhood does not have additional significance in terms of another aspect of his troubled sexuality. Perhaps his repressed desire for sexual contact with a woman was sublimated into the desire to be a father. Certainly Paul's predilection for the use of the parent-child metaphor to convey some of his ideas about what constitutes right Christian behaviour seems to have been in some danger of leading him into those dangerous waters where the love of punishment endemic in all authoritarian control systems becomes entangled with sadistic and masochistic impulses of a sexual nature. It would be too simplistic to blame just Paul's sexually repressive influence for the behaviour of those (mostly celibate) clergy whose longstanding physical and sexual abuse of children is increasingly becoming public knowledge, but it certainly has not helped.

I am not writing this to make you ashamed, but to admonish you as my beloved children. For though you might have ten thousand guardians in Christ, you do not have many fathers. Indeed in Christ Jesus I became your father through the gospel. I appeal to you, then, be imitators of me. For this reason I sent you Timothy, who is my beloved and faithful child in the Lord, to remind you of my ways in Christ Jesus, as I teach them everywhere and in every church. But some of you, thinking that I am not coming to you, have become arrogant. But I will come to you soon, if the Lord wills, and I will find out not the talk of these arrogant people but their power. For the kingdom of God depends not on talk but on power. What would you prefer? Am I to come to you with a stick, or with love in a spirit of gentleness? (I Corinthians 4:14-21).

This was not Paul at his impressive best as an expositor of the teachings of Jesus. The idea of Paul threatening to come with a stick to beat into submission any of those "arrogant" enough to disagree with some of his religious ideas, is ludicrously inappropriate, and shows that Paul's ideas about power and its uses and abuses have almost nothing in common with those of Jesus.

Not quite so extreme as the above but of the same general tone, is Paul's threatening demand for obedience, again from the Corinthians, in verse 10 of Chapter 13 of his second Epistle to them. There we find, "So I write these things while I am away from you, so that when I come, I may not have to be severe in using the authority that the Lord has given me". In the light of that, words such as Paul uses in II Corinthians 10:1 have a hollow ring to them; "By the meekness and gentleness of Christ, I appeal to you". People who have truly understood the meekness and gentleness of Christ do not carry sticks with which to engage in a trial of strength with their opponents, any more than they carry swords to cut off the ears of their enemies.

Perhaps most clearly indicative of the authoritarian arrogance of Paul's overvaluation of his own level of spiritual development are his boastful appeals to his readers, to be, not like Jesus, but rather like himself.

Friends, I beg you, become as I am. (Galatians 4:12)

For I would that all men were as I myself. (I Corinthians 7:7)

Be imitators of me, as I am of Christ. (I Corinthians 11:1)

Brothers and sisters, join in imitating me, and observe those who live according to the example you have in us. (Philippians 3:17)

Paul seems to have been so addicted to the idea of the huge benefits to be derived from the process of authoritarian submission that he extended the principle from submission to God, Jesus, and Paul to submission to secular authorities. His attempts to justify this extension involve him in such nonsensical reasoning that one cannot help but wonder whether what he wrote in Romans 13:1-6 was written because he believed in the spiritual value of submitting to the dictates of any persons in authority, or whether it was just to placate any secular authorities from whom he might have been in danger of persecution. Paul writes,

> Every person must submit to the supreme authorities. There is no authority but by act of God, and the existing authorities are instituted by him; consequently anyone who rebels against authority is resisting a divine institution, and those who so resist have themselves to thank for the punishment they will receive. For government, a terror to crime, has no terrors for good behaviour. You wish to have no fear of the authorities? Then continue to do right and you will have their approval, for they are God's agents working for your good. But if you are doing wrong, then you will have cause to fear them; it is not for nothing that they hold the power of the sword, for they are God's agents of punishment, for retribution on the offender. That is why you are obliged to submit. It is an obligation imposed not merely by fear of retribution but by conscience. That is also why you pay taxes. The authorities are in God's service and to these duties they devote their energies (Romans 13:1-6).

It is hard to believe that Paul really held such a naïve view of political reality. It is even harder to believe that Paul thought that the authorities who were responsible for the crucifixion of Jesus, and those in the occupying Roman power who ordered the execution of hundreds, if not thousands of Jewish citizens, were really "in God's service" and acting as "God's agents of punishment for retribution on the offender." If Paul did write those words, and believed them, then his thought processes at the time of writing were, to say the least of it, highly disordered. If he did not believe what he wrote in that passage then there is no other way to honestly describe his behaviour than to say that he was lying. One wonders, had he lived in the twenty-first century, where Paul's sympathies would have lain in the uprising of ordinary citizens against the totalitarian oppression of some of their rulers in the "Arab Spring" revolts that have sprung up recently in so many Middle Eastern countries. Fortunately a very large segment of the Christian Church in South Africa rejected Paul's views about the need for submission to the political authorities of the day. Had they not done so the church could never have made the impressive contribution it did to the ending of apartheid.

Paul has wielded immense power in the development of Christian thinking, but as Dag Hammarskjöld, from his powerful position as Secretary-General of the United Nations once reflected in his diary, "Only he deserves power who everyday justifies it."[116] Too often the spiritual value of Paul's ideas are not of a quality which justifies the power the Christian Church has allowed him to have in shaping its theology. It behoves us all to critically evaluate what aspects of Paul's thought deserve the powerful place in Christian thinking they have enjoyed for nearly two thousand years, and which do not.

In many ways the personalities of the pre-conversion Saul and the post-conversion Paul are little different from each other.[117] Saul hated the followers of Jesus who constituted the early Christian Church with a vengeance, and participated in a reign of terror against them which served as a channel through which much of his cruel punitive energies flowed. Paul, the Christian 'saint', became part of the sect he had previously persecuted, but much of his cruel, punitive way of thinking remained with him after his conversion, only it was now directed at those fellow Christians who challenged aspects of his formulation of what the new religion was all about. Pre-conversion Saul and post-conversion Paul both had the same burning desire for power, to play a dominant role in whatever they were doing. For Saul it was to be the most effective persecutor of Christians.

You have heard no doubt, of my earlier life in Judaism. I was violently persecuting the church of God and was trying to destroy it. I advanced in Judaism beyond many among my people of the same age, for I was far more zealous for the traditions of my ancestors (Galatians 1:13-14).

The converted Paul's dominant motive was to become very powerful in the leadership of the very church he had earlier tried to destroy.

It is doubtless to a considerable extent the fact that Paul had a very authoritarian personality which underlies the agitation reflected in the many times in his epistles where he tries to put a stop to disagreements among church members and to plead (or press) for an end to disharmony among them. He obviously had had many unhappy experiences of conflict within the churches and in his relationships with them. In Paul's second Epistle to the Corinthians he repeatedly expresses his desire to visit the Corinthians again, but in the penultimate verse of the penultimate chapter voices his fears that the experience might not be an entirely happy one.

For I fear that when I come, I may find you not as I wish, and that you may find me not as you wish; I fear that there may perhaps be quarrelling, jealousy, anger, selfishness, slander, gossip, conceit and disorder.

Paul seems to have been completely unaware of how the autocratic, hectoring tone of his preaching predisposed towards the disharmony among his hearers that so distressed him. Conflict will very rarely if ever be meaningfully resolved by saying things such as Paul said in Philippians 4:2, "I urge Euodia and I urge Syntyche to be of the same mind in the Lord", and telling people to, "Do all things without murmuring and arguing so that you may be blameless and innocent, children of God without blemish" (Philippians 2:14), has even less chance of success, and is indeed likely to increase whatever disharmony there already was among those to whom such orders are addressed.

The dice are loaded against highly authoritarian people in their attempts to resolve conflict. Unless they modify their autocratic style they will experience much frustration when they try to do that. Encouraging free-flowing discussion with the honest expression of feelings rather than issuing orders and using emotional blackmail to get people to comply is an absolute requirement for the achievement of peace and harmony in human relationships. It is hardly surprising that Paul's life was marked by so much conflict if he believed, as stated in the KJV of the English Bible at Romans 1:29, that being "full of ... debate" (or "strife" as the NRSV translation has it), was one of the human behaviours which put people in the category of those who "deserve to die". "Let's compromise and say I'm right" would seem to have been a very apt motto for Paul.

Paul's attitude to the ethical principles propounded by Jesus

One indication of how little changed in Paul's thinking after his conversion is to be found in the minimal role the ethical principles of Jesus played in what we know of his preaching as a Christian and, very strikingly, the way in which he modified some of those principles so that they lost much of the ethical significance they had originally had in the teaching of Jesus.

We know very little of the pre-conversion life of Saul. Almost all that we do know is that he came from a family of tent-makers, a craft through the income from which he largely supported himself in his adult life. His father was a Pharisee, and he himself was a most zealous Pharisee who until his conversion (somewhere around 31 to 36 CE when he was in his late twenties to very early thirties) was an especially active and enthusiastic persecutor of Christians. His early religious life was therefore much preoccupied with punishment, suffering and death, and although with his conversion he changed from being a persecutor of Christians to being a leading protagonist for the religion, his thinking, as illustrated in this chapter, continued to be dominated by obsessive ideas of the necessity at times for cruel behaviour, not least by God himself.

In marked contrast to the author of the Old Testament book of the *Song of Solomon*, Paul seems to have taken little interest in the pleasures and potential for enjoyment of the physical side of life. Sex was a no-no, and he seemed to take little interest in any of the details of Jesus' earthly life. In Philippians 3:19-20, having disparaged those "who mind earthly things," he asserts that, "our conversation is in heaven," (unlike the conversations of Jesus, who rarely if ever lost sight of the manifestations and applicability of the ethical principles he taught in the here-and-now world of flesh and blood reality), and Paul lost no opportunity to stress to his readers the emphasis he placed on "Christ crucified": "For the Greeks seek after wisdom: But we preach Christ crucified" (I Corinthians 1:22-23), the implication being, 'and nothing else'. This implication is strengthened nine verses later when Paul writes, "I determined not to know any thing among you, save Jesus Christ, and him crucified" (I Corinthians 2:2). Paul makes these bold assertions, not as the 'admission of guilt' which might have been more appropriate, but as a proud boast.

Of course Paul did not stick rigidly to this agenda to the complete exclusion of everything else. He was able to find some space to boast of his achievements and quite a lot of space to expounding his very restrictive views on sexual morality, and the importance of authoritarian submission by those with less power to the dictates of those with most power. But perhaps the most unfortunate consequence of Paul's obsession with "Christ crucified" was the way in which that topic dominated his letters at the expense of any significant emphasis on the ethical teachings of Jesus. Of the 1494 verses of the seven epistles which modern scholars are generally agreed were fairly certainly written by Paul (Romans, I and II Corinthians, Galatians, Philippians, I Thessalonians, and Philemon), only 43 make reference to any of the ethical principles taught by Jesus (which had nothing to do with his death), and which we discussed in Chapter 5. In other words a mere 2.9% of the verses in those seven epistles make any reference to the spiritual insights of the man whose teachings most Christians thought were at the heart of their religion.

Perhaps even more surprising is the fact that although he clearly regarded his letters to young churches as an important teaching device to keep new converts on track in their under-standing of the implications of being a Christian, in none of the verses in them dealing with the ethical principles taught by Jesus does he give any credit to Jesus for bringing them to our attention. Anyone whose introduction to Christianity was via the Pauline epistles would be most surprised to eventually discover that, at least as far as Christianity is concerned, they all originate with Jesus and not with Paul. The feeling this generates in us, that Paul was more interested in claiming credit for the quality of those principles than in the principles themselves, is heightened by the way in which in writing about them he sometimes intro-duces an additional idea of his own which is in some way discordant with the clear intention of Jesus' formulation of the principle.

At one end of the scale are those relatively innocuous cases where Paul quotes Jesus, but adds a thought of his own which adds nothing to the ethical profundity of what Jesus urged upon us. For example in verse 17 of Chapter 12 of his Epistle to the Romans he provides an accurate and helpful summary of Jesus' teaching (as expressed in Luke 6:27-35 amongst other places), when he writes, "Do not repay anyone evil for evil", but unfortunately undermines the strength of this principle by adding his own thought, "Be careful to do what is right in the eyes of everybody". Seeking the approval of others rather than acting in the ways dictated by one's own conscience and principles is precisely one of the things that Jesus so strongly criticised the Pharisees for, as discussed in Chapter 5.

Again, in I Corinthians 10:24, Paul's very appropriate restatement of Jesus' simple urging of us to do good to others, as reported in Acts 20:35, is preceded by a piece of self-denying psychopathology proclaiming that which was no part of what we know of Jesus' thinking from scholarly study of the gospel records. Paul writes, "Nobody should seek his own good, but rather the good of others" (I Corinthians 10:24). Similarly although Jesus did urge us not to try to lord it over others and think ourselves better than they, he most decidedly did not say that we should put ourselves down as worse than others, and yet Paul writes, "Do nothing from selfish ambition or conceit, but in humility regard others as better than yourselves" (Philippians 2:3).

Even less admirable are the two verses (12 and 13) of Chapter 4 of Paul's first Epistle to the Corinthians where he adds a distinctly self-congratulatory, "What a good boy am I?" flavour to Jesus' simple, "Blessed are ye, when men shall revile you, and persecute you, and shall say all manner of evil against you falsely, for my sake" (Matthew 5:11). Paul's version (in I Corinthians 4:12-13) reads, "Being reviled, we bless; being persecuted, we suffer it; being defamed we intreat". These words are set in a self-abasing masochistic context of, "Poor me, but I do love my suffering", the passage quoted above being preceded in verse 11 and the beginning of verse 12 by, "Even unto this present hour we both hunger, and thirst, and are naked, and are buffeted, and have no certain dwelling place; and labour, working with our own hands", and followed by, "we are made as the filth of the world, and are the offscouring of all things unto this day" (I Corinthians 4:13).

Paul's words in I Corinthians 4:12-13 quoted above are a reference back to the words of Jesus as recorded in Matthew 25:42-45,

> I was an hungred, and ye gave me no meat: I was thirsty, and ye gave me no drink: I was a stranger, and ye took me not in:
> Naked, and ye clothed me not: sick, and in prison, and ye visited me not.

At the same time they are an indirect covert claim to the state of blessedness of Jesus himself when, through empathetic identification with the sufferings of humanity, he felt their pain as though it was his own.

The exaggerated, self-depreciating way of reporting (in verse 13 above) the unpopularity of Christians in the wider society in which they lived, is a proudly masochistic wallowing in the pleasure Paul obviously got from abusing himself and the whole human race as worthless rubbish. Such a view has nothing to do with any spiritual insight and everything to do with the splits in Paul's authoritarian psyche, one of the most unfortunate effects of which is a splitting off from the human being of the divine within us all, "the light within", as the Quakers like to call it, which part of ourselves is then seen as a distant, remote, "God out there".

Most serious of the distortions which Paul sometimes introduces into his statement of the ethical principles preached by Jesus are those which give an unpleasantly punitive twist to the simple humanistic, non-punitive ideas of Jesus. One of the most misleading of those is to be found in Romans 12:20. In Proverbs 25:21-22 we find the words, "If thine enemy be hungry, give him bread to eat; and if he be thirsty, give him water to drink; for thou shalt heap coals of fire upon his head, and the Lord shall reward thee". In Matthew 5:44 Jesus is reported to have said, "But I say unto you, Love your enemies, bless them that curse you, do good to them that hate you, and pray for them which despitefully use you; and persecute you". (See also Luke 6:27-28). At this point the ideas expressed in the quote from Proverbs and in Jesus' summary of them diverge significantly. The words of Proverbs 25:21-22 go on to explain that the reason for the desirability of this selfless generosity towards one's enemies is actually a punitive one. It is to be done in order to "heap coals of fire" on the head of our enemy, in terms of the principle of "killing 'em with kindness". For this, according to the writer of Proverbs, God will reward us. Jesus supplies a quite different reason for recommending that we love our enemies. We are urged to do this,

> That ye may be the children of your Father which is in heaven: for he maketh his sun to rise on the evil and on the good, and sendeth rain on the just and the unjust. For if ye love them which love you, what reward have ye? do not even the publicans the same? And if ye salute your brethren only, what do ye more than others? do not even the publicans so? Be ye therefore perfect, even as your Father which is in heaven is perfect (Matthew 5:45-48).

In other words Jesus urges us to love our enemies, to do good to those who hurt us, not in order to punish them and hurt them for their bad behaviour, but because the fundamental ethical principle of the Kingdom of God is to love, to love God and to love our neighbour, the only thing in the universe which has the power to transform any negative situation into a positive one. When we love our neighbour (which is sometimes one of the most difficult things in the world to do), we are one with God. As long as we harbour anger and a desire for revenge towards our enemies, we are out of touch with that compassionate, generously-forgiving Spirit, some sort of awareness of which is the common bond which unites all human beings in one common humanity. Sadly this fundamental principle of Jesus seems to have been rarely present in Paul's thinking, and in his statement of the principle of treating kindly those who despitefully use us, he reverts to the fundamental idea in Proverbs 25; 21-22, that the reason for behaving in this seemingly compassionate way is actually in order to "heap coals of fire" on the wrongdoer's head.

Before we leave this topic, let us look at one further example of how deeply ingrained in Paul's mind a judgemental, punitive approach to ethically unacceptable behaviour is. Instead of the friendly warning that Jesus gave us of the danger we place ourselves in, the danger of being judged by others when we become judgemental towards them, Paul magisterially thumps the table and proclaims,

> Therefore you have no excuse, whoever you are, when you judge others; for in passing judgement on another you condemn yourself, because you, the judge, are doing the very same things. You say, 'We know that God's judgement on those who do such things is in accordance with truth'. Do you imagine, whoever you are, that when you judge those who do such things and yet do them yourself, you will escape the judgement of God? Or do you despise the riches of his kindness and forbearance and patience? (Romans 2:1-4).

Paul seems to be blissfully unaware of how, according to that reasoning, he is condemning himself in condemning those who condemn others. Perhaps in some largely unconscious way he felt that his exalted spiritual status put him above the law he is expounding to others. Goodness knows how Paul squares his pretty robust condemnation of those who judge others with the "against judging others" content of his message. Self-awareness was not in general one of Paul's strong points! Even twelve chapters later, in Romans 14:10 the penny does not seem to have dropped: "But why dost thou judge thy brother? Or why dost thou set at nought thy brother?" Paul demands to know; seemingly unaware that this is a behaviour that he himself engages in on a grand scale in respect of those who do not share his views on appropriate sexual behaviour and various theological niceties. (Interestingly, in Romans 3:4 Paul quotes without disapproval the words of Psalm 51, verse 4, "So that you may be justified in your words, and prevail in your judging"). Throughout his epistles rarely does Paul miss an opportunity to condemn the behaviour of those who do not follow his teachings to the letter. As for the sentence which follows the two quoted above from Romans 14:10, "For we shall all stand before the judgement seat of Christ", what logic connects it with the rest of the verse, and quite where the Doctrine of the Atonement fits in with any of it is, to say the least of it, obscure.

Against this background of an apparent eagerness to put his own distinctive stamp on the ethical principles proclaimed by Jesus, three passages in Paul's epistles stand out with refreshing ethical clarity. In I Thessalonians 5:15, despite being slightly marred by the autocratic tone in which he paraphrases Jesus' words, Paul does state (albeit without acknowledging Jesus as his source for the idea), one of Jesus' very important ethical principles, "See that none of you repay evil for evil, but always seek to do good to one another, and to all". Paul repeats much the same idea, but in a form closer to Jesus' original statement of the principle in Romans 12:14 where we find him writing, "Bless those who persecute you; bless and do not curse them". His untouched-up quoting of the recommendation of Jesus to, "Love your neighbour as yourself", in Romans 13:10 and Galatians 5:14 is a pleasant surprise, although again Paul gives no acknowledgement of the source of that principle in either the teachings of

Jesus or in the Old Testament where it was first stated (in Leviticus 19:18).

Insecurity and inferiority

As already pointed out, Paul's version of the Christian message rarely makes any reference to Jesus' ethical teachings, and when Paul does refer to those teachings it is without even mentioning the name of Jesus[118]. That Paul should fail to mention the name of the man whose formulation of the system of ethical principles he is ostensibly promoting in his work of "preaching the gospel to all nations," can hardly be an oversight. It does, however, make sense if Paul had serious feelings of insecurity and inferiority in his new role of promoter rather than persecutor of the Christian Church. And any sense of inadequacy Paul might have felt in that regard would further explain the desire which he admitted to (in II Corinthians 10:16), of doing his gospel-spreading work in virgin territory rather than building on a foundation laid by others. His professed reason for this, not wanting to boast "of work already done in another's sphere of action", sounds somewhat like a rationalisation. Perhaps Paul felt this way because he was aware that there was all too often unseemly conflict between himself and other co-workers in the field, but perhaps a more compelling reason was that he felt so insecure that he was unwilling to share whatever glory attached to the foundation of new churches in faraway places. "I make it my ambition to proclaim the good news, not where Christ has already been named, so that I do not build on someone else's foundation" (Romans 15:20).

It would be surprising if Paul did not at times feel inferior to those of the disciples who formed the early church in Jerusalem who had known Jesus as a person and who could speak from personal experience of what they remembered of his life and teaching. Paul had no such data bank to draw on, and it is not impossible that this was one of the psychological factors which drove his greater interest in the development of theological theories about Jesus as Christ, rather than in Jesus as teacher and healer, in which aspects of Jesus' life he seems to have had very little interest.

The concept of Christ, the Messiah, is a purely intellectual construct. The word *Messiah* is a term used in Judaism, Christianity and Islam for the redeemer figure expected in one form or another by each religion. In Jewish tradition the term *Messiah* refers to a leader, a future King of Israel, physically descended from King David, who will rule the people of a united tribes of Israel and usher in the Messianic Age of global peace. *Khristós* is the Greek version of the Hebrew word *Mašía* (Messiah) used in the Septuagint (the Greek version of the Hebrew bible). The word *Christ* is the English equivalent of the Greek word *Khristós*. It is not a personal name, but rather a title, the appellation Jesus Christ (or Christ Jesus) meaning, "Jesus who is the Messiah".[119]

Paul played a highly significant part in the early Christian Church's development of a theology which identified Jesus as that long-awaited Messiah. The extent to which, for Paul, Jesus primarily fulfilled a theological function is to be seen in the choice of names he made when referring to Jesus.

In the seven New Testament epistles which most modern scholars agree were almost certainly written by Paul himself, the plain, unadorned name Jesus appears only 13 times while the title *Christ* is used as the sole name for Jesus 166 times. The name Jesus with some additional title (either Christ, the Lord, the Lord Christ, or Christ our Lord) appears 132 times, ten times as frequently as the single unadorned name "Jesus". In addition to the 166 times the appellation "Christ" appears on its own, that title appears a further 118 times with the addition of some other word as in "Christ Jesus", "Jesus Christ", "Christ the Lord", or "The Lord Jesus Christ". In other words Paul mentions the name "Jesus" at all in less than a third of his references to him, and in only 13 of these cases does he use his name plain and unadorned, without some additional descriptor of his theological status. In more than two-thirds of his references to Jesus Paul does not mention his human name at all.

Why?

It may be that at times in discussion with the surviving disciples, especially where a conflict of opinions arose, Paul felt inferior to those who had spent many months in Jesus' company and could discuss his teaching from first-hand experience of it. Perhaps it is not too fanciful to imagine Paul in such situations, muttering under his breath something along the lines of, "Well I never met the man myself, but I yield to no man in my understanding of his cosmic significance". The extent to which he rather arbitrarily claims some of his opinions to be the edicts of God, suggests some degree of inner insecurity on Paul's part about the rightness of those views. The breathtaking conceit of his aggressively defensive outburst in I Corinthians 14:37, "If anybody thinks he is a prophet, or spiritually gifted, let him acknowledge that what I am writing to you is the Lord's command," is just one strong indicator of this.

But there is more direct evidence that Paul did harbour significant feelings of inferiority. In I Corinthians 15:9, in a moment of rare self-reflective honesty he writes, "For I am the least of the apostles, unfit to be called an apostle, because I persecuted the church of God". Those feelings of guilt are unlikely to have arisen entirely spontaneously within Paul, who was clearly often at loggerheads with some of his fellow Christian teachers and proselytisers. Some of those rival evangelists probably publicly denigrated Paul in the same way that he attacked them from time to time in his epistles to young churches. Paul's rather desperate plea in I Corinthians 9:2, ("For though I may not be an apostle to others, surely I am to you! For you are the seal of my apostleship in the Lord") throws some light not only on the reason for some of the anxiety about retaining his authority over his readers that permeates Paul's two epistles to the Corinthians, but also on the degree to which early Christian evangelists were in conflict with each other.

The New Testament record gives only a few tantalising hints as to the scale of that conflict. Of particular interest in the present context is the relationship between Peter and Paul. Chapter 15 of Acts reports on a highly significant meeting held in Jerusalem in the early years of Paul's ministry. The background to this meeting is given in the first two verses of the chapter.

> Then certain individuals came down from Judea and were teaching the brothers, "Unless you are circumcised according to the custom of Moses you cannot be saved." And after Paul and Barnabas had no small dissension and debate with them, Paul and Barnabas and some of the others were appointed to go up to Jerusalem to discuss this question with the apostles and the elders.

Peter's contribution to the debate starts in Acts 15:7 with the words,

> My brothers, you know that in the early days God made a choice among you, that I should be the one through whom the Gentiles would hear the message of the good news and become believers.

There is an intriguing gap in the New Testament record of what happened in the relationship between these two men Peter and Paul subsequent to that meeting, which gave its full support to the position of Paul and Barnabas in not requiring the circumcision of male Gentiles upon their conversion. Peter's statement quoted above is the last we hear of Peter playing a major role in bringing the Christian gospel to the Gentiles, it being Paul who takes on this task with vigorous enthusiasm. It *could be* that Peter was so impressed by Paul's performance at that meeting that at some point thereafter he handed his Gentile portfolio over to him. If he in fact did that, it was possibly also because he was relieved to no longer have to carry this burden, particularly in the light of the sometimes heated conflict which kept erupting among Jewish Christians about the necessity for the circumcision of male Christian converts. On the other hand perhaps he was gradually edged out of this role by Paul and his followers. After the huge time lapse we shall probably never know exactly what happened, but it is clear from the passage in Galatians 2:11-14 discussed a little further on in this chapter, that there remained definite tension between Paul and Peter for many years.

What we shall also never know is whether any power-play between Peter and others among the apostles might have been involved in determining the future leadership of the church. What we do know is that James seems to have been the leader of the early Christian Church in Jerusalem at the time of the meeting discussed above, in which the views of Paul and Barnabas prevailed, and yet at some point in those early years it was Peter who was regarded in that light, and recognised by the Church as the first Pope (from CE 32 to 67).

However little we know of Paul's relationships with his fellow Christians we know enough of the feelings of inferiority that Paul carried, to understand at least a little of the somewhat frosty and often conflict-filled relationship which seems to have existed between him and the remnant of Jesus' disciples who had formed themselves into the early Christian Church in Jerusalem. Certainly there are some aspects of Paul's post-conversion behaviour and the way he writes about it at the beginning of his Epistle to the Galatians (Galatians 1:11-24 and 2:1-10) which become explicable on the assumption that he suffered serious feelings of inferiority.

In the first place it is very strange that, according to Paul's account, he did not immediately after his Damascus Road conversion experience hasten to Peter, James the brother of Jesus, and the other disciples gathered into the embryonic Christian Church in Jerusalem. One would have thought Paul would have wanted to meet them and express his regret about the vendetta he had waged against their church and those within it he had persecuted so strongly, and to assure them of the sincerity with which he held his newfound convictions. One would have thought that he would have wanted to find out how they felt about this new situation and to seek their opinions about how he could best repair the damage he had done. But no, according to Paul he chose to, "not consult any man, nor did I go up to Jerusalem to see those who were apostles before I was, but I went immediately into Arabia and later returned to Damascus" (Galatians 1:16-17). It was to be three years before Paul, "went up to Jerusalem to get acquainted with Peter and stayed with him fifteen days. I saw none of the other apostles – only James the Lord's brother. I assure you before God that what I am writing to you is no lie" (Galatians 1:18-20). We shall look at those three verses more closely a little later in this chapter.

It is to be noted, however, that Chapter 9 of the Acts of the Apostles tells a somewhat different story of Paul's immediate post-conversion activities. According to Acts 9:7-9, immediately after his Damascus Road experience of being blinded by a flashing light and hearing the voice of Jesus talking to him, he could see nothing even though his eyes were open. His companions led him by the hand into Damascus where, "For three days he was without sight, and neither ate nor drank". During a visit from a Damascus disciple, Ananias, "something like scales fell from his eyes, and his sight was restored" (Acts 9:18). The account of Paul's subsequent behaviour continues in verses 18 to 20,

Then he got up and was baptized, and after taking some food he regained his strength. For several days he was with the disciples in Damascus, and immediately he began to proclaim Jesus in the synagogues, saying, 'He is the Son of God'.

With two exceptions these two accounts are not necessarily incompatible: the account in Acts can be seen as filling in some of the detail which is missing from Paul's very sketchy account in Galatians of his movements after his conversion experience. The one exception is Paul's claim that he did "not consult any man" about the developing church doctrine about the meaning of Jesus' life and death before he started preaching about him. There is no reason to doubt his claim in Galatians 1 that it was three years before he went up to Jerusalem and met any of the apostles. However, if the account in Acts is historically accurate (which again there is no reason to doubt) it is inconceivable that in the several days he spent with the disciples in Damascus while he was recovering his sight, "regaining his strength", and being baptised, he would not have been told of the developing early Christian doctrine about the significance of Jesus' life and death. Indeed, would the Damascus disciples have baptised him without such "education" having taken place? If this did happen then Paul's claim that he, "did not consult any man", and that, "the gospel that was proclaimed by me is not of human origin; for I did not receive it from a human source, nor was I taught it, but I received it through a revelation of Jesus Christ" (Galatians 1:11-12), is at best a gross distortion of the truth – and a distortion of the truth which for those who believe it, would put Paul's version of Christian theology head and shoulders above that of any other Christian.

A more serious discrepancy lies in the fact that there is no mention in Chapter 9 of Acts (the chapter which describes Paul's post-conversion history), of any visit to Arabia or of a three-year wait before he visited Jerusalem. His visit to that city is described in Acts 9:23 as having taken place, "after some time had passed", a choice of words which hardly suggests a three-year time lapse.

Acts reports that when he got to Jerusalem, Paul "attempted to join the disciples; and they were all afraid of him, for they did not believe that he was a disciple". It took the intervention of Barnabas (who became Paul's very close friend until a bitter dispute led to their parting company for ever), to get the apostles to accept his bona fides. It seems though that the addition of Paul to their ranks was not universally regarded as a blessing by the Jerusalem church who, after it became known that there were plots to kill him, "brought him down to Caesarea and sent him off to Tarsus"[120], his birthplace (Acts 9:30).

Although it is difficult to know exactly where the historical truth lies in this matter, the above considerations do make Paul's strangely inappropriate statement that, "I assure you before God that what I am writing to you is no lie" (Galatians 1:18-20) look decidedly suspect.

Another example of the sort of thing which suggests that Paul may have felt insecure of his status in the leadership hierarchy of the infant Christian Church is the conflict he embroiled himself in, in respect of his taking the intended-for-the-Jews gospel of Jesus to the Gentiles. Although on every count an intention of impeccable ethical and spiritual quality, one cannot help wondering whether at least part of the powerful emotional driver for this development was not the fact it afforded Paul the chance to be an unchallenged leader in virgin territory. Working among the Jews, having himself no personal knowledge of Jesus, he probably felt he would always be a Johnny-come-lately, whereas in the relatively uncharted territory of gentile Christianity the brightness of his own star would be undimmed by the light from any other possibly more charismatic leaders.[121]

If there is any truth in this speculation about the real emotional driver of Paul's missionary work it does not in any way detract from the value of whatever good Paul's preaching may have done in the world, but it should alert us to the need to critically evaluate the quality of his theological ideas and not

simply accept them as an exposition of the "mind of God". It is
relatively easy for most twenty-first century Christians to smile at
the sex phobia of a man who could recommend total abstinence
from sex for everyone, even for couples who are married to each
other, but the even more damaging ideas contained in his
denigrations of the spiritual beauty of the human body and in his
tedious repetition of the misguided idea that there is an
unavoidable fundamental adversarial relationship between our
'carnal mind' and our 'spiritual mind' are not always so easily
rejected.

A third point that makes one wonder about the possibility of
Paul entertaining above-average feelings of insecurity and inferiority is his rather cocky put-down of Peter, which Paul reports in
his Epistle to the Galatians.

> But when Cephas 122 came to Antioch, I opposed him to the
> face, because he stood self-condemned; for until certain
> people came from James, he used to eat with the Gentiles. But
> after they came, he drew back and kept himself separate for
> fear of the circumcision faction. ... But when I saw that they
> were not acting consistently with the truth of the gospel, I said
> to Cephas before them all, "If you, though a Jew, live like a
> Gentile and not like a Jew, how can you compel the Gentiles to
> live like Jews" (Galatians 2:11-12, 14).

This reads like the overblown, self-righteous response of
someone delighted to have found a chink in the armour of a well-
armed adversary. One can all too easily imagine Paul mentally
addressing Peter with a further put-down along the lines of,
"Jesus may have regarded you as the rock on which his church
was to be built, but for one held in such high regard your
behaviour is pretty disappointing. You're no paragon of virtue.
I'm holier than thou when it comes to Christian righteousness."

Galatians 1:18-20

So what are we to make of those three verses from the first chapter of Paul's Epistle to the Galatians quoted above? Three things are particularly worthy of remark. Firstly it is strange that this new firebrand Christian chose to preach and proselytise for the first three years of his post-conversion life independently of the leaders of the early church who had actually worked with Jesus. Secondly, and relatedly, it is apparent that Paul was wanting to make it very clear to his readers that he owes no man anything in respect of the content of the gospel which he preaches. He doubtless felt that had he spent fifteen days in discussion with all the leaders of the church at the start of his ministry, people might think that that was where he had got his ideas from, that they had been teaching him what Christianity was all about. But Paul is determined to try to get people to realise that the whole content of his message was a divine revelation (and that therefore Paul was uniquely favoured and his religious views beyond criticism).

> The gospel that was proclaimed by me is not of human origin; for I did not receive it from a human source, nor was I taught it, but I received it through a revelation of Jesus Christ (Galatians 1:11-12).

Speaking about his only other self-reported visit to the Jerusalem-based Christian Church, made fourteen years after his first visit, he arrogantly asserted,

> Those who were supposed to be acknowledged leaders (what they actually were makes no difference to me; God shows no partiality) – those leaders contributed nothing to me (Galatians 2:6).

Beneath the surface of Paul's arrogant dismissal of the idea that he could possibly have anything to learn from his co-religionists lurks more than a suspicion of envy of the superior status of those men, "who were supposed to be acknowledged leaders". His insecurity and sense of inferiority is even more clearly revealed when a few verses later (according to the NIV translation of the bible) he almost sarcastically describes James, Peter, and John as, "those reputed to be pillars" of the church (Galatians 2:9). Even more telling is Paul's arrogant description of the content of his preaching in Romans 16:25 as "my gospel". He used this term on a number of other occasions in his epistles (e.g. in Romans 2:16) in preference to his more usual, "the gospel of Christ". Despite his expressed confidence in the impeccable credentials he has for his version of "the Gospel of Christ", in verses 6 to 8 of the first chapter of his Epistle to the Galatians he shows a bitter contempt for those fellow evangelists who differ from him in some of the details of their understanding of what constitutes that Gospel. He writes,

> I am astonished that you are so quickly deserting the one who called you in the grace of Christ and are turning to a different gospel – not that there is another gospel, but there are some who are confusing you, and want to pervert the gospel of Christ. But even if we or an angel from heaven should proclaim to you a gospel contrary to what we proclaimed to you, let that one be accursed (Galatians 1:6-8).

It seems that even pronouncing this curse was not enough to abate Paul's anger and in the next verse (9) he vents his spleen with a repetition of it.

> As we have said before, so now I repeat, if anyone proclaims to you a gospel contrary to what you have received, let that one be accursed.

This doubly vicious attack on his fellow workers in the field adds significantly to the evidence provided by Paul's proud assertion of the source of his knowledge as to what constitutes the "Gospel of Christ", that he felt insecure and inferior to the apostles and former disciples of Jesus in respect of his status in the hierarchy of the embryonic early Christian Church.

Arrogance is always the outward and visible sign of inner insecurity and perceived inferiority. Through the defence mechanism of Reaction Formation that inner insecurity is transformed into its exact opposite in our presentation of ourselves to the world – our Persona. It is an (often totally unconscious) attempt to cover-up and hide, even from ourselves, the real emotional truth of our psychological state – fear and anxiety about what is actually a feeling of humiliating inadequacy about ourselves.

By dismissing the idea of any possible contribution by existing church leaders to his own spiritual growth, Paul is in effect asserting his own spiritual superiority to them, and assigning them to a lower place in the hierarchy of true Christian commitment. From what we read elsewhere in the New Testament, the idea that, "Attack is the best means of defence", was by no means foreign to Paul's nature. Unfortunately such Reaction-formation-driven behaviour, although actually coming from a sense of inner psychological weakness, comes across to outside observers as an arrogant overvaluation of our good qualities, and a lack of appropriate recognition of the positive qualities of others, whatever their faults may be.

A major contributory factor to Paul's arrogance towards the leaders of the Jerusalem church might well have been the guilt he must have felt towards them for the way he had treated Christians before his Damascus Road experience. The seventh chapter of the book of Acts gives a chilling account of the stoning to death of the apparently very highly regarded early Christian martyr Stephen. Paul, or rather Saul as he was before his conversion, was complicit in this: "And Saul was there, giving approval to his death" (Acts 8:1). The chapter continues,

> On that day a great persecution broke out against the church at Jerusalem, and all except the apostles were scattered throughout Judea and Sumeria. Godly men buried Stephen and mourned deeply for him. But Saul began to destroy the church. Going from house to house, he dragged off men and women and put them in prison" (Acts 8:1-3).

Guilt about the many instances of that sort of behaviour there must have been will have sat very heavily on Paul, and he would have required much evidence of the forgiveness of those within the church in order to feel accepted by them, and in particular by its leaders. Since it seems that Paul himself avoided much contact with those who could have reassured him on this point he is unlikely to have received evidence of that forgiveness for some considerable time after his conversion.

The third aspect of the verses we have been looking at that is worth examining is to be found in verse 20: "In what I am writing to you, before God, I do not lie!". Paul's interpolation of this into his account of his relationship with the Jerusalem church seems decidedly odd. Phrases of this 'True as Bob' type seem to belong less to a religious context than to a secular one, where they often arouse an uncomfortable feeling that the person using them is "protesting too much" the truth of what he or she is saying. To be charitable, perhaps what motivated Paul to say what he did was not an attempt to hide any distortion of the truth in what he had said in the previous two verses, but rather an awareness that his avoiding contact with the leaders of the Jerusalem church must seem strange to many people, and that some might find it hard to believe that he had in fact kept away from them for so long. However one looks at it, Galatians 1:20 retains some air of oddity.

In passing it is worth noting that Galatians 1:20 is not the only place we find Paul assuring us of the truthfulness of what he is saying in what feels like a somewhat inappropriate way. In Philippians 1:8 he writes, "For God ... is my witness, how I long for all of you", and in Romans 1:9, again calls on God as a witness to the truth of what he is saying, "For God is my witness, whom I serve with my spirit in the gospel of his Son, that without ceasing I make mention of you always in my prayers". A little later in that Epistle he again assures us that he is being truthful, "I speak the truth in Christ. I am not lying, my conscience confirms it in the Holy Spirit" (Romans 9:1). In II Corinthians 1:23, he writes, "But I call on God as witness against me: it was to spare you that I did not come again to Corinth", and in II Corinthians 11:31 again protests his honesty, "The God and Father of the Lord Jesus (blessed be he forever!) knows that I do not lie". It is as though some 'still small voice' was stirring within Paul and causing him some doubt as to whether, although he was telling the truth, it might perhaps not have been the whole truth.

Inconsistencies between what Paul practised and what he preached

Although it really requires detailed scholarly study of the earliest surviving original sources of Paul's epistles to be absolutely clear on this point, Paul's self-reported behaviour does seem at times to contradict his own rules about what Christians should and should not do. Boasting is a case in point. On the one hand Paul pontificates, "Then what becomes of boasting? It is excluded. By what law? ... By the law of faith" (Romans 3:27), and tells readers of that same Epistle, "I say to everyone among you not to think of yourself more highly than you ought to think" (Romans 12:3).

But these strictures do not prevent Paul from proudly proclaiming in II Corinthians 1:14, "On the day of the Lord Jesus we are your boast even as you are our boast", and in I

Thessalonians 2:19, "For what is our hope or joy or crown of boasting before our Lord Jesus at his coming? Is it not you? You are our glory and joy!" In II Corinthians 5:12 he unashamedly writes, "We are not commending ourselves to you again, but giving you an opportunity to boast about us". Later in that same Epistle he states, "I often boast about you; I have great pride in you" (II Corinthians 7:4), and a little later in that chapter, talking about some conversations he had had with Titus about the Corinthians, says, "If I have been somewhat boastful about you to him, I was not disgraced; everything we said to Titus ... has proved true" (II Corinthians 7:14). In Philippians 3:3 he further writes, "We ... who worship in the Spirit of God and boast in Christ Jesus," and in I Corinthians 9:15 he angrily insists that, "No one will deprive me of my ground for boasting!", repeating more or less the same idea in II Corinthians 11:10, "As the truth of Christ is in me, this boast of mine will not be silenced".

Furthermore, in II Corinthians 12:1 he makes the most extraordinary statement that, "It is necessary to boast; nothing is to be gained by it, but I will go on". What he goes on to write in the rest of that verse and subsequent ones is, about "visions and revelations of the Lord", writing of a person whom he knows "in Christ" (most probably himself), who fourteen years earlier was "caught up to the third heaven" (II Corinthians 12:2). This person, according to Paul, "was caught up into Paradise and heard things that are not to be told, that no mortal is permitted to repeat" (II Corinthians 12:4). Paul then uses his account of this strange, 'out of this world' event as a point of departure for a most convoluted bit of writing in which, while claiming not to be boasting, he is very obviously promoting himself as a man of exceptional qualities. He writes, "On my own behalf I will not boast, except of my weaknesses. But if I wish to boast, I will not be a fool, for I will be speaking the truth. But I refrain from it, so that no one may think better of me than what is seen in me or heard from me, even considering the exceptional character of the revelations" (II Corinthians 12:5-7).

One does not know quite what Paul hoped to achieve by that bit of tortuous 'reasoning', but certainly the whole question of the rights and wrongs of boasting seems to be one he could not easily let go of. The confusion in his thought on the subject is undoubtedly to be at least partially explained by the splits in his personality. In II Corinthians 11:18, as part of a sarcastic attack on the Corinthians for having allowed a rival Christian teacher to shake their confidence in the rightness of Paul's teaching, he writes, rather surprisingly for the stern moralist he can be at times, "Since many boast according to human standards, I too will boast", and goes on in II Corinthians 11:21-31, to give effect to the freedom he has given himself in this respect by presenting with relish the credentials by which he claims his status as no less 'kosher' than that of any other apostle.

But whatever anyone dares to boast of ... I also dare to boast of that. Are they Hebrews? So am I. Are they Israelites? So am I. Are they descendants of Abraham? So am I. Are they ministers of Christ? I am talking like a madman – I am a better one: with far greater labours, far more imprisonments, with countless floggings, and often near death. Five times I have received from the Jews the forty lashes minus one. Three times I was beaten with rods. Once I received a stoning. Three days I was shipwrecked; for a night and a day I was adrift at sea; on frequent journeys, in danger from rivers, danger from bandits, danger from my own people, danger from Gentiles, danger in the city, danger in the wilderness, danger at sea, danger from false brothers and sisters; in toil and hardship, through many a sleepless night, hungry and thirsty, often without food, cold and naked. And, besides other things, I am under daily pressure because of my anxiety for all the churches. Who is weak, and I am not weak? Who is made to stumble, and I am not indignant? If I must boast, I will boast

of the things that show my weakness. The God and Father of
the Lord Jesus (blessed be he forever!) knows that I do not lie.

Reading the above verses and the similar masochistic
outpourings in Chapter 4, verses 8 to 10 and in Chapter 6, verses
4 and 5 of the same Epistle, one can see that Paul does indeed
quite often stick to his resolve, stated in II Corinthians 12:9, "So,
I will boast all the more gladly of my weaknesses, so that the
power of Christ may dwell in me"[123]. However, he doesn't quite
manage to stick to his determination to limit his boasting to just
those weaknesses, as he said he would a few verses earlier, ("On
my own behalf I will not boast, except of my weaknesses" (II
Corinthians 12:5)). In II Corinthians 1:12 he writes, "This is our
boast, the testimony of our conscience: we have behaved in the
world with frankness and godly sincerity".

At several places in his epistles Paul reveals the inner
insecurity which lies beneath the seeming arrogance which
drives both his boasting and his neurotic anxiety that the
Corinthians should not abandon his version of the Gospel in
favour of those of rival Christian teachers. In Philippians 2:16 he
writes, "It is by your holding fast to the word of life that I can
boast on the day of Christ that I did not run in vain or labour in
vain". Attacking those rival evangelists who did not share Paul's
views that the circumcision of male gentile converts to
Christianity was both unnecessary and undesirable, we find an
exasperated Paul saying, in Galatians 6:13-14, "The circumcised
… want you to be circumcised so that they may boast about your
flesh. May I never boast of anything except the cross of our Lord
Jesus Christ". Nevertheless, despite this self-denying determination, in II Corinthians 10:7 he tells his readers to,

Look at what is before your eyes. If you are confident that you
belong to Christ, remind yourself of this, that just as you
belong to Christ, so also do we. Now even if I boast a little too

much of our authority, which the Lord gave for building you up … I will not be ashamed of it.

Despite all his attempts to justify the acceptability of his boasting, Paul does not seem to have entirely convinced even himself in that regard. In II Corinthians 12:11, he again defends himself in an 'it wasn't my fault' way, but this time not putting the blame for having done what he was not proud of having done onto his carnal mind, but this time on the hapless Corinthians to whom he was writing an unsolicited letter. He writes,

I have been a fool! You forced me to it, indeed you should have been the ones commending me, for I am not at all inferior to those super- apostles.

Although the way in which Paul at least later in his ministry stuck to his guns in the matter of his enlightened belief that male circumcision (like its female counterpart) brings no spiritual benefit to those who suffered under it, his opposition to what at first seems to have been a majority view among the leaders of the early Christian Church was probably not driven solely by passionate religious belief, but also to some extent by other less worthy motives. In carving out for himself a niche as the champion of Gentile conversion to Christianity (of which crusade his objection to circumcision was a part) he established a unique place for himself in the hierarchy of the Church, a prestigious position that he was not going to let go of lightly. The reason he gives in II Corinthians 11:12-13 for continuing to act as he had been doing since his conversion, is hardly an example of Christian Ethics at its best.

And what I do I will … continue to do, In order to deny an opportunity to those who want an opportunity to be recognised as our equals in what they boast about. For such boasters are false apostles, deceitful workers disguising themselves as apostles of Christ.

Such a rebellious outburst seems very out of place coming from someone who laid claim to being a leading figure in the Christian Church of the time, especially one who could write in his Epistle to the Galatians (Chapter 5, verse 26), "Let us not become conceited, competing against one another, envying one another".

In the same sort of way, whilst the confused feelings of inferiority and insecurity underlying Paul's occasional displays of boastfulness excite our compassionate sympathies, his Reaction-Formation-driven immodesty is not an example of either psychological or spiritual maturity. A mild form of his self-congratulatory style is to be found in II Corinthians 1:16, where he describes his plan to visit the Corinthians (who seem to have by no means all been bursting with excitement to see him at all) twice in a short space of time. "I wanted to visit you on my way to Macedonia, and to come back to you from Macedonia and have you send me on to Judea". This plan, he explains in verse 15, was motivated by the desire that the Corinthians "might have a double favour" from him.

Even less modest is the claim with which he follows his II Corinthians 11:5 outburst about not being in the least inferior to "these super-apostles". As an explanatory note to that assertion he writes, "I may be untrained in speech, but not in knowledge; certainly in every way and in all things we have made this evident to you" (II Corinthians 11:6). In doing so he seems to have forgotten what he wrote in the previous chapter of this Epistle, "Let the one who boasts, boast in the Lord. For it is not those who commend themselves that are approved, but those whom the Lord commends" (II Corinthians 10:17-18).

The lack of consistency between some of the rules Paul lays down for 'good behaviour', and his unabashed reporting of cases where, without any attempted justification for what he is saying, he does not obey his own rules, is quite striking. Consistency is not one of Paul's strengths and his lack of it can probably be explained by the splits in his personality and his anguished experience of sometimes doing what he believes to be 'wrong things', even though he doesn't want to do them, and failing to do the good things that he wants to do, as discussed earlier in this chapter. Whatever the reason for the inconsistencies we encounter in Paul's teaching (for example in his confused views about the doctrine of the Atonement and his own salvation status), those inconsistencies should caution us to critically evaluate all of Paul's pronouncements (not just on religious matters, but, for example his uncritical acceptance of the institutions of slavery and the concept of the divine rights of rulers) and not just accept them as, 'The Word of God', which many of them most certainly are not.

Paul, Money and Emotional Blackmail

Paul seems to have often been disappointed by the poor financial support he and his co-workers received from the churches he visited. In his first Epistle to the Corinthians he felt obliged to remind them (in verse 14 of Chapter 9) that, "The Lord commanded that those who proclaim the gospel should get their living by the gospel". He gives no detail as to when "The Lord" commanded this, or where that alleged command is recorded. He returns to the question of the need for generous giving several times in the course of his letters. For example, in II Corinthians 9:6 he writes, "The point is this: the one who sows sparingly will also reap sparingly, and the one who sows bountifully will also reap bountifully", assuring his readers that, "You will be enriched in every way for your great generosity" (II Corinthians 9:11).

There seem to have been two reasons why not all the churches he visited delivered on the requirement to fund the work of Paul and his co-workers; either they didn't have the ready cash available when it was needed, or they didn't take their 'obligation' to finance the work of the Evangelists seriously enough.

In respect of the first problem of ready cash not being available "for the saints" when needed, Paul asserts his autocratic authority and tells the Corinthians that they,

> should follow the direction I gave to the churches of Galatia. On the first day of every week, each of you is to put aside and save whatever extra you earn, so that collections need not be taken when I come (I Corinthians 16:1-2).

To try to persuade those who weren't shouldering their responsibilities to see the error of their ways, Paul used a number of different approaches. It is one of his less endearing characteristics that he sometimes cloaked his anger at others for not doing what he thought they should be doing in emotionally manipulative words which are clearly designed to make the recipient of the message feel either guilty or sorry for him (or both). The unedifying, moralistic way in which Paul uses emotional blackmail to try to influence those in the churches who did not do what he regarded as appropriate to meet the physical needs of himself and his co-workers is sometimes quite distasteful. The ability to express his anger (when he feels it) in straightforward, non-judgmental language rather than in overt or covert moralistic criticisms of those who have offended him, is not an interpersonal communication skill that was highly developed in Paul. He could have benefited greatly had he been born much later than he was, and had had the opportunity to ponder those wise words of an anonymous sage of more modern times, "Never demand as a right what you can ask for as a favour" – a piece of great psychological wisdom which is entirely consistent with the ethical teachings of Jesus.

How does Paul go about loosening the purse strings of those

he felt should be giving financial support to his work?

Firstly by telling them that it is their duty to give financial support to the visits of the evangelists who convert them.

> At present ... I am going to Jerusalem in a ministry to the saints; for Macedonia and Achaia have been pleased to share their resources with the poor among the saints at Jerusalem. They were pleased to do this, and indeed they owe it to them; for if the Gentiles have come to share in their spiritual blessings, they ought also to be of service to them in material things (Romans 15:25-27).

In Paul's Epistle to Philemon he asks Philemon (who in response to Paul's preaching had some time before converted to Christianity) to forgive one of his former slaves, Onesimus, who had run away from him in order to escape punishment for a theft he was alleged to have committed. The fleeing Onesimus made his way to Paul who at the time was imprisoned (probably either in Rome or Caesarea) and followed in his master's footsteps in converting to Christianity, in response to Paul's preaching. Following this event Paul wrote a letter to Philemon (preserved for posterity as the Biblical Epistle to Philemon), trying to effect a reconciliation between him and his former slave. In this he was successful. Philemon forgave Onesimus and released him from bondage, the two having henceforth become "fellow workers for Christ". In part of his appeal to Philemon, Paul wrote of Onesimus's impending visit,

> welcome him as you would welcome me. If he has wronged you in any way, or owes you anything, charge that to my account. I, Paul, am writing this with my own hand: I will repay it. I say nothing about you owing me even your own self. I do wish, brother, that I may have some benefit from you in the Lord; refresh my heart in Christ (Philemon 17-20).

In his second Epistle to the Corinthians Paul goes further than just pointing out the new converts' indebtedness to those who had brought the gospel to them. He tells the Corinthians that if they do not give him financial support for his work among them they are effectively forcing him to rob the other churches of the benefits those other churches have paid for.

> Did I commit a sin by humbling myself so that you might be exalted, because I proclaimed God's good news to you free of charge? I robbed other churches by accepting support from them in order to serve you (II Corinthians 11:7-8).

Although in that second Epistle to the Corinthians Paul is at pains at times to stress that he has never sought and does not want any material help from the Corinthian church, there is reason to doubt his sincerity in making that claim.

> And when I was with you and was in need, I did not burden anyone, for my needs were supplied by the friends who came from Macedonia. So I refrain and will continue to refrain from burdening you in any way (II Corinthians 11:9).

The tone of this verse is very different from that of the verses quoted above from the epistles to the Romans and to Philemon (Romans 15:25-27, and Philemon 17-20) and even from that of the two verses (7 and 8) preceding this one (II Corinthians 11:9). The probable reason for this shift in attitude from the, "You ought to be ashamed of yourselves for neglecting me," of verses 7 and 8, to the, "I won't make any demands on you," of verse 9 becomes clear in what Paul wrote in the next chapter of that Epistle.

> How have you been worse off than the other churches, except that I myself did not burden you? Forgive me this wrong! Here I am, ready to come to you this third time. And I will not

be a burden, because I do not want what is yours but you; for children ought not to lay up for their parents, but parents for their children. I will most gladly spend and be spent for you (II Corinthians 12:13-15).

In this second Epistle to the Corinthians Paul was clearly angling for an invitation from them for another visit and did not want any demand from himself for financial support to diminish the church's desire to have him back again. Perhaps when he had written verses 7 and 8 he felt he might have gone too far in demanding financial support from the Corinthians and sought to dissipate any antagonism that might have been created by taking refuge in his dishonest claim that he wanted only to give and not to receive. Whether or not for the same sort of reason Paul makes a similar protestation in his first Epistle to the Thessalonians of his not seeking any pecuniary advantage in his visits to the gentile churches.

As you know and as God is our witness, we never came with words of flattery or with a pretext for greed; nor did we seek praise from mortals, whether from you or from others, though we might have made demands as apostles of Christ. … You remember our labour and toil, brothers and sisters; we worked night and day, so that we might not burden any of you while we proclaimed to you the gospel of God (I Thessalonians 2:5-7, 9).

It is quite clear that, notwithstanding some protestations to the contrary on Paul's part, he was not happy with a state of affairs where any of the churches he visited did not contribute towards his upkeep. It is entirely reasonable that Paul should feel this way, but unfortunately rather than honestly admit his personal hurt at the neglect he had suffered, he too often claims that he is quite happy with the state of deprivation this puts him in. To what extent he did this because he enjoyed being an ascetic martyr (or giving the impression of being one), and to what extent he did it with the intention of making those who had been neglecting his welfare feel guilty, and thereby motivated to do something to make amends for their neglect, is something we shall never know.

What we do know is that being nurtured by his flock did very understandably give Paul pleasure. In Philippians 4:10 he writes, "I rejoice in the Lord greatly that now at last you have revived your concern for me", although in the next three verses he makes the dubious claim that he is equally content with a state of deprivation.

> Not that I am referring to being in need; for I have learned to be content with whatever I have. I know what it is to have little, and I know what it is to have plenty. In any and all circumstances, I have learned the secret of being well-fed and of going hungry, of having plenty and of being in need. I can do all things through him who strengthens me (Philippians 4:11-13).

If that were true it is hard to see why Paul ever alluded to the issue of the neglect he has suffered, except in the strange case of Philippians 4:16-17, where he manages to simultaneously maintain his self-pitying stance, with an emotionally manipulative prodding of the Philippians to continue to be generous in their giving towards his upkeep. The trick he uses is to claim that while it is a matter of indifference to him whether or not he receives any material support from the Philippians, he does want them to give to him because of the benefits they will receive from God for their generosity if they do so. Expressing his appreciation for what they did in the past, he writes, "You sent me help for my needs more than once. Not that I seek the gift, but I seek the profit that accumulates to your account" (Philippians 4:17).

This is, of course, a distorted form of the truth that, "It is more blessed to give than to receive", which here provides a clever, but not very convincing rationalization of his reasons for wanting the Philippians to continue giving him continuing financial support – "It's only for your own good. Personally I don't mind any degree of suffering nor how much I give to you without receiving any recompense for my efforts". Now really, Paul! We weren't born yesterday!

Some further examples

A further example of Paul's use of emotionally manipulative pressure to achieve his objectives is to be found in II Corinthians 9:7. Whilst doing his best in the preceding verses, and indeed in the whole Epistle, to make the recipients of his message feel guilty if they do not perform according to his expectations, Paul here lays another obligation on them – not to give because they feel they must, but to do so of their own free will, thereby putting them into a catch 22 situation.

> Each of you must give as you have made up your mind, not reluctantly or under compulsion, for God loves a cheerful giver (II Corinthians 9:6-7).

This is not the only time that the strength of Paul's desire to persuade people to a certain course of action is matched only by his desire that they should not feel that they are complying with his wishes because of pressure from himself. In Philemon 14, writing to Philemon to try to secure his forgiveness of Onesimus, and having told Philemon in verse 8 that he was, "Bold enough in Christ to command you to do your duty", Paul says,

> I preferred to do nothing without your consent, in order that your good deed might be voluntary and not something forced.

Bringing his request to an end in verse 21 he writes, "Confident of your obedience, I am writing to you, knowing that you will do even more than I say". So much for free will and the importance Paul attaches to giving as a voluntary behaviour! Perhaps he would have approved of the generous offer Henry Ford has been reported to have made to his early customers to the effect that they could have their Model T Ford cars in any colour they liked as long as it was black!

On the positive side?

Paul is by no means one-sidedly negative about the issue of financial support "for the saints", and does express his gratitude when he encounters generous giving. True to form though, he is not slow to use his expressions of gratitude for mercies past as an opportunity for encouraging further giving from the churches. In II Corinthians 8:1- 3, we find,

> We want you to know, brothers and sisters, about the grace of God that has been granted to the churches of Macedonia; for during a severe ordeal of affliction, their abundant joy and their extreme poverty have overflowed in a wealth of generosity on their part. For, as I can testify, they voluntarily gave according to their means, and even beyond their means, begging us earnestly for the privilege of sharing in this ministry to the saints.

Paul uses this example of the magnificent generosity of the Macedonians to encourage the Corinthians to "excel" in a similarly "generous undertaking" (II Corinthians 8:7) that they had given to Paul. He advises the church that in his opinion it is appropriate to now bring this project to fruition. However, Paul had obviously encountered disappointments before when promised support failed to materialize, and whilst expressing his delight at the "bountiful gift" that the Corinthians had promised, he explains to them that he is sending "the brothers" to them (an almost Mafia-like threat!) to make sure they are ready with their gift when it is needed, lest it seem that it was being exacted under duress.

Now it is not necessary for me to write you about the ministry to the saints, for I know your eagerness, which is the subject of my boasting about you to the people of Macedonia, saying that Achaia has been ready since last year; and your zeal has stirred up most of them. But I am sending the brothers in order that our boasting about you may not prove to have been empty in this case, so that you may be ready, as I said you would be; otherwise if some Macedonians come with me and find that you are not ready, we would be humiliated – to say nothing of you – in this undertaking so I thought it necessary to urge the brothers to go on ahead to you and arrange in advance for this bountiful gift that you have promised, so that it may be ready as a voluntary gift not as an extortion (II Corinthians 9:1-5).

The Response of the Churches to Paul's visits

It is clear from his epistles that Paul's visits to the gentile churches were not always a resounding success. His visit to the Philippians seems to have been a particularly low point. In his first Epistle to the Thessalonians, Paul writes,

But although we had already suffered and been shamefully mistreated at Philippi, as you know we had courage in our God to declare to you the gospel of God in spite of great opposition (I Thessalonians 2:2).

Paul's second letter to the Corinthians in particular indicates that the Corinthians were not all eager to see him again after his first visit. Paul himself admits that it had crossed his mind, "… not to make you another painful visit" (II Corinthians 2:1). There may be many reasons for the lack of unanimous delight sometimes exhibited by the churches he visited. An important one of these could well be that, to judge from his writings, the tone of much of his preaching was very probably oppressively authoritarian and badgering, rather than inspiring. Paul's proud assessment of his preaching in I Thessalonians 2:5, "Our words have never been flattering words, as you have cause to know", may be a simple statement of fact, but reads more like a slightly embarrassed admission that it is not unknown for him to go beyond calling "a spade a spade", and to call it "a bloody shovel". One particular aspect of the frequently oppressive tone of his preaching which may well have irked some of the Corinthians is the rather obsessional disapproval Paul was clearly not slow to express of some of the sexual goings-on in their community. In II Corinthians 12:21, referring to a planned third visit to the Corinthian church he writes,

> I fear that when I come again, my God may humble me before you, and that I may have to mourn over many who previously sinned and have not repented of the impurity, sexual immorality, and licentiousness that they have practised.

To Paul's highly negative views on sex and sexual immorality we now turn.

Paul and sex

No psychological survey of the mind of Paul, even a brief one, would be complete without looking at his attitudes towards, and beliefs about sex.[124] Paul's anxieties about sex and sexual behaviour cohere around three themes: the 'badness' of the human body and the sinfulness of taking any pleasure in it, the inferiority of women and the need to keep them constantly in their subordinate place, and his beliefs about how we should deal with the sexual urges that arise within us from time.

Paul's feelings about the body and sexual desire

Here once again the splits in Paul's psyche seem to be operating to cause him to hold two very different and incompatible views, this time about the ethical status of the body. Although doubtless believing that the body-mind-spirit unity of the human being was created by God who, according to Genesis 1:31, pronounced his creation to be 'very good', and despite describing the body in I Corinthians 6:19 as "a temple of the Holy Spirit," and having asked his readers in I Corinthians 3:16, "Do you not know that you are God's temple and that God's Spirit dwells in you?", Paul was able at the same time to write about our "vile body" (Philippians 3:21), and to write, in I Corinthians 9:27, "I beat my body and make it my slave so that after I have preached to others, I myself will not be disqualified for the prize".

The parallel themes of the unacceptability of the human body and human sexual activity feature prominently in Paul's epistles. In Romans 1:24 he writes, "Therefore God gave them up in the lusts of their hearts to impurity, to the degrading of their bodies among themselves," and warns, "For if you live according to the flesh, you will die; but if by the Spirit you put to death the deeds of the body, you will live" (Romans 8:13). In Romans 13:14 he commands, "Put on the Lord Jesus Christ, and make no provision for the flesh, to gratify its desires", and in Galatians 5:16 sends the same message, "Live by the Spirit, I say, and do not gratify the desires of the flesh".

Presumably what leads Paul to forget his description of the body as a temple of the Holy Spirit and drags him down from his lofty spiritual plane is the realisation that the body is the place of operation of the drive for sexual satisfaction. It is here in our mortal bodies that sinful "evil desires" arise (Romans 6:12), where "sinful passions" are at work (Romans 7:5), and therefore where "the misdeeds of the body", have to be "put to death"

(Romans 8:13). Not one word of anything like this puritanical attempt to deny people the enjoyment of sexual and sensual pleasure is to be found in the teachings of Jesus. Paul by contrast urges upon us a life of sacrifice which eschews the seeking of such delights. Invoking "the mercies of God" (which bizarre and seemingly pointless bit of pious verbiage is presumably intended to strengthen his appeal to his readers for self-sacrifice), he writes: "I appeal to you therefore, brothers and sisters, by the mercies of God, to present your bodies as a living sacrifice, holy and acceptable to God, which is your spiritual worship" (Romans 12:1).

Why should anyone's sacrifice of sexual pleasure be acceptable to God? Indeed from the standpoint of Albert Schweitzer's concept of God as a being in whom the Will to Live and the Will to Love are intimately bound up, such self-denial on the part of any member of the human race in the twenty-first century is more likely to be unacceptable than acceptable to God. Paul does not even attempt a rational argument as to why he holds the views he does about the sacrificing of bodily pleasure being 'God's will', and what evidence he has to substantiate his vehemently expressed belief that, "Those who belong to Christ Jesus have crucified the flesh with its passions and desires" (Galatians 5:24). This is neither the first nor the last time that Paul explicitly or implicitly makes the arrogant claim, unsupported by any evidence beyond his say-so, that he knows the mind of God better than any of those who have a different vision of the truth from himself.

In Romans 6, verses 12, 13, and 19 and in I Corinthians 6:15-17 Paul becomes more specific about actual body parts.

Therefore, do not let sin exercise dominion in your mortal bodies, to make you obey their passions. No longer present your members to sin as instruments of wickedness but present yourselves to God as those who have been brought from death to life, and present your members to God as instruments of righteousness. Just as you once presented your members as slaves to impurity and to greater and greater iniquity, so now present your members as slaves to righteousness for sanctification (Romans 6:12-13 and 19).

Do you not know that your bodies are the members of Christ? Should I therefore take the members of Christ and make them members of a prostitute? Never! Do you not know that whoever is united to a prostitute becomes one body with her? For it is said, "The two shall be one flesh." But anyone united to the Lord becomes one spirit with him (I Corinthians 6:15-17).

In Romans 7:18-20, Paul gives a clue as to one important reason why he hates his body so much.

For I know that nothing good dwells within me, that is, in my flesh. I can will what is right, but cannot do it. For I do not do the good I want but the evil I do not want is what I do. Now if I do what I do not want, it is no longer I that do it, but sin that dwells within me, therefore I am innocent.

In Galatians 5:17 he further explains that, "The flesh lusteth against the Spirit and the Spirit against the flesh: and these are contrary the one to the other: so that ye cannot do the things that ye would". By splitting his concept of himself into two warring parts, his body and his spirit, identifying his "real self" with the spiritual part of himself, and rejecting his body as bad, he is able to disclaim responsibility for any wrongdoing or failure to say or do the right thing on his part.

The theme of the disreputability of sexual feelings runs as a background thread throughout the 1018 words of the 39 verses of Chapter 7 of Paul's First Epistle to the Corinthians, the chapter in the first verse of which Paul states, "It is well for a man not to touch a woman"[125], (or as the New English Bible translation has it, "It is a good thing for a man to have nothing to do with women"!) and in verse 17 of which occurs the revealing phrase, "This is my rule in all the churches". 35 verses (933 words) of the 39 in that chapter, (from which I shall quote extensively in what follows), are devoted entirely to Paul's statement of the rules and regulations which he believes should govern human sexual behaviour. The remaining 4 verses are devoted to telling slaves "not to be concerned" about their status.

As already remarked earlier in this chapter, Paul's conception of freedom seems to be of a state where the individual can do anything they like as long as they do not transgress any of God's (and for 'God's' read 'Paul's) rules.

> For you were called to freedom, brothers and sisters, only do not use your freedom as an opportunity for self-indulgence, but through love become slaves to one another (Galatians 5:13).

Some freedom!

From what Paul wrote in his epistles it is easy to see the main outlines of his belief in the endemically adversarial relationship which he believed exists between sexuality and spirituality, but there are layers of complex pathology in his often disordered thought on the subject which, for lack of sufficient data we shall never be able to fully understand. Occasionally, however, we do get a brief glimpse into something of that psychopathology.

In II Corinthians 11:2 we find, "I feel a divine jealousy for you, for I promised you in marriage to one husband, to present you as a chaste virgin to Christ." Given Paul's views about the negative spiritual impact any form of sexual activity has on those who engage in it, it is not surprising that he would think that nothing less than a chaste virgin would be suitable as a bride for Christ. But given his grudging toleration of marriage as little more than a necessary evil, it is strange why he should want to find a bride for Christ at all.[126] Even stranger at first sight is why he, Paul, should see himself as the person arranging this marriage, and presenting his 'daughter' as the chosen bride to Christ. Upon deeper consideration this is not so strange.

In II Corinthians 11:1 Paul precedes the sharing of his fantasy with the words, "I wish you would bear with me in a little foolishness. Do bear with me!" In other words Paul was aware that there was something not quite kosher about his wish to present his Corinthian converts, "in marriage as a chaste virgin to Christ".

No wonder! Implicit in this fantasy is the idea that it is not just the Corinthian Church but the whole Christian Church which Paul is imagining himself as handing over to Christ as a virginal bride. There are two striking implications hidden in the scenario Paul has constructed. The first is that if Christ were to accept Paul's offer of the Christian Church as his bride, he would be acknowledging Paul as the father of the Christian Church, the ultimate authority therein. So much for Peter, James the brother of Jesus, and the rest of that motley crew of whose status in the early church as former disciples of Jesus, Paul was clearly very envious, as discussed earlier in this chapter.

But more than just implying that he, rather than Peter, is the real head of the Christian Church, what raises Paul's creation of the image of himself as the father of the bride of Christ to the level of a masterstroke is the fact that, as the father of the bride, Paul would of course become the father-in-law of her husband, Christ himself. What a powerful wish-fulfilling fantasy – God the father, and Paul the father-in-law of Jesus Christ would make Paul only one step away from becoming the most powerful being in the universe! The only potential fly-in-the-ointment in that scenario would be if the Christian Church were not found to approximate closely enough to the image of a "chaste virgin" to make her acceptable as a "bride of Christ". Perhaps one of the more powerful unconscious motivations[127] that drove Paul's self-imposed celibacy and his relentless, obsessional crusade against sexual activity among church members was some vague fear of that type. Abolish, or at least cut to the absolute minimum all sexual activity among Christians, and he would be home and dry as second-in-command of the universe, at least in his own imagination.

To what extent this "little foolishness" has played a significant role in subsequent developments in the Christian Church it is impossible to say but it has certainly had some influence on the church's preoccupation with virginity and sexual abstinence. One of the most bizarre of recent developments in this regard has been the emergence in the right-wing of the authoritarian face of Christianity in the United States of "Purity Balls" in which girls as young as 4 "pledge their virginity to their father". Below is an extract from one of the 24 660 000 responses to a Google search with the probes "Purity Balls", "Purity Rings", and "Purityrings".

In a chandelier-lit ballroom overlooking the Rocky Mountains one recent evening, some hundred couples feast on herb-crusted chicken and julienned vegetables. The men look dapper in tuxedos; their dates are resplendent in floor-length gowns, long white gloves and tiaras framing twirly, ornate updos. Seated at a table with four couples, I watch as the gray-haired man next to me reaches into his breast pocket, pulls out a small satin box and flips it open to check out a gold ring he's about to place on the finger of the woman sitting to his right. Her eyes well up with tears as she is overcome by emotion.

The man's date? His 25-year-old daughter. Welcome to Colorado Springs' Seventh Annual Father-Daughter Purity Ball, held at the five-star Broadmoor Hotel. The event's purpose is, in part, to celebrate dad-daughter bonding, but the main agenda is for fathers to vow to protect the girls' chastity until they marry and for the daughters to promise to stay pure. Pastor Randy Wilson, host of the event and cofounder of the ball, strides to the front of the room, takes the microphone and asks the men, "Are you ready to war for your daughters' purity?"

Wilson's voice is jovial, yet his message is serious—and spreading like wildfire. Dozens of these lavish events are held every year, mainly in the South and Midwest, from Tucson to Peoria and New Orleans, sponsored by churches, nonprofit groups and crisis pregnancy centers. The balls are all part of the evangelical Christian movement, and they embody one of its key doctrines: abstinence until marriage.[128]

The issue of Time Magazine of the 17th July, 2008 reported on another similar event as follows:

There are some mothers and some uncles among the 150 people in the ballroom of the Broadmoor hotel, but the night belongs to fathers and daughters. The girls generally range in age from college down to the tiny 4-year-old dressed all in purple who has climbed up into her father's arms to be carried. Some are in their first high heels—you can tell by the way they walk, like uncertain baby giraffes. Randy Wilson, co-inventor of the Father-Daughter Purity Ball, offers a blessing ...[129]

One wonders whether Paul would have offered his blessing too, or whether he might have felt uncomfortable at such a brazen display of father-daughter sexuality. One also wonders if the name of the co-inventor of the Purity Ball institution, Pastor Randy Wilson, would have raised a smile or even a chuckle from Paul, or whether he shared the belief of the second-century Church leader Clemens of Alexandria that "Laughter does not become a Christian".

There is one final aspect of Paul's crusade for the ending of all sexual activity by Christians which is worth noting, although it would take us too far into the field of Depth Psychology to explore it fully here. This is that Paul's crusade has something of the nature of a death wish for the future of the religion about it. If all Christians were to cease having sex, no children would be born to Christian parents. Whilst such an eventuality would not necessarily lead to the extinction of Christianity in the short-term, the more successful the Christian Church became in creating new converts the smaller the pool of potential converts would become. Should the objective of converting all the world ever be reached, the religion would become extinct together with the whole human race within one generation.

The inferiority of women

The second theme around which Paul's pathological concept of sex clusters lies in the realm of gender relationships, and funda-mental to his views in that regard are his frequently expressed beliefs about the inferiority of women. Paul's views on this subject are of a piece with those reflected in the second (rather than in the first) Genesis account of the Creation of the Universe. The words of Genesis 1:27 imply equality between the sexes, that first account stating simply, "God created man in his own image, in the image of God he created him; male and female he created them". By contrast in the second account of the Creation in Genesis 2:4-25, woman was created as an afterthought. The impression given by that second Creation account is that when God had created man he thought his creation tasks were finished, but after a while the thought struck him that, as reported in the NIV of the English Bible,

It is not good for the man to be alone. I will make a helper suitable for him. ... So the Lord God caused the man to fall into a deep sleep; and while he was sleeping, he took one of the man's ribs and closed up the place with flesh. Then the Lord God made a woman from the rib he had taken out of the man, and he brought her to the man.

The only stated reason for the existence of women in that second Creation account is that she was to be "a helper suitable for (men)".

This appalling relegation of the female sex to the status of second-class citizen whose only purpose in life is to be "a helper of men" is clearly of a piece with Paul's thinking about the role of women in the world, and specifically in the church. The second Genesis Creation account and Paul's lingering influence are probably important factors in maintaining the strenuous objection of many within at least the Roman Catholic and Anglican churches to the ordination of women and their elevation to any positions of real authority in the church.[130] Echoing the words of Genesis 2:4-25, Paul states categorically that,

Man was not made from woman, but woman from man. Neither was man created for the sake of woman, but woman for the sake of man (I Corinthians 11:8-9).

Seeking to firmly establish the inferior status of women which puts them under an obligation to be submissive, (especially to their husbands, if they are married), Paul thunders,

Women should be silent in the churches. For they are not permitted to speak, but should be subordinate, as the law also says. If there is anything they desire to know, let them ask their husbands at home. For it is shameful for a woman to speak in church (I Corinthians 14:34-35).

One of the most breathtaking examples of the extent and depth of Paul's authoritarian arrogance is to be found in verses 37 and 38 which almost immediately follow those two verses. Almost unbelievably he unashamedly asserts those male chauvinist ideas to be not just his own, but to be "a command of the Lord".

> Anyone who claims to be a prophet, or to have spiritual powers, must acknowledge that what I am writing to you is a command of the Lord. Anyone who does not recognize this is not to be recognized (I Corinthians 14:37-38).

Of course the real reason for trying to silence the voice of women in the church, whatever 'religious' rationalisation may be given for such attitudes, is male insecurity in the face of the power of a woman's sexuality – the divine feminine within the female body – one manifestation of what the Quakers talk about as the 'divine light' within us all.

Not content with trying to silence women in church Paul seeks to ensure that they also do not appear there with their hair visible to other worshippers Presumably his motivation for this is his not entirely unjustified belief that the sight of a woman with a beautiful head of hair is likely to arouse sensual thoughts and feelings in those who see it. This in turn might stimulate thoughts of 'carnal pleasures' in those whose minds Paul believed should be filled with thoughts about theology and the worthlessness of human beings.

Rather than state this simple truth about what was going on in his mind when he wrote this (and which was probably based on the feelings aroused in himself by the sight of a beautiful head of hair adorning a woman's body), Paul produced what ought to be called a rationalisation of his reasons for wanting to stop women appearing in church with their heads uncovered. However, Paul's attempt to justify his belief in this respect in I Corinthians 11:3-15 is so lacking in rationality, and so full of logical gaps and illogical non-sequiturs that it seems inappropriate to dignify what he writes with any other label than that of "a failed attempt at ratio-nalisation". Paul pontificates,

> I want you to understand that Christ is the head of every man, and the husband is the head of his wife, and God is the head of Christ. Any man who prays or prophesies with something on his head disgraces his head, but any woman who prays or prophesies with her head unveiled disgraces her head – it is one and the same thing as having her head shaved. For if a woman will not veil herself, then she should cut off her hair; but if it is disgraceful for a woman to have her hair cut off or to be shaved, she should wear a veil. For a man ought not to have his head veiled, since he is the image and reflection of God; but woman is the reflection of man. Indeed, man was not made from woman, but woman from man. Neither was man created for the sake of woman, but woman for the sake of man. For this reason a woman ought to have a symbol of authority on her head because of the angels. ... Judge for yourselves: Is it proper for a woman to pray to God with her head unveiled? Does not nature itself teach you that if a man wears long hair, it is degrading to him, but if a woman has long hair, it is her glory? For her hair is given to her for a covering (I Corinthians 11:3-15).

Much could be said about this extraordinary display of male chauvinistic conceit masquerading as spiritual guidance. The arrogant and irrational belief in male superiority and entitlement expressed in verse 7 of the New Revised Standard Version of the English Bible quoted above is even more forcefully brought out in the New International Version translation, which reads, "A man ought not to cover his head since he is the image and glory of God: But the woman is the glory of man". And what a woman having "a symbol of authority on her head" has to do with the angels is a puzzlement, as is the question of why, if a woman's hair has been "given to her for a covering", long hair should be "her glory" while long hair in a man, which serves the same heat-conserving biological function in a man as in a woman, should be "degrading to him". As for judging for ourselves, "whether it is proper for a woman to pray to God with her head unveiled?" and whether "nature itself" teaches us "that if a man wears long hair, it is degrading to him", Paul might have been very surprised (not to say alarmed) could he have known how relatively few Christians over the centuries have shared his strange views in these matters.

After Paul's lengthy diatribe against allowing women the same behavioural freedoms as those very largely granted to men in the Christian community, it is amusing to read again his statement (in II Corinthians 3:17) that, "Where the Spirit of the Lord is, there is freedom". I believe that in saying that Paul is expressing a profound spiritual insight, but it is one which largely invalidates his strictures about the rightness and wrongness of various aspects of both male and female human sexual behaviour, hairstyle, and modes of dress and personal adornment.

One cannot but wonder sometimes just what Paul's concept of freedom was. In I Corinthians 7:32 he explains to his readers that, "I want you to be free from anxieties". In pursuit of that aim he argues strongly against getting married because of how that state gets in the way of men being, "anxious about the affairs of the Lord, how to please the Lord" (I Corinthians 7:32), and of women, "being anxious about the affairs of the Lord, so that they may be holy in body and spirit" (I Corinthians 7:34). In the next verse Paul writes, "I say this for your own benefit, not to put any restraint on you, but to promote good order and unhindered devotion to the Lord." Did Paul really think that he was bringing the freedom of the "spirit of the Lord" to his readers by warning them off the idea of getting married? I shall have more to say more about this a little further on in this chapter.

Paul's views about the rightness and wrongness of various forms of sexual activity

The third theme running through Paul's pontifications about sex and related matters comprises a set of injunctions giving effect to Paul's fundamental belief that sexuality is the enemy of spirituality, and should be suppressed as far as possible. Paul operationalises this belief by laying down a number of prohibitions against certain specific sexual behaviours. He asserts that either it is God's will or his own belief – without explaining how he knows the difference between these two situations – that the following behaviours should not be engaged in.

Fornication

Fornication refers to sexual intercourse between two unmarried persons, and is a particular target of Paul's attempts to persuade people to suppress their sexual instincts. Verse after verse proclaims the sinfulness of such behaviour.

> The body is meant not for fornication but for the Lord, and the Lord for the body (I Corinthians 6:13).
>
> Shun fornication! Every sin that a person commits is outside the body; but the fornicator sins against the body itself (I Corinthians 6:18).
>
> For this is the will of God, your sanctification: that you abstain from fornication; that each one of you know how to control your own body in holiness and honour, not with lustful passion, like the Gentiles, who do not know God (I Thessalonians 4:3-5).

Given pride of place in I Corinthians 6:9-10 at the head of a ten-item list of those who "shall not inherit the kingdom of God", are fornicators. Those two verses read:

Do you not know that wrongdoers will not inherit the

kingdom of God? Do not be deceived! Fornicators, idolaters, adulterers, male prostitutes, sodomites, thieves, the greedy, drunkards, revilers, robbers – none of these will inherit the kingdom of God.

It is noteworthy that whilst male prostitutes are singled out for special mention as one particular type of wrongdoer, female prostitutes escape specific attention. Presumably this is not because they are not excluded from inheritance of the Kingdom of Heaven, but because they also fall into the excluded categories of fornicators or adulterers, on which grounds they are to be excluded anyway. The same reasoning applies to male prostitutes however, so why they get additional specific mention and female prostitutes do not, is something of a mystery. Perhaps Paul for all his disapproval of their profession had something of an uncharacteristically soft spot for them, or perhaps he regarded them as so far beyond the pale that he could not bear to mention them here, admittedly an unlikely possibility.

In Galatians 5:19-21, fifteen 'works of the flesh' are listed, of which Paul says, "I am warning you, as I warned you before: those who do such things will not inherit the kingdom of God." Again heading the list of proscribed activities is 'fornication', but surprisingly, apart from that item and the two sins of 'idolatry' and 'drunkenness', the two lists have nothing in common. In full, the Galatians 5:19-21 listing reads as follows,

Now the works of the flesh are obvious: fornication, impurity, licentiousness, idolatry, sorcery, enmities, strife, jealousy, anger, quarrels, dissensions, factions, envy, drunkenness, carousing, and things like these.

Interestingly in neither of these lists does murder appear as something the committing of which will exclude us from the kingdom of God. However murder does feature in the twenty-one-item list of 'bad behaviours' in Romans 1:29-31, of which Paul says, "God's decree" is "that "those who practise such things deserve to die". Even more interestingly that list does not include any specific sexual behaviours, although from the context in which the list appears it is fairly clear that most, if not all of them are subsumed under the heading of, "every kind of wickedness". The full list reads:

> They were filled with every kind of wickedness, evil, covetousness, malice. Full of envy, murder, strife, deceit, craftiness, they are gossips, slanderers, God-haters, insolent, haughty, boastful, inventors of evil, rebellious towards parents, foolish, faithless, heartless, ruthless. They know God's decree, those who practise such things deserve to die (Romans 1:29-32).

What is clear from these three extracts from his letters is that Paul has no consistent listing in his head as to what constitutes sin. The list varies with the church he is writing to, and presumably with the mood he is in at the time of writing. It appears that Paul believes that fornicators cannot enter the Kingdom of God, and probably that they deserve to die. Either way Paul gives absolutely no explanation as to why sex between two unmarried persons should be regarded as a sin – he seems to regard his autocratic assertion to that effect (on no evidence at all) as the statement of a self-evident truth, which it most certainly is not. In Paul's day, two thousand years ago, the danger of a woman becoming unwantedly pregnant was a powerfully important factor to be taken into account in the sexual behaviour of any couple. Today, with the advent of several alternative forms of reliable contraception, there is absolutely no logical, psychological, or spiritual reason why sex between unmarried persons should be regarded as sinful. Even if it were granted that fornication is a sin, Paul's view of the harsh penalty God imposes for sexual transgression is far removed from the spirit of Jesus' "Let he who is without sin cast the first stone" approach to sexual wrongdoing.

The sexual mores of the hapless Corinthians seem to have aroused particularly strong anxiety in Paul. In his first Epistle to the Corinthians he writes,

> I am writing to you not to associate with anyone who bears the name of brother or sister who is sexually immoral ... Do not even eat with such a one ... 'Drive out the wicked person from among you' (I Corinthians 5:9, 11, 13).

Paul's outburst in I Corinthians 5:1-5, part of which I quoted earlier in this chapter, is even more radically incompatible with Jesus' way of dealing with unsatisfactory sexual behaviour.

> It is actually reported that there is sexual immorality among you, and of a kind that is not found even among Pagans; for a man is living with his father's wife. You are to hand this man over to Satan for the destruction of the flesh, so that his spirit may be saved in the day of the Lord (I Corinthians 5:1-5).

Quite where Paul's beliefs about "the atoning death of Christ" fit in with this astonishing display of unchristian viciousness is, to say the least of it, not immediately obvious. As to how Satan would go about his assigned task of destroying the flesh of this particularly wicked fornicator, the mind boggles.

Marriage

Paul identifies a number of different types of situation where marital status is involved in determining how acceptable or otherwise a particular sexual encounter might be.

The situation where two people are married to each other

Whilst probably most people regard this as the one situation in which there is unambiguously nothing wrong with seeking the gratification of sexual desire with a partner, there are at least two different situations which must be distinguished in regard to the sexual behaviour of married persons with each other – the one being where at a particular time both partners desire such an encounter, and the other the case where one partner does desire such an experience and the other, for whatever reason, does not.

One of the unfortunate consequences of adopting a rigid sex-outside-marriage-is-always-wrong morality is that for some people it is too easy to move from that position to what they regard as a corollary view that sex within marriage is always right. Thrusting unwanted sexual intimacy on anyone, whether one is married to them or not, is for many people, whatever their religious convictions or lack of them, a completely unacceptable behaviour. However that is a view not shared by everyone, and not by all Christians. How much influence the views of Paul have had in this matter it is impossible say, but the best that can be said about the second of the two verses of I Corinthians 7:3-4 is that it could easily be interpreted as supporting the view that if one married partner wants sexual contact with their spouse, that spouse must submit to the wishes of their partner whether they want such contact at that time or not.

In the KJV, verse three of Chapter 7 of the Epistle in question contains the ethically impeccable injunction, "Let the husband render unto the wife due benevolence: and likewise also the wife unto the husband", benevolence meaning (according to the Shorter Oxford English dictionary), "Disposition to do good, kindness, generosity, affection, goodwill towards another". This injunction, however, is followed by a verse with a very different flavour to it, and which appears to justify any infractions within marriage of the Golden Rule with its urging to compassionate behaviour which was so important to Jesus, and to justify marital rape. Paul writes, "The wife hath not power of her own body, but the husband: and likewise also the husband hath not power of his own body, but the wife." It is difficult to understand these words as being anything other than yet another attempt by an oppressive autocrat to entrench the acceptance of authoritarian structures in society, even in marriage, a state which for generations has been seen by many as the one place on earth where they could experience mutual respect, compassionate love, and nurturance.

It is instructive to compare the KJV translation of those two verses quoted above, with three modern English translations which do not refer to benevolence but state (with varying degrees of specificity) that the duty of married couples is to satisfy each other's sexual needs, and disempoweringly, to deny the right of either partner to be in control of what they do with their bodies and what is done to them. Collectively these four translations tell us something about Paul's thinking, but they also tell us perhaps even more about the minds of the translators, and the dangers of attaching any rigid interpretation to the specific wording of any particular translated bible text. Although all four translations reflect a very authoritarian approach on the part of Paul, the original writer, the King James Version (1611) is the only one which emphasises the need for a loving relationship between married couples which goes beyond a merely sexual one.

Let the husband render unto the wife due benevolence: and likewise also the wife unto the husband. The wife hath not power of her own body, but the husband: and likewise also the husband hath not power of his own body, but the wife.

The New English Bible translation (1961) reads,

The husband must give the wife what is due to her, and the

wife equally must give the husband his due. The wife cannot claim her body as her own; it is her husband's. Equally, the husband cannot claim his body as his own; it is his wife's.

and the New International Version (1973),

The husband should fulfil his marital duty to his wife, and likewise the wife to her husband. The wife's body does not belong to her alone but also to her husband. In the same way the husband's body does not belong to him alone but also to his wife.

The choice of words in the New Revised Standard Version (the English translation favoured by the majority of modern biblical scholars) strongly suggests that the translators of that edition of the Bible believed that what Paul had in mind in writing those verses was sex rather than love. Their translation suggests, in an even more extreme form than the other translations, that the sex act is to be seen as one of a meeting between two disempowered bodies who have no right to seek their own pleasure – each partner's role is not "to make love", but to participate in a mutual 'being done to'.

The husband should give to his wife her conjugal rights, and likewise the wife to her husband. For the wife does not have authority over her own body, but the husband does; likewise the husband does not have authority over his own body, but the wife does.

Whichever translation we feel most accurately reflects Paul's thinking, his 'ruling' in this matter is a quite startling reminder of how deeply ingrained authoritarian attitudes are in his psyche. It is also another example of the breathtaking arrogance of Paul that he should have thought that as an unmarried male, with no personal experience of marriage, he had the right to pontificate on the subject of how married persons should think about, and conduct themselves in their relationship with their partners.

The idea that people should have empowered control over how they live their lives seems to have aroused great anxiety in Paul, who wasted a lot of time and energy in trying to promote an attitude of mind of authoritarian submission in those whose thinking and behaviour he sought to influence. In I Corinthians 6:19-20 he writes,

Or do you not know that your body is a temple of the Holy Spirit within you, which you have from God, and that you are not your own? For you were bought with a price; therefore glorify God in your body.

And of course Paul reserves for himself, as self-appointed supreme representative of God on earth, the right to decide which behaviours glorify God and which do not.

Whatever ambiguities there may be about the details of what Paul's views may have been about sexual freedom within a marriage, he is unambiguously clear about one thing, and that is that those aiming for the highest state of spiritual perfection should not be sexually involved with anyone, whether they are married to them or not. Paul stops short of condemning sex between married partners as wrong, but puts up with it for quite the wrong reasons. He grudgingly tolerates sexual behaviour between married partners if one or other of them cannot "control themselves", but makes it clear that such people exist in a lower state of spiritual grace than those who do succeed in stifling the sexual impulse within themselves altogether. In I Corinthians 7:2 he writes, "To avoid fornication, let every man have his own wife, and let every woman have her own husband" (I Corinthians 7:2), and in I Corinthians 7:9 urges those who "are not practising self-control" to marry, "For it is better to marry than to be aflame with passion". What a miserable justification for entering the marital state – no joy, no sense of delight in enjoying the company of one's partner and the possibility of working together to achieve a common goal. For Paul, it seems, the purpose of marriage is to ensure that no one has more than one sexual partner in their lives.

Despite his conviction that it is praiseworthy for married partners to abstain from sexual encounters for a while, he does recognise the dangers inherent in either party making unilateral decisions to refrain from sex with their partner for too long. At the same time he makes it clear that his toleration of any sexual encounter in marriage is a concession to the weak-willed, and that it is his view that it would be best if any agreement by married partners to abstain from sex for a while were to become their permanent way of being. In I Corinthians 7:5-7 he writes,

> Do not deprive one another except perhaps by agreement for a set time, to devote yourselves to prayer, and then come together again, so that Satan may not tempt you because of your lack of self-control. This I say by way of concession, not of command. I wish that all were as I myself am.

Adultery

This refers specifically to a situation in which one (or both) of the parties to a sexual engagement is married to someone other than the person they are involved with in that particular sexual act. Paul has surprisingly little to say specifically about this beyond very appropriately getting those who preach against it to examine their own behaviour very honestly. In Romans 2:22 he writes, "You that forbid adultery, do you commit adultery?" Perhaps he felt that the prohibition against it contained in the Ten Commandments made further comment from himself superfluous, although such reticence is unlike Paul who generally was not backward in coming forward with unambiguous endorsement of views expressed elsewhere in the bible with which he strongly agreed.

Perhaps there was a deeper reason for his relative silence on this subject. It is no more than a wild speculation, but perhaps the pre-Christian Saul, who may well have had an active sex life before his conversion, was on at least one occasion involved in a relationship with a married woman and had more of a conscience in the matter than some of the more colourful figures among later Christian clergy and televangelists, whose vehement condemnation of sexual immorality was later found to have been a smokescreen behind which to hide their own adulteries. Whatever the reason, Paul was certainly far more restrained in his comments on adultery than he was in his condemnation of fornication, an 'offence' which probably most other Christians regard as, at worst, less heinous than adultery.

Divorce

In I Corinthians 7:10-11 we find,

> To the married I give this command – not I but the Lord – that the wife should not separate from her husband (but if she does separate, let her remain unmarried or else be reconciled to her husband), and that the husband should not divorce his wife.

After brazenly declaring this to be 'the Lord's view', it is somewhat of a surprise to find Paul in the next verse giving further rulings in respect of situations where one of the marital partners is a believer and the other is not, explicitly saying that those further views are his own and not 'the Lord's'. As usual Paul gives us no clue as to how he knows what are merely his own ideas, and which he believes are God's. Perhaps it is that Paul believed that any of his own views which echoed any opinion expressed in the Old Testament was "the Lord's view", while he was content to regard any opinions that he held which did not have that Old Testament backing as just his own. If so his faith in the Old Testament as a whole as carrying the voice of God was naively misplaced.

Re-marriage

Relatedly it is notable how despite Paul's frequent disparagement of 'the law' in contrast with the freedom which he said ought to be experienced by the Christian ("Where the Spirit of the Lord is, there is freedom." II Corinthians 3:17), he himself readily accepts the strictures of Judaic law when the ideas contained therein coincide with his own personal opinions. Indeed, especially in the area of sexual morality, he cheerfully adds to them, encouraging (even decreeing) rule-bound behaviour, in complete contrast to the compassionate, not-sacrificing-a-person-to-a-principle teachings of Jesus.

In Romans 7:2-3 he writes,

> Thus a married woman is bound by the law to her husband as long as he lives; but if her husband dies, she is discharged from the law concerning the husband. Accordingly she will be called an adulteress if she lives with another man while her husband is alive. But if her husband dies, she is free from that law, and if she marries another man, she is not an adulteress.

How many people's lives have been miserably ruined by autocratic pronouncements of this callous, uncompassionate, "You made your own bed, now lie in it" type. Significantly, providing further evidence of Paul's bias in favour of trying to restrict the spontaneous behaviour of women more than that of men, Paul has nothing to say about the situation where the male half of a divorced couple lives with another woman while his former wife is still alive. If what is sauce for the goose is sauce for the gander, then the two verses following Romans 7:2-3 should have read something along the lines of, "And a married man is bound by the law to his wife as long as she lives; but if his wife dies, he is discharged from the law concerning the wife. Accordingly he will be called an adulterer if he lives with another woman while his wife is alive. But if his wife dies he is free from the law, and if he marries another woman, he is not an adulterer". Paul is, however, silent on that score. The implications of that silence are obvious, and do not redound to the credit of Paul as a spiritual leader.

The same male-biased, one-sided expression of belief is expressed in I Corinthians 7:39-40,

A wife is bound as long as her husband lives. But if the husband dies, she is free to marry anyone she wishes, only in the Lord. But in my judgement she is more blessed if she remains as she is. And I think that I too have the spirit of God.

Where two single persons desire to marry each other

In general Paul is pretty discouraging of anyone's desire to marry under any circumstances at all, although he graciously 'permits it' in some situations. There are doubtless many reasons for Paul's anti-sex stance, and they lie on a continuum of believability. At one end are the really powerful emotional drivers of his opinions, whose true nature lies buried deep in Paul's unconscious. At the other end are more straightforward, practical ones. In between lie at least some unsatisfactory explanations which are either based on ignorance or rationalisation – or both.

One of the more acceptable considerations that probably influenced Paul in his crusade against sexual behaviour, given that reliable contraception was not available in his lifetime, is that Paul, like Jesus and many of their Jewish compatriots, was living in a state of eager expectation of the imminent end of the world. It was commonly understood that this would be a time of chaos which would inevitably cause hardship and misery until the

Parousia (the return of Christ, the Messiah), marked the inauguration of the Kingdom of God upon earth. No one who believed that this was about to happen would be under any illusion that this would be other than a horrendous time for pregnant women and those nursing babies or caring for young children. Whether or not Jesus actually described this prophesised time in the words attributed to him in Matthew 24:16-21, they undoubtedly capture the feelings of anxiety that must have abounded in the Jewish world in the first half of the first century CE. Jesus is reported to have said of this end of the world chaos,

> Then let them which be in Judaea flee into the mountains: Let him which is on the housetop not come down to take any thing out of his house: Neither let him which is in the field return back to take his clothes. Woe unto them that that are with child, and to them that give suck in those days! But pray ye that your flight be not in the winter, neither on the Sabbath day: For then shall be great tribulation, such as was not since the beginning of the world to this time, no, nor ever shall be.

Although certainly not the whole story of Paul's obsession with the suppression of sexual behaviour, these issues may well have been in his mind when he wrote,

> Now concerning virgins, I have no command of the Lord, but I give my opinion as one who by the Lord's mercy is trustworthy. I think that, in view of the impending crisis, it is well for you to remain as you are. Are you bound to a wife? Do not seek to be free. Are you free from a wife? Do not seek a wife. But if you marry, you do not sin, and if a virgin marries, she does not sin. Yet those who marry will experience distress in this life, and I would spare you that. I mean, brothers and sisters, the appointed time has grown short; from now on, let even those who have wives be as though had none (I

Corinthians 7:25-29).

Another issue, briefly touched on earlier in this chapter, which probably played some part in Paul's attitude to sex was something which at first sight seems to have some religious justification, but which on closer inspection turns out to be absolute nonsense. Paul writes,

> I want you to be free from anxieties. The unmarried man is anxious about the affairs of the Lord, how to please the Lord; but the married man is anxious about the affairs of the world, how to please his wife, and his interests are divided. And the unmarried woman and the virgin are anxious about the affairs of the Lord, so that they may be holy in body and spirit: but the married woman is anxious about the affairs of the world, how to please her husband (I Corinthians 7:32-34).

It is hard to believe that Paul really believed that unmarried persons spend all their time being "anxious about the affairs of the Lord", and that married persons spend all their time thinking about how they can please their spouse. Would that things were so simple! The inevitable frustrations of married life and the anger that those frustrations generate, all too often lead married couples to spend less and less time even thinking about their partners, let alone thinking about what they can do to please them. And most unmarried persons spend a considerably greater proportion of their time thinking about how to achieve a happy sexual relationship with a partner than they do about "the affairs of the Lord". If Paul really thought that remaining unmarried would cause people to think less about sex than if they were married, he was extremely naïve. The effect would, for most people be exactly the reverse. The unmarried Paul himself seems to have devoted a disproportionate amount of his time to thinking and writing and preaching about sex, albeit from a very negative point of view.

Notwithstanding the aforegoing, Paul does give some grudging 'permission' to some 'special cases' to marry.

> If anyone thinks that he is not behaving properly towards his fiancée, if his passions are strong, and so it has to be, let him marry as he wishes; it is no sin. Let them marry. But if someone stands firm in his resolve, being under no necessity but having his own desire under control, and has determined in his own mind to keep her as his fiancée, he will do well. So then, he who marries his fiancée does well: and he who refrains from marriage will do better (I Corinthians 7:36-38).

It is clear from the foregoing that Paul's general attitude to sex is overwhelmingly negative with absolutely no celebration of the 'Joy of Sex' in any of its aspects. For the most part his writings on the subject are all about condemnation, prohibitions, and attempts to control the sexual behaviour of those who call themselves Christians. Even within marriage, sex is only grudgingly granted a place as the lesser of two evils. This being so it is quite strange that two forms of sexual behaviour, homosexuality and masturbation, which have come in for more than their fair share of vituperative condemnation from the Christian Church over the nearly two thousand years of its existence, receive relatively scant attention from Paul.

Homosexuality

Towards the end of the twentieth century attitudes to homosexuality became something of a hot potato in some sections of the Christian Church, the clash of views on the subject at one time threatening to cause a major schism in the Anglican Church. Perhaps predictably, Paul had nothing but moralistic condemnation for those whose sexual desires sought satisfaction in this way. What he said on the subject was,

For this reason God gave them up to degrading passions. Their women exchanged natural intercourse for unnatural, and in the same way also the men, giving up natural intercourse with women, were consumed with passion for one another. Men committed shameless acts with men and received in their own persons the due penalty for their error (Romans 1:26-29).

Not surprisingly in view of those comments, Paul pronounced his judgement that "sodomites" ("homosexual offenders" in the NIV translation), along with idolaters, thieves, drunkards, fornicators, adulterers and four other assorted wrongdoers will not "inherit the Kingdom of God" (I Corinthians 6:9-10). All in all Paul's condemnation of homosexuality is pretty extreme in its intensity, but short on quantity.

But it is not just overt homosexual behaviour which arouses Paul's ire. Anything which might be associated with such behaviour is regarded as a grave defect. One such characteristic is long hair in a male. At different times in different cultures long hair on a male has been regarded in either a positive or a negative light. For Paul it was unambiguously a no-no. "If a man have long hair it is a shame unto him", he writes in I Corinthians 11:14. Wisely he stops short of claiming this to be one of God's opinions. Perhaps it is so obviously true to Paul that long hair in a male is a disgrace that he feels it unnecessary to bring God in on his side. "Does not the very nature of things teach you that if a man has long hair, it is a disgrace to him?" (I Corinthians 11:14). It is strange that a man who courageously, in the teeth of much opposition in the early church, could argue, and successfully argue the case for the irrelevance of male circumcision to a man's spiritual state, could get so hung up on the length of a man's hair.

Masturbation
Even more surprising than the relatively small number of refer-

ences Paul makes to homosexuality is his failure to even mention, let alone erect any prohibitions against masturbation. It is surprising because he does not hesitate to condemn just about every other form of sexual behaviour, and parts of the Christian Church have been quite vicious in their attempts to suppress what is for both men and women, an entirely natural and healthy activity. Those who have tried to do this have caused a great deal of psychological harm to those who have been intimidated by their unhealthy repressive views on this subject, which many people have been led to erroneously believe is, 'the Christian Church's position'.

Whether Paul said nothing on this subject because he subsumed masturbation under labels such as, "sexual immorality", and, "every kind of evil," is hard to say, but certainly with most other aspects of sexual behaviour he did not shy away from being very explicit about what he was crusading against. Perhaps a more likely reason for Paul's silence is that he recognised, at least unconsciously, that, for the individual for whom all other avenues for the release of sexual energy have been coercively closed, denial of that 'last resort' outlet would seriously put at risk their ability to function as a reasonably normal human being. Our bodies are not designed for sexual abstinence in the prime of life, and do not react well to the enforced inhibition of sexual energy. Various forms of impaired physical and/or psychological functioning are very often the result. Very probably Paul himself indulged in masturbation as a safety valve for the release of his own pent-up sexual energies from time to time.

Sex and love

One final comment needs to be made about Paul's attitude to sex, and that is that sex for Paul seems to mean a purely genital act of animal lust. But such a concept lies at one end of a continuum at the other end of which lies the experience of complete physical, mental, and spiritual integration through the loving exchange of the mutual giving and receiving of pleasure, an experience which seems to have been unknown to Paul, and which far from taking one further away from the spiritual depths of life, brings one closer to them. The essence of such a peak experience of sexuality was beautifully captured in a short poem by the 13th-century Sufi[131] poet Rumi.

> Out beyond ideas of wrongdoing and rightdoing,
> there is a field. I'll meet you there.
>
> When the soul lies down in that grass,
> the world is too full to talk about.
> Ideas, language, even the phrase each other
> doesn't make any sense any more – Jelaluddin Rumi
> (Translated by Coleman Barks).

What distinguishes rape from all forms of consensual sex is not the extent to which the satisfaction of animal lust appears to be the driving force of the encounter, but whether the behaviour of each partner is sensitively attuned to the pleasure (or lack of it) their partner is getting from the experience, and where necessary adjusts their behaviour accordingly. With such an attitude of mind even 'pretend rape' and the experience of the giving and receiving of 'raw animal pleasure', are not rape and can be very exciting for both parties involved. Without it, even low-key sexual encounters and even those between married partners, are to a greater or lesser extent, and consciously or unconsciously, if not quite rape, at least a poor second best to what any sexual encounter has the potential to be.

Paul's obsession with sex and almost complete ignoring of sexual love makes his epistles worse than useless as any sort of guide for those involved in a sexual relationship who want to deepen the spiritual side of that relationship. It is a great pity that

Paul had no sensitivity-enhancing ideas to offer his readers comparable with D. H. Lawrence's poem, *All I ask*. Being a man, Lawrence uses language which expresses what a male longs for in a relationship, but all those longings are not just the deepest wishes of men in respect of a sexual partner, but of women too.

All I ask of a woman is that she shall feel gently
towards me
when my heart feels kindly towards her,
and there shall be the soft, soft tremor as of unheard
bells between us,
It is all I ask.

Christian leaders need to offer those of their flock who are in relationship with a partner much more than bible study classes if they are to be any help in making marriage a source of mutual joy and delight, and to do anything to minimise the extensive distress caused by the now nearly 50% of couples whose marriages end up on the rocks. Paul's belief that for those who wish to attain the highest levels of spiritual development, total abstinence from sex is a *sine qua non* makes much of his writing not just unhelpful but a serious hindrance to the attempts of those Christians who seek for themselves and others, joyful human relationships.

Further explorations
There is much more that could be said about Paul's religious ideas, but to go into them here would unbalance the structure of this book, whose primary emphasis is on the ideas of Jesus. Much of Paul's writing outside the themes that I have dealt with in this chapter does not stand up to careful critical analysis. As just one example of this, verses 11 to 13 of the seventh chapter of Paul's Epistle to the Romans read,

For sin, seizing an opportunity in the commandment, deceived me and through it killed me. So the law is holy, and the commandment is holy and just and good. Did what is good, then, bring death to me? By no means! It was sin, working death in me through what is good, in order that sin might be shown to be sin, and through the commandment might become sinful beyond measure.

Those words are not difficult to understand because they are profound, but because they are the poor expression of confused thinking. Indeed, at times what Paul has to say is just meaningless nonsense. Two such examples are to be found in the fifth chapter of Paul's second Epistle to the Corinthians. In verse 14 he writes, "We are convinced that one has died for all; therefore all have died", and in verse 21, "For our sake he made him to be sin who knew no sin, so that in him we might become the righteousness of God." Many more similar examples of the same sort of thing are to be found scattered throughout Paul's epistles.

Some final points on the mind of Paul
Paul's triumphal resolution of the paradox of his sometimes doing what he didn't want to do and not doing what he wanted to do which so haunted him, gives a valuable clue to the way in which his salvation theology was shaped by, indeed driven by, his attempt to understand himself and his temptations, and to escape the consequences of the doubtless many times he succumbed to some of those temptations.

I thank God through Jesus Christ our Lord. So then with the mind I myself serve the law of God; but with the flesh the law of sin (Romans 7:25).

Unable to bear the idea that thoughts and behaviours belonging 'to the flesh' were actually part of his own psyche, Paul (as many both before and after him have done) splits his being into two separate parts which are radically different from each other – his mind and his body, and identifies himself with his mind (the real Paul) and rejects his body as a foreign entity, against which he has to fight because it keeps asserting itself in a manner which would, if he allowed it to have its way, lead him into behaviours of which he believed God disapproved. Unable to grasp the significance of Jesus' teaching that, "it is in forgiving others that we ourselves are forgiven", and believing that sinful behaviour must be punished, he played a major role in developing the early foundations of the Doctrine of the Atonement – that because of Jesus' sacrificial death, humankind (and therefore Paul as well) was free of punishment for the thoughts and behaviours for which his 'carnal mind' was responsible.

The result was that in Paul's troubled mind his pathological resolution of his personal psycho-spiritual problems became inflated to cosmic proportions. It wasn't just Paul who was experiencing a destructive conflict between what he judged to be his good and bad selves. Human life in general became seen as a battlefield between the forces of Good (embodied in whatever parts of ourselves submit to 'the will of God', as defined of course, by powerful leaders within the Christian Church) and those of Evil, embodied in our 'carnal mind', defined as a way of being in which our biological nature is allowed to express itself freely.

For the flesh lusteth against the Spirit, and the Spirit against the flesh: and these are contrary the one to the other: so that ye cannot do the things that ye would (Galatians 5:17).

From this flowed a logically flawed theological structure which different branches of the Christian Church have tinkered with in different ways for nearly two thousand years, a theological structure which is doomed to eventual collapse because of the psychopathological foundations on which it has been built.

Underpinning that whole theological structure is fear – fear of an 'omnipotent' supernatural being who has all the qualities of a cruel medieval absolute ruler. This 'God' sacrificed his "dearly beloved son" as "the propitiation for our sins" (I John 2:2, and 4:10), or at least, according to many of those of an authoritarian turn of mind, for all our sins except the greatest sin of all, not accepting the truth of church teachings about the significance of Jesus' "atoning death" (Romans 3:25). Such a being has no objective, real world existence. He exists only in the minds of confused and frightened people and whatever 'experience' people have of him has a remarkable resemblance to whatever fears we may have, or have had in our childhood, of our father, conflated with any similar fears we have had of our mother and other persons in authority. In the course of the last few chapters of this book I shall sketch the outline of a more satisfactory concept of the nature of God.

For it is just here that the root of the intellectual mess which Christianity has become lies. Christianity, which many of its adherents believe was founded by Jesus the Jew of Nazareth, does to some extent preach the message of love, compassion and toleration proclaimed by that spiritual genius. It does to some extent seek to listen to, and try to understand the teachings of that real flesh and blood human being who walked this earth 2000 years ago, and whose life and teachings provide a window into a profound understanding of the nature of God. When it does so, we see its humanistic face. But the church also and often more vociferously follows the example of Paul in "preaching Christ crucified". When it does that we see the authoritarian face of the religion. The thought worlds of these two faces are poles apart.

It is not just the biblical writings of St Paul which have corrupted the insights into spiritual reality of those to whom the thought-world of authoritarian Christianity is congenial. In Appendix 4, I give a brief outline of some of these additional sources.

I am well aware that in writing as I have about Paul, treating him as an entirely flesh and blood human being rather than as some sort of junior member of the God family (not quite of the status of Jesus as God's son, but rather as something like a nephew or a godson), some people will be scandalised by my irreverence towards some of his beliefs and ideas. What I have written is not intended to diminish in any way our appreciation of the value of the profound spiritual ideas which he did express from time to time, and for which I have the deepest respect, as I repeatedly acknowledge throughout this book. But there is an ever-present danger that for some devout Christians all his ideas will become idols before which they feel they must intellectually prostrate themselves and which they feel they dare not question or criticise.

But Paul was not a God. He was entirely human, and I do not believe we can evaluate the quality of his religious ideas without evaluating to what extent psychopathology was present in his thinking. As is the case with all of us, theology is inextricably bound up with psychology in Paul, and all the other writers of books in the Bible.

Chapter 8

Humanistic and Authoritarian Christianity compared

Progress in truth – truth of science and truth of religion – is mainly a progress in the framing of concepts, in discarding artificial abstractions or partial metaphors, and in evolving notions which strike more deeply into the root of reality.[4]
– Alfred North Whitehead. *Religion in the Making*

The previous chapter of this book was dominated by a discussion of the ideas of St. Paul and how they differ from those of Jesus. In this chapter I want to add to that a broader perspective on the differences between the humanistic and authoritarian faces of Christianity and shall look at a number of specific areas where those differences show up particularly strongly. I shall do this under seven broad headings: Respect for Authority, The Nature of God, Innate Goodness versus Innate Wickedness, The Relationship between Human Beings and God, Forgiveness versus Punishment, The Acceptance of Rigid Dogma, and The fate of Christian Ethics at the hands of authoritarian Christianity.

Respect for authority

Although the question of respect for authority is very much in one's face in thinking about authoritarian Christianity, it is no less an issue with humanistic Christianity. One fundamental difference between these two branches of Christianity is in the different beliefs they hold about the source of the authority which each believes it has for the rightness of its ideas. Those of us who are happy to align ourselves with humanistic Christianity do so because we believe that the ethical teachings of Jesus derive whatever authority we are prepared to grant them from the intrinsic quality of the ideas they encapsulate: we believe in the power of human behaviour which is guided by such principles to transform the world from one which contains much pain, frustration and sadness into one which will more and more become an earthly paradise of more realised than dashed hopes, of more peace than conflict, of more love than hate, of more pleasure than pain.

By contrast authoritarian Christianity derives its authority from the positional power of its self-appointed leaders, who have built defensive barricades around their dogmas to preserve themselves as far as possible from effective challenge. An important component of the defences authoritarian Christians have built for themselves is the proscription of any significant independent thinking or feeling by adherents of the religion. There is only one right way to think and feel where religion is concerned, and that is the way church leaders prescribe.

Sometimes the pronouncements of the Top Dogs in authoritarian Christianity are honestly expressed as being just their personal opinion (however divinely inspired). However, the temptation to a religious leader to claim that ideas that he (or very occasionally she) feels particularly strongly about are in fact not just personal opinions, but privileged communications direct from God, sometimes gets the better of them. The real psychological motivation for that manoeuvre is of course to put those ideas beyond criticism. But whether or not a church leader honestly admits that the views they are expressing are just their own, or claims that they are a direct message from God of what he 'wants', or 'wishes', or 'demands', or 'thinks', the fact is that all those pronouncements are the personal opinions of the leaders.

The only intelligent grounds we have for regarding one person's opinions as being more profoundly true than those of another, is that they speak with the authority, not of the church in which they hold positional power, but with the authority we grant them because of what we perceive to be the quality of their ideas, and the authenticity of their presentation of those ideas. There is nothing like any suspicion that a speaker is (consciously or otherwise) not being entirely honest with us, or that they do not respect us as sensible adults, able and empowered to make our own decisions about the truth of what they are saying, for us to lose respect for the probable truth and value of any communications from them. The personal qualities of a speaker are powerful determinants of how much the psychologically mature person regards them as speaking authoritatively. It is too often the case where religious people are concerned, that people feel, to quote again those perceptive words of Emerson, "Who you are shouts so loudly in my ears that I cannot hear what you are saying".

In some denominations and sects (especially those reacting against the supreme power granted to the Pope in Roman Catholicism), ultimate authority in all matters of religion is on the face of it transferred to the bible, but of course in practice, for even the most strongly fundamentalist Christians, it is not the actual words of the bible which are regarded as an unassailable authority, but rather those words as interpreted by the Top Dogs in their particular denomination. Whilst it may suit the particular psychological needs of a rigid fundamentalist to believe that the universe and everything in it came into existence in just six days, as recorded in verses 3 to 31 of the first chapter of the book of Genesis (although, significantly, not in the other Creation account reported in Genesis 2: 4-25), believing in the same literal truth of the words Jesus is reported to have spoken to those standing around him about the imminence of his 'second coming', (namely that, "There be some standing here, which shall not taste of death, till they see the Son of man coming in his kingdom"[132]) presents fundamentalist Christians with a problem that most would prefer not to face.

The nature of God

Sigmund Freud was an Austrian Neurologist who gradually turned his attention from neurological processes to mental ones, and developed the once very popular approach to the treatment of psychological disorders known as Psychoanalysis. In his day he undoubtedly made important contributions to the study of human psychology, and some of the ideas he introduced (such as the concept of Defence Mechanisms) have been of lasting importance and value. However, advances in other approaches to dealing with mental problems, and the discovery through meticulous scholarly research of serious discrepancies between Freud's case notes and his published accounts of some of those cases, has been one among a number of factors which have rather knocked him off the pedestal he once stood on in the fields of psychology and psychiatry.[5]

Freud was a firmly convinced atheist, and claimed that the concept of God was a purely human creation which did not refer to anything which has any objective, real existence. He believed that humankind developed the concept on the basis of the universal human experience of having at least one parent, whom in our earliest childhood years most of us experienced as all-good, all-powerful and all-knowing, which in contrast with our helpless and largely ignorant infant selves they almost were. Certainly for several years we were almost totally dependent on at least one of them for our continued existence – that parent (or parent-substitute) was in almost total control of our lives, of the only part of the universe of which we had any direct personal experience.

As we daily grew in physical strength and intellectual understanding, we gradually realised that our parents were far from perfect – they were not all-powerful, they were not all-knowing and they were certainly not all-good. No matter what virtuous people, what devoted parents they were, they let us down from time to time, being powerless to provide us with immediate relief from the pains of colic, nappy rash, and things like our teeth cutting their way through our gums. Sometimes they made no attempt to comfort us in our distress, indeed sometimes adding to it by deliberately hurting us. The gradual realisation of the limitations of our earthly parents must have been a devastating experience and have left each of us with an acute sense of vulnerability and a longing for a more totally reliable form of protection. Freud believed that out of that longing for a totally reliable source of protection and comfort was born the rudimentary idea of God. We wished for such a being to exist, and were able to help each other to believe that there was a real 'something out there', who, just like our earthly father and mother but far more powerfully effectively, could protect and comfort us when we were in need, BUT (just as with most of our parents), only IF WE WERE GOOD, which usually meant being obedient to their commands. According to Freud, the individual's conception of God, "Is in every case modelled after the father … God is at bottom nothing but an exalted father".[133]

The further parallels between the traditional authoritarian concept of God and our relationship with that being, and our concept of an earthly father and our relationship with him are fairly obvious, but not appropriate to go into here. As to why God should in general in the Western world be seen as a father figure rather than a mother figure, there is much debate, but a significant factor in that may well be that crucially important though what a child gains from its mother may be, in the Western world at least, it is male figures which wield the most power.

What is certain is that Freud's explanation of the origin of the concept of God is not the whole story. What is almost as certain is that there is some truth in his theory in some, perhaps in many cases. What is not at all certain is just how much of any particular person's concept of God is to be accounted for in terms of Freud's theory. What is also clear is that it is a widespread part of the traditional Christian conception of the nature of God, and particularly of that to be found in the authoritarian face of Christianity, that he behaves like an earthly father, in that much of the time he is not present in our everyday life, but every so often appears on the scene and does things (like condemning our behaviour, or forgiving us when we have done wrong).

For those who believe in this concept of God, he is not an integral part of the universe, but an outsider to it who occasionally intervenes in it, and makes something happen. That situation is rather like that of a child playing with a Lego village he or she has created. There is the village all beautifully laid out, and there is the child looking at it and thinking about it, but not continuously involved in everything going on there. The child and the village are two quite separate things. Then the child suddenly reaches forward and moves a car, or one of the figures, and suddenly the child and the village become one thing. Then the child stops rearranging things and goes off to tea, and again there are two separate things, the child and the Lego village, and they remain that way until the child returns and starts doing things with his or her Lego creation, when they once again become a single child-Lego-village unit.

Freud and his latter-day atheistic fellow-travellers, Richard Dawkins and company, have made a most valuable contribution to the liberation of the human race from the tyranny of belief in the existence of some controlling, cruel, despotic, omnipotent, invisible being. The God they have tried to liberate us from is, however, only one conceptualisation of the entity to which the verbal label God has been applied.

Limiting ourselves to the Christian tradition to keep the discussion as brief as possible, many different concepts as to the nature of God are to be found in the thinking, writings and preachings of those who have placed themselves within the Judeo-Christian tradition over the past 2000 years or so. These concepts have cohered around four different themes.

Firstly the idea of God as the creator and sustainer of the

universe and all that lies in it, an omnipotent, omniscient, and omnipresent being who has potential autocratic control of every aspect of our lives except our wrongdoing, which he is impotent to prevent. Secondly the idea of God as the ultimate moral authority in the universe, the supreme judge of all humanity who after our physical death will decree for each of us either a life of eternal bliss with him in heaven, or one of eternal suffering in the company of the devil and his angels in hell. Thirdly, and very differently, the idea of God as a being with all the best qualities of a loving parent, who seeks what is best for his children, as reflected (amongst other ways) in the frequently occurring biblical image of God, in the form of Jesus, as a caring shepherd tending his flock.

All three of these types of concept of God have something of the human about them. The all-powerful, controlling, authoritarian and moralistic types have at their heart a being who does physical things in the physical world, creating things, making things happen (such as causing some armed criminals to fire shots which miss some (but not all!) of their intended targets), pronouncing judgement and allocating people to different sorts of eternal living quarters. However metaphorically intended, it is very difficult for some people not to see such a being as in fact a person, albeit one with a transparent body – some sort of super-scientist, or super-engineer or super-policeman, who being so clever, so all-knowing, and so all-powerful, has been able to make his body invisible.

It is but one small step from talking about such a being as 'thinking', 'feeling', 'wanting', and being possessed of a whole range of very human emotions, (and even ascribing a gender to 'him') to speculating as to the nature of the body 'he' must surely have – an invisible body, true, but surely a body. Under the influence of the belief that this being is omnipresent, it is again but a further small step to entertain grotesque images of this God as being of huge size.

The tendency to ascribe human qualities to God is one that has waxed and waned in both Judaism and Christianity over the centuries. One example of what must surely be this anthropo-morphising[134] tendency near its peak is to be found in a book written somewhere in the period of the seventh to the tenth centuries CE called Shi'ur Koma (Estimation of the height), in which God is described as a huge being in human shape. The measurement of his various body parts, eyes, ears, lips, neck, beard, ankles, etc. is given in parasangs. The Shorter Oxford English Dictionary defines a parasang as "a Persian measure of length, usually reckoned as between 3 and 3½ English miles", but the writer of Shi'ur Koma hastens to inform us that the measurements he gives for God's body parts are not in earthly but rather in heavenly parasangs, each of which "measures a million cubits, each cubit four spans, and each span reaches from one end of the world to the other".[135]

Although presumably few people today would take such extreme flights of fancy seriously, for many people who talk and think about God as a controlling and judgemental being, 'he' is a person who has all the good qualities of the human being, including a body, (a male one of course, albeit an invisible one), but none of their all-too-human faults.[136]

The concept of God as a loving heavenly father, whilst clearly strongly related to our knowledge of the best of earthly fathers, places the emphasis on the non-physical emotional relationship between a parent and a child. Jesus, in those sayings which can be fairly reliably attributed to him, used this metaphor of 'our heavenly father' extensively in talking about God, reflecting the warm emotional bond and sense of unity that existed between himself and God, rather than describing him as engaged in any physical activities.

This de-emphasis on God as a person in favour of God as the source of warm, caring love is carried even further in some of the examples of the fourth type of concept of God in the Judeo-

Christian tradition, in which God is seen as a being with purely spiritual properties rather than physical ones. Because of the thought world of the times in which the various books of the bible were written, this type of concept of the nature of God is less prominent in the Christian scriptures and thinking than the other three, but is nevertheless strongly present. Although the statement, "God is a spirit", appears only once in the New Testament (in verse 24 of the fourth chapter of John's gospel), that is probably because that simple but powerfully true concept has been conflated with other less spiritually pure ideas in the Dogma of the Holy Trinity. This strange concept of God as three co-equal persons in one (which is about as easy to grasp as it is to visualise a square circle or a square every point on the perimeter of which is equidistant from the point of intersection of its diagonals) has obsessively intrigued the Christian Church for centuries. Perhaps it is the impossible-to-fully-grasp, koan-like quality of this doctrine which is responsible for the huge contrast between the single New Testament statement of the straight-forward belief that "God is a spirit", and the nearly three million hits a Google search unearthed in response to the probe, "Bible. God is a spirit and the Trinity".

Exploring the complex and often confused thinking that lies behind that doctrine would take us too far away from the central thrust of this book to be undertaken here. For present purposes let us just simplistically summarise the situation by saying that we find two very different types of concept of God in the bible: an authoritarian, moralistic one (with some aspects of the 'God as our father' concept) on the one hand, and on the other an Abstract-Spiritual one (with other aspects of the 'God as our father' one) on the other.

The concept of God implicit in the authoritarian face of Christianity belongs to the first category. It is the idea of a powerful ruler who created and sustains the universe and all that is in it. He stands apart from his creation, judging how we behave, intervening here and there (not always on the most rational grounds it would seem), and observing the moral qualities of the behaviour of his children, upon whom he will one day, when he feels the universe has gone on long enough, sit in judgement and either admit to the joys of heaven or consign to an eternity of horrible punishment (or if you are a Roman Catholic believer, to a time-limited period of punishment in Purgatory).

This is a concept of a being for whose existence there is not one shred of objective evidence, but which many adherents of many religions have been brow-beaten into believing does exist, and before whose power all humanity ought to quake. The most striking aspect of this being is his (and it nearly always is 'his' rather than 'her') close resemblance to a cruel psychopath. He has a firm belief in the necessity of punishment in controlling human behaviour, a blood lust, and very ambivalent feelings towards his 'dearly beloved son'. He has a (once highly effective) hierarchically organised PR team whose selling of the demand for obedience to the dictates of authority, and the forbidding of any questioning of that authority, is as much in their own interests as they proclaim it to be in God's.

The view from the humanistic face of Christianity is quite different: As briefly touched on in Chapter 5 of this book, the concept of God implicit in the humanistic face of Christianity is squarely in the camp of the Abstract-Spiritual concepts of God. God and man, and God and woman are one. God is part and parcel of every aspect of life – is part of the way the universe functions. The word God is just a verbal label to describe one aspect of how the world works, just as the words 'The Force of Gravity' and 'The Laws of Thermodynamics', are verbal labels identifying particular parts of the way the universe works in its physical aspect.

Water turns to ice if its temperature drops below a certain point, and to steam if its temperature rises above another certain point. It doesn't do so because any Law of Physics *makes it happen*. Scientific laws are a description of certain sorts of cause and effect relationships, which scientists have formulated as a result of meticulous and repeated observation. Those laws don't *make things happen* in the physical world. They are just a description of the 'way things are', which highlights some of the general principles operating in the physical world.

Similarly God doesn't *make things happen*. The term 'God' is just a symbol for the way the world works in its spiritual aspect. It is because the universe has the properties reflected in the concept of God of the humanistic face of Christianity, that living our lives in accordance with the ethical principles which Jesus urged upon us has such positive effects on human happiness. In the remaining chapters of this book I shall return to this topic several times to give a somewhat fuller description of this entity called 'God'.

Innate goodness versus innate wickedness

One of the rationalised justifications many persons of an authoritarian cast of mind rely on to justify their controlling behaviour, is that they are in some way a superior being, who knows better and behaves better in respect of the matter which has provoked their controlling behaviour, than the person they are trying to force into conformity with their own thinking. However, authoritarian controlling behaviours, contrary to the impression they create in outsiders, are always driven by a sense of inadequacy and some sort of inferiority. The person who is quietly confident about their good qualities is respectful of the rights of others to hold different views from themselves, and does not try to force theirs onto other people.

The holier-than-thou attitude which so frequently seems to underlie the anxious, often angry attempts at the control of others (rather than the more-likely-of-success attempt to gently influence them), is there because the person feels anything but better, stronger, 'holier' than the person whose behaviour they are trying to control. There are many layers of the personality where a deeply disturbing sense of inadequacy which drives the person to try to control others may exist, but to a large extent understanding these is a matter for psychological rather than purely religious concern.

The one aspect of the issue which is of considerable spiritual significance though, is the belief (discussed at some length in Chapter 6) that many people have, that in the deepest core of their being they are bad, or even evil. This is a view that is by no means restricted to Christians, or even to religious people in general. The eminent atheistic philosopher Bertrand Russell is just one high-profile example of this phenomenon among the unambiguously non-religious. Religion, and specifically the authoritarian face of Christianity with its doctrine of *Original Sin,* is however, very strongly implicated in the prevalence of this view among many of its adherents. According to this doctrine, because the first man, Adam, committed the sin of disobedience to God's instructions, the whole human race ever since has been tainted with sin – we are all "miserable sinners" and, "there is no health in us".

Authoritarian Christianity has as one of its fundamental assumptions, that human beings are all rotten at the core, born in sin, and were it not for the sufferings and death of Jesus on the cross, would all be headed for an eternity of unending suffering as a punishment for the original sin with which we are saddled, not because of anything we have done, or failed to do, but because we were born (through no wish of our own) into this world, and have Adam, the man who disobeyed God, as our ultimate ancestor.

It is this view which fuels much of its theology, particularly the Doctrine of the Atonement. One of the fundamental assumptions of that doctrine is that not only did the wrongdoing of that aboriginal man Adam deserve punishment, but also that Adam's guilt has been passed down to his children and thence to their children and so on throughout all generations. The fact that in Ezekiel 18:20 it is unambiguously stated that, "A child shall not suffer for the iniquity of a parent, nor a parent suffer for the iniquity of a child", is conveniently overlooked by those who believe that every statement in the bible is "the word of God".

Humanistic Christianity takes as a fundamental given, that we humans are all fundamentally good and beautiful people. Those of us who are happy to identify ourselves as humanistic Christians are not in the habit of using quotations from the bible to justify the rightness of our beliefs, but it is interesting to note that the view that human beings in their aboriginal core are good, lovely people has strong support in the biblical record. The first book of Genesis is devoted to an account of God's Creation of the universe and all the plants and animals that exist within it, culminating in the creation of human beings. Verse 27 of this first chapter of Genesis reads (in the original King James version of the English bible), "So God created man in his own image, in the image of God created he him; male and female created he them", and the last verse of the chapter (31) announces unequivocally, "And God saw everything that he had made, and, behold, it was very good". Nowhere in this first chapter of the first book of the bible, is there any suggestion that human beings are anything other than fundamentally "very good", and nowhere in the gospel accounts of the life and sayings of Jesus is there any record of Jesus ever even implying any contradiction of that view.

This view of the essential nature of the 'made in the image of God' human being as pure unadulterated goodness, deeply embedded in the heart of humanistic Christianity, is in stark contrast to the pathological *original sin* view of human beings as fundamentally wicked, to be found in authoritarian Christianity.

Considering the widespread prevalence of this negative view of the essential nature of humanity among Christians, it is quite surprising to find little justification for the concept in the scriptures. Psalm 51, verse 5 seems to simply accept the self-evident truth of this fact, "Behold I was shapen in iniquity; and in sin did my mother conceive me", but neither there nor anywhere else in the Old Testament is there any explanation as to why this is the case. Even the long rambling discussion of sinfulness (and its relationship to death) in verses 12 to 21 of the fifth chapter of Paul's Epistle to the Romans which deals with this issue, gives no sort of explanation of how original sin is transmitted. In fact it gives nothing more than a repetitive, superficial description of the transmission of guilt *fact*. In verse 12 we find the words (referring to Adam's eating of the fruit of the Tree of the Knowledge of Good and Evil – against God's strict instructions), "Sin came into the world through one man". In verse 18 we find, "Therefore just as one man's trespass led to condemnation for all, so one man's act of righteousness leads to justification and life for all", and in verse 19, "For just as by one man's disobedience the many were made sinners ...".

Given that disobedience to the orders of authority is the cardinal sin in all authoritarian systems (and yet sometimes a very psychologically healthy, necessary and commonly-occurring human response to attempts to enforce conformity to the will of another), it is hardly surprising that the concept of the inherent sinfulness of humankind found in authoritarian Christianity fertile ground in which to flourish. It is an idea which is totally devoid of any logic. It is just as ludicrous as the idea that had my mother or father been a convicted criminal I would have been born with a criminal record.

But is Original Sin only about disobedience, or is there more than immediately meets the eye lying beneath the concept? The few lines from Psalm 51 quoted above give a possible clue. "Behold I was shapen in iniquity, and in sin did my mother conceive me". Since in the psalmist's day conception only took place during or shortly after sexual intercourse, the conclusion is inescapable that for the psalmist sexual intercourse is sinful. He is unlikely to have been alone in believing that. Certainly several centuries later St Paul held a closely similar view. Bearing in mind that a key aspect of the concept of Original Sin is that everyone is tainted by it, and that having sexual desires is a universal part of our biological nature, it is entirely reasonable to suppose that the idea of original sin arose from humanity's widespread anxiety about its sexuality.

Such an hypothesis could also rather neatly make sense of the idea that original sin is always inevitably transmitted to children from their parents. It is a striking fact that biologically and psychologically speaking, before the development of the medical techniques of artificial insemination and *in vitro* fertilisation, probably the only common factor linking the births of all children at all times and in all places with the character and actions of their parents was the fact that all those births took place as a result of sexual intercourse between the baby's parents. And it is a further fact that when, as a result of sexual contact between a man and a woman, one or more sperm penetrate a female ovum, a process is set in motion which (unless medical problems arise or there is some human intervention), leads to the birth of a child with the same fatal weakness as its parents – the desire for sexual contact with another human being. If having sexual desires is defined as a sin (as it more or less was by St Paul for one), then we are all indeed born sinners, and whenever acting to satisfy our sexual desires results in the birth of a baby we shall inevitably, because of the nature of human biology, be passing on that sinfulness to the next generation.

Some people may find such a theory that it is in sperm-ovum contact that 'original sin' is transmitted to the newly-conceived far-fetched, but it is for most people much more believable than the doctrine of the Virgin Birth (that Mary conceived Jesus without engaging in sexual intercourse with any human being), an idea which makes no biological sense whatsoever. However, even that biological miracle is perhaps easier to believe in than the still more way-out Roman Catholic Doctrine of the Immaculate Conception. Many people seem to be under the misapprehension that the claim that this bit of dogma makes is that Jesus "was born of a virgin". In fact it makes an even more extraordinary claim. It is defined in the COED as the belief that "God preserved the Virgin Mary from the taint of original sin from the moment she was conceived". One wonders whether those who formulated this doctrine agonised over the precise meaning of the concept of "from the moment of her conception". Had God intervened a split second too early Mary would not have existed and his intervention would have been wasted on thin air. Had he intervened a split second after conception his intervention would have come too late – just by being conceived she would already have contracted original sin.

Of course, since "all things are possible to God" he could have retroactively altered Mary's medical history, so that although she started out life tainted by original sin, she wasn't tainted by original sin. What intellectual gymnastics the omnipotent God of authoritarian Christianity has to get up to preserve the illusions of some of his humble servants on earth. But it is not the fact that human intelligence is limited that makes it difficult to accept the truth of the whole package of Original Sin, Virgin Birth, and Immaculate Conception, together with St Paul's weird idea that celibacy generates a state of superior spirituality. It is simply that those ideas are irrational, illogical, and at their root rest on the same psychopathological foundation – the belief that sex is intrinsically sinful.

The relationship between human beings and God

Flowing naturally from the fear-based concept of God as a punitive tyrant whose anger has to be appeased if we are to escape eternal punishment from him for our misdeeds, is the idea that there is a great gulf fixed between God and Man. God is all good, while sinful man, despite longing to attain a similar state of perfect goodness, has a strong inclination to do wrong, to rebel against the demands God makes on us to 'be good'. For those who live under the influence of authoritarian Christianity there is a fundamentally adversarial relationship between God and humankind – life is a continuous battle to lead a virtuous life according to the principles 'God' has laid down.

The more restrictions the narrow-minded dogmatism of the authoritarian wing of the Christian Church places on the natural, spontaneous manifestations of our 'God-given' biological nature,[137] the more frequently we are likely to experience the temptation to ignore some of those restrictions. For many devout Christians, succumbing to any particular temptation is followed by feelings of guilt, and unless they have despairingly given up the attempt to 'be good', will redouble their efforts to resist temptation in the future. But attempts to 'be good' which are driven by guilt and fear are never successful for very long, and those who go this route are destined to fail over and over again. The more successfully the particular branch of the Christian Church to which they belong has sold itself and its priests, ministers, or pastors as a necessary intermediary in the process of At-one-ment, the bridging of the gap between the human race and God, the more quickly such failure will send them scurrying back into the arms of their church to perpetuate an endless cycle of sin, repentance, penance, and yet more sin.

Psychologists working as therapists are often advised to try to work themselves out of a job as quickly as possible with each of their clients. In other words they are recommended to see an important part of their function as being to empower those clients with the skills and attitudes of mind necessary for them to cope happily and successfully with any issues that arise in their life without further therapeutic help.

Far from encouraging any similar idea of self-sufficiency in spiritual matters, the authoritarian face of Christianity promotes a concept of its own indispensable and continuing role in bridging the hypothesised great divide between God and humankind. How would the confused Christian know what to believe if the church did not tell him or her? How would the sinful pilgrim ever re-establish a relationship with God if the church were not there to provide guidance and instruction about how to live 'the good life', to prescribe punishments for disobedience to the will of the church leaders, and to monitor the state of repentance which has to be achieved in order to get back into God's good books. The relationship thus re-established is of necessity always a tenuous one, no one caught up in such a system of thought being under any illusion that they will not repeat their wrongdoing over and over again. On this view, life is one long struggle to achieve union with God despite our repeated disobedience to what we have been persuaded are his orders.

The temptation to sin in defiance of the Church's definition of right behaviour comes from what St Paul referred to as our carnal mind, which for him was something which the Christian was constantly at war with. Once the view of ourselves as inherently wicked has taken root, the authoritarianly-minded system of thought ensures a self-sustaining vicious cycle of self-denigration and idealisation of the perfection of God. In this frame of mind, the more we are aware of our faults, the more keenly we feel how far short we fall of the perfection of the all-good God whose approval we desperately seek. The more that is the case, the more many Christians are tempted to believe that their virtues are 'not really me', and project them onto God. And so the gulf between ourselves and God widens – God becomes more and more 'perfect' and we become more and more impoverished and beset by a sense of worthlessness Eventually some people drop into a bottomless pit of despair where they echo St Paul's anguished cry, "O wretched man that I am! Who shall deliver me from the body of this death?" At which point representatives of the authoritarian face of Christianity rush in with their simplistic salvation formulas, offering us the priceless experience of God's love, the only cost of which is the abandonment by the sinner of any independent thinking, and blind obedience to the dictates of the church.

The very, very different view of the fundamental nature of the relationship between God and humankind which pervades humanistic Christianity is well expressed in the story of the old Quaker who, on his deathbed was asked by a caring friend, but one who was part of a more authoritarian Christian tradition, whether he had made peace with his maker. The old man's reply beautifully encapsulates the non-adversarial way of thinking which characterises humanistic Christianity – "I didn't know we had ever quarrelled," he said. One of Father de Mello's delightful whimsical cameos expresses much the same idea:

> To newcomers the Master would say, 'Knock and the door will be opened to you.' To some of them he would later say conspiratorially, 'How would you expect the door to be opened when it has never been shut?'

Forgiveness versus punishment

There is no record, biblical or otherwise, of Jesus having ever prescribed any punishment for any of the cases of wrongdoing which were brought to his attention. On the contrary his response to the case of "the woman taken in adultery" that had aroused the ire of the community was (as reported in the eighth chapter of St John's gospel), "Go, and sin no more", (John 8:11), while his reaction to those who would have violently punished her by stoning her to death was, "He that is without sin among you, let him first cast a stone at her" (John 8:7). Very different is the reaction of many within the Christian Church who are of an authoritarian disposition whose response to wrongdoing is to condemn it in a holier-than thou manner, and to arrogantly dish out punishments on what they claim to be God's behalf, in complete contradiction of the practice of Jesus.

These punishments range from the torture and murder of presumed 'witches', heretics and other 'wrongdoers' in the past, to the demand for the recitation of prayer after prayer still beloved of the Catholic confessional today. The use of the frequent repetition of the Lord's Prayer (with its profound statement of the fact that it is in forgiving others that we ourselves are forgiven) as a punishment for our wrongdoing through which we shall obtain forgiveness of our sins is particularly oddly illogical. Is it really necessary to batter the ears of God with constant repetition of those wise words of Jesus which proclaim that it is not through the enduring of punishment that we obtain forgiveness of our sins, but rather through the process of forgiving others? (Matthew. 6:12 and 14-15, and Luke 6:37). If the Catholic priesthood had spent half as much time helping their flock to master the often very difficult art which Jesus exhorted us to practise, of forgiving those who have wronged us, as they have on prescribing penances, (i.e. "punishments for wrongdoing"), the incidence of the "manifold sins and wickednesses" of their own clergy, which is now costing them billions of dollars, would have been greatly reduced, and a great deal of Christian-Church-imposed human suffering would have been avoided.

The acceptance of rigid dogma

In authoritarian Christianity the demand for obedience to the dictates of higher authority means that everyone lower down the power hierarchy must believe exactly what the leaders of the organisation want them to believe, and do whatever those leaders want them to do. Of course this requires that there should be an agreed clear statement of belief to which all members of the community can and must give their assent.

The attempts by competing leaders within the early Christian Church to impose their particular beliefs upon the whole church has led to much conflict. One of the most significant differences among those competing views was between those who believed that Jesus was simply a man, albeit a uniquely spiritually-inspired man, and those who believed that he was both God and man, ("Of one substance with the Father"). As discussed in Chapter 3, the Roman emperor Constantine's intervention in the dispute (undertaken because for purely political reasons he wanted the Christian Church to be a united one) was a major factor in the eventual triumph of the view that Jesus was both God and man. This belief, and other associated ones, became enshrined in the Nicene Creed in 325 CE.[21]

Constantine's authoritarian influence still lingers in the modern church in many ways, not least in the habit in at least most mainstream churches, of encouraging the congregation to repeat the words of that creed at nearly every church service. Although often presented as giving the congregation a chance to affirm what they believe, of greater importance to the authoritarian Church is the fact that it provides their flock with a constant reminder of what they are supposed to believe if they want to call themselves Christians, and to retain the remission of punishment benefits that that status confers upon them.

The most serious problem with this approach to religion is that placing such emphasis on the acceptance of rigid dogma implies that 'Right Belief' is more important than the quality of spiritual experience. The implication is that if you have the right ideas in your head you will experience the right sort of religious feelings.

From a psychological and spiritual perspective this is a disaster. As A. N. Whitehead put it in the passage quoted at the beginning of Chapter 6, "Religions commit suicide when they find their inspirations in their dogmas".[27] It is the experience of oneness with the divine which is of value to the individual, not his or her intellectual ideas about any aspects of that experience. Feeling must come first, and theoretical formulations about what is going on when the person feels contact with the deepest ethical principles in the universe are of secondary importance, and inevitably only capture a small part of that spiritual experience. Thoughts, ideas, theories and all forms of intellectual constructions in the field of religion are only of value if they help the individual to make sense of what they are feeling, and thereby help them to attain a more profound level of spiritual experience.

The seventeenth-century French mathematician, physicist, inventor, and Catholic philosopher Blaise Pascal expressed this truth rather delightfully when he wrote,

> It has pleased God that divine verities should not enter the heart through the understanding, but the understanding through the heart.

For authoritarian Christianity religious thought comes before spiritual feeling. Emotional experience is only spiritually valid if it flows from acceptance of the correct dogma (usually involving something to the effect that Jesus suffered and died for our sins). The spiritual experiences of those who have not accepted the 'truth' of such a belief are discounted as inauthentic and worthless. At one stroke the religious life of all those outside the Christian religion is written off (and even that of those Christians who have not met such church-ordained requirements as being 'born again'/attending the right church services/Mass or Confession) demanded by a particular sub-group).

For humanistic Christianity, spiritual experiences which flow from living one's life in harmony with the ethical principles taught by Jesus are of primary importance when and wherever they may occur: all forms of Theology and creed-making are secondary. Experiencing feelings of compassion, humility, of being interconnected with everything that is, of inward peace, is what is really important. The development of new thought structures, of intellectual ideas in the religious domain (even those articulated in this book!), can really only be justified if they help us make more sense of our spiritual experience (or lack of it), and help us to find ways of deepening in an ever more-satisfying way whatever positive experiences we have in that area of our lives.

Apart from the above considerations, the demand of authoritarian Christianity for the acceptance of rigid dogma has a number of other very negative side effects. Most regrettably it acts as a deterrent to new thinking and the development of new religious insights. Self-contradictory as it is, every new denomination that develops its own identity and new orthodoxy has done so by doubting some aspect of a previous orthodoxy. The leaders of each such group have permitted themselves to doubt, and then to reject some aspect of the dogma and/or practices of the parent body from which they have sprung, but then (very often) do not permit their newly acquired adherents to deviate an inch from the newly-proclaimed orthodoxy.

Inevitably almost all the members of any group will have some doubts about the validity of some of the group-beliefs, and in an environment where such doubts are strongly disapproved of, the person harbouring them will in general feel guilty about doing so. Unless and until their doubts develop to such a point that they leave the church they are in, the chances are that any burden of guilt that they are already suffering under will be increased by the fear that they are being 'disloyal' and/or thinking 'wicked thoughts'. Far from recognising that being a 'doubting Thomas' is often a virtue, such people often feel pressured into believing that the fact that they are not swallowing everything they are told they ought to believe hook, line, and sinker, indicates some grave moral and/or spiritual defect in their character.

Of course to the leaders in the authoritarian face of Christianity such an increase in guilt levels will seem a good thing, as it is likely to increase sales of their 'Salvation package'.

To those making up the humanistic face of Christianity, and doubtless to most psychologists, anything which raises people's guilt levels, undermines their self-confident belief in the value of their own independent thinking, and makes them distrustful of their own spiritual instincts is regrettable and contrary to the whole thrust of Jesus' recommendations about what sort of life we should live if we want to be in the Kingdom of Heaven. The demand for the acceptance of rigid dogma, the constant repetition of the Nicene Creed, and various slogans around the theme of 'the blood of Jesus' made in the name of authoritarian Christianity has nothing to do with spirituality, nor with Jesus' vision of what it means to be living in the Kingdom of God.

The demand for obedience to authority and the unquestioning acceptance of the truth of the ideas of persons in authority is to be found in many areas of life other than the religious one. In all of them it has the same stunting effect on mental flexibility, psychological sensitivity, and human happiness. It makes people more likely to be more accepting of the status quo, and more critical of new ideas and ways of doing things when they encounter them.

Such a fearful approach to life is not good for business, professional development or more generally for personal growth towards psychological maturity, and simple human happiness. It pressures people away from authenticity of action and exploring what is right for themselves. The poem, *The School*, in Appendix 1 is well worth frequent re-reading.

The Fate of Christian Ethics at the Hands of Authoritarian Christianity

The Christian Church could have played a very powerful role in spreading the influence of the ethical principles promoted by that reforming Jewish religious genius Jesus of Nazareth. To some extent it has done this, but the efforts of those within its ranks who have succeeded in that task have in many ways been

303

undermined by those whose Christian beliefs have struggled, not entirely successfully, to find a place within their authoritarian personality structure. Referring back to the components of the ethics of Jesus identified in Chapter 5, in brief summary what has happened with the intrusion of authoritarian attitudes into the ethics of Jesus is:

1. Love and Compassion

The fundamental importance which Jesus placed on love has been watered down by those of an authoritarian disposition by statements such as, "God is loving but he is also just", and "Spare the rod and spoil the child", and the introduction of ideas such as 'loving punishment' which make a mockery of the concepts of love and compassion as preached by Jesus, and provides an attempted justification for all manner of aggressive cruelty.

2. Meekness and Humility

The meekness and humility of the man who made his final, 'triumphal' entry into Jerusalem on a donkey has in many branches of the Christian Church been replaced by a desire for self-aggrandizement and the achievement of a superior status in the eyes of the world by those at the top of, or trying to climb up the power hierarchy in their particular branch of the church. Although the rich vestments worn by powerful religious leaders in churches like the Roman Catholic and Anglican ones at pageants associated with special occasions can sometimes undoubtedly be impressive from a purely aesthetic point of view, there is a thin line between what creates beauty and what looks like a vulgar ostentatious display of unseemly wealth, if not in fact like such a caricature of the normally fairly restrained desire to 'dress to impress' as to be laughable. The reversal of the attempt by Vatican II, the reforming congress of the Roman Catholic church called by the reforming Pope John XXIII, to limit the length of the chasuble, the trailing peacock tail worn by the

Pope on special occasions must be a disappointment to those reforming Catholics who find the ostentatiousness of a twenty-three metre gold embroidered train an embarrassment.

Another aspect of the pressures within the Christian Church away from attitudes of meekness and humility is to be seen in the almost universal custom in Christian Churches to have sermons delivered from an elevated pulpit. Although the practice does sometimes have some practical benefits, it is undeniable that having a congregation looking up at a preacher rather than down on him, or on the level with him has some symbolic significance. Most people, whether they are conscious of the fact or not, and whether they like the situation or not, feel a greater sense of power and confidence when people have to literally physically 'look up to them' when they talk, just as they would feel more impressively powerful when riding on a horse than when riding on a donkey. When (as is all too often the case) a sermon is delivered with a pompous and arrogant air of moral superiority on the part of the preacher, literally over the heads of his (and it nearly always is 'his' rather than 'her') audience, the total message received by the congregation is hardly one of encouragement to a mental attitude of meekness and humility, or that the preacher believes those words of Jesus that, "Blessed are the meek, for they shall inherit the earth."

3. People before principles

The more of an authoritarian personality anyone has, the more they will regard 'obedience' as the greatest virtue and 'disobedience' as the greatest sin. After all what greater disaster has ever befallen the human race than that one person's wrongdoing has placed every member of it (including those not yet born) in jeopardy of eternal suffering and torment. Even a nuclear holocaust would seem relatively unimportant compared to that disaster which has befallen humanity. And what was that wrongdoing? It was Adam's sin of disobeying God's orders.

Disobedience is so fundamentally wicked that instances of it can trigger cosmic calamities and deserves the most extreme of punishments.

That attitude of mind is what permeates the thinking of those who make up the authoritarian face of Christianity. It is diametrically opposed to Jesus' teaching about what is right and wrong. "The Sabbath was made for man, not man for the Sabbath", means that the rules and regulations surrounding Sabbath observance and other religious practices should be regarded as being there to enhance the quality of life of human beings. If strictly observing any code of conduct in any particular situation does not achieve that humanistic objective, then those rules should not be applied. To do otherwise is to disregard that fundamental principle of Jesus' vision of the ethics that reign in the Kingdom of God, of (in Albert Schweitzer's words) "never sacrificing a person to a principle", a neat paraphrase of Jesus' belief that, "The Sabbath was made for man, not man for the Sabbath".

4. Non-judgementalness

Perhaps nothing more is needed to emphasise the contrast between Jesus' approach to wrongdoing and the beliefs and behaviours of those in the authoritarian branch of Christianity than the passage from Cardinal Newman already quoted in Chapter 5. John Henry Newman was an important figure in the religious history of nineteenth-century England. Originally an evangelical Oxford academic and clergyman, he converted to Roman Catholicism in 1845 at the age of 44. He was a self-confessed life-long opponent of liberalism in religion. In 1863, in an exchange with Thomas Allies, a nineteenth-century English historical writer who specialised in religious subjects and like himself converted to Roman Catholicism from Anglicanism, Newman refused to publicly condemn slavery as 'intrinsically evil' on the grounds that it had been tolerated by St Paul. He asserted instead that, "slavery is a condition of life ordained by

God in the same sense that other conditions of life are".[138]

On 12th May, 1879, at the age of 78 he was elevated to the rank of Cardinal, becoming (though a Birmingham resident) Cardinal Deacon of San Giorgio al Velabro. Just over a hundred years after his death in 1890 he passed the first hurdle on the path to Sainthood, being proclaimed (in 1991) *venerable* after a thorough examination of his life and work by the Sacred Congregation for the Causes of Saints. On 19th September, 2010 during his highly controversial official visit to Britain, Pope Benedict XVI announced the beatification of Cardinal Newman who, therefore, now has only one more hurdle to clear before achieving Canonisation as a Christian Saint. His having reached this status presumably means that the Vatican-based Roman Catholic Church endorses the views Cardinal Newman expressed in the quote to which I referred earlier, in which he writes,

The Church holds that it were better for sun and moon to drop from heaven, for the earth to fail, and for all the many millions who are upon it to die of starvation in extremist agony than ... that one soul, I will not say should be lost, but should commit one single venial sin.

The attitude of vicious moralistic judgementalness underlying that piece of writing is totally incompatible with what we know of Jesus' attitude to wrongdoing. Christianity is indeed not a single religion, but two radically different ones sharing the same generic name.

5. Mutuality/Reciprocity

The idea that we will be rewarded for good behaviour is an important part of both the humanistic and authoritarian faces of Christianity but the hypothesised mechanism by which this happens is very different in each case. Flowing from the concept of God embedded in the authoritarian face of Christianity is the idea that rewards and punishments are doled out by a super-human, super-policeman God who spends much of his time monitoring human behaviour and arranging appropriate conse-quences to befall us, in either this world or the next.

In complete contrast, the concept of God embedded in the humanistic face of Christianity is not one of an active agent who either intervenes in human affairs when he feels so inclined, or keeps a record of our misdeeds to bring out on the 'Day of Judgement'. For those who find their spiritual home in the humanistic face of Christianity, God is a being whose existence determines the fact that behaviour in accordance with ethical principles such as those we discussed in Chapter 5 brings a here-and-now reward. It is because God is, because the universe is the way it is, that "It is in giving that we receive", and that, "it is in forgiving others that we ourselves are forgiven". As Emerson once said,

It is one of the most beautiful compensations of this life that no man can sincerely try to help another without helping himself. … Serve and thus you shall be served.

6. Inversion of the power hierarchy

One of the core beliefs of those whose religious affiliation is with the authoritarian face of Christianity is that those at the top end of the religious power hierarchy are entitled to unquestioning obedience and uncritical respect for the truth of their opinions, often not just in religious matters, but in other aspects of life as well (such as having sex with a partner before marriage, and the use of birth control methods, which are not primarily matters of spiritual significance). The thinking of those people who believe that just because of the positional power they hold in a church, their views on these matters should carry more weight than those of rank and file church members, has obviously not been touched by what Jesus had to say about the inversion of the power hierarchy in the Kingdom of God from that which prevails in earthly kingdoms. For Jesus, it was those who give up earthly power and become as little children, and see themselves as the servants of the least rather than of the most powerful members of the human race, who are greatest in the Kingdom of Heaven, and therefore whose views on spiritual matters are likely to be of more profundity than those of many of the churchmen who wear the richest robes and the biggest hats in religious ceremonies.[139]

To be fair, even if some priests and other clergy do love their presumed elevated religious and (as it was once thought) moral status in society, the sycophantic way in which some of their followers treat them is probably not their fault. The psychological phenomenon their authoritarianly-submissive behaviour demonstrates is of a piece with the fawning adulation with which royalty, pop stars and sports heroes are often treated by those who see themselves as lesser mortals. It is sad if a person's religion does not empower them with a greater sense of their own worth, and the knowledge that in terms of our humanity we are all equal.

7. The need for authenticity

Two key values espoused by those who make up the humanistic face of Christianity are those of Autonomy and Authenticity. The COED gives two definitions of the word 'autonomy': "Freedom of action," and "The possession or right of self-government". Although the second definition seems on the face of it to apply more in the political realm, it does also make sense in the psychological field. To feel that one has autonomy means to feel that one has the right to be oneself rather than a clone or vassal of someone else; that one has the right to control one's own life, to think for oneself, to make one's own decisions, and not to have to obey any rules which other people try to impose on us against our will, but rather to behave in ways which in our opinion further our own best interests, whilst being duly respectful of the needs and wishes of others. Having autonomy is an essential requirement for living one's life authentically, 'authentic' being defined by the COED as "of undisputed origin or veracity; genuine". In other words it is the opposite of hypocrisy and pretence. When someone is behaving authentically, the behaviour that people see them engaging in is an honest expression of their feelings – they are not pretending (to be more intelligent or more virtuous than they really are). As already discussed, Jesus had harsh words for those religious leaders who did not behave with authenticity, but put on a show of piety to impress lesser mortals with their own superiority in the spiritual realm.

The demands made by authoritarian Christians for uniformity of belief and doctrinal purity in the religion of their choice runs completely counter to Jesus' urging of us to live our lives in such a way that there is complete harmony between what we inwardly think and feel, and our outward behaviour, not to be 'whited sepulchres', clean and beautiful on the outside but full of rotting old bones on the inside. The more we achieve that state of harmony between our inner and outer selves the more influence we shall exert on those we interact with.

The ethics of Jesus embodied in the humanistic face of Christianity embrace a vision of ways of behaving that will make it possible for us all to be fully authentic, in other words honest about our thoughts and feelings. The authoritarian face, however, is very different and produces results diametrically the opposite of those aimed at by the ethical principles encouraged by Jesus. The prevalence of 'Holier-than-Thou' moral judgements, together with the fear engendered by the urgency with which the need for 'salvation' is touted, are absolutely guaranteed to produce exactly the opposite effect from communications which spring from a non-judgemental compassionate view of life. To be authentic in the emotional environment generated by authoritarian Christianity is not safe. It opens one up to the possibility of being judged and condemned for any moral shortcomings our judges feel they can spot in us. Much better to be whatever the religious equivalent of 'politically correct' may be, and say and do whatever one is told to by church leaders.

Factors responsible for the intrusion of authoritarian thinking into the intellectual fabric of the Christian Church

What is it about authoritarian structures which attracts people to them where they exist, and motivates them to create them where they have not existed before? Two factors are particularly important: firstly the drive for personal power. There are always those looking for a congenial environment in which to exercise the power they feel they do not have in their everyday lives. For some people the church offers a good opportunity for that. The fundamental psychopathology in the drive to feel invincibly powerful at the top of the hierarchy of an authoritarian organisation is a deep inner feeling of weakness and inadequacy. The process of Reaction Formation creates in our Persona a false picture of strength and self-confidence when in reality we are in a vulnerable emotional state. Unfortunately, as has often been said, "All power corrupts, and absolute power corrupts absolutely". It is not possible for the ethical principles of Jesus to remain uncorrupted in the minds of those whose lives are governed by organisational values which are in flagrant contradiction of some of the most basic of those principles.

The other factor involved in the development and perpetuation of authoritarian religious attitudes is that the absolute nature of the demands for obedience to orders from on high, takes away a considerable measure of personal responsibility for their actions from people who respond with authoritarian submission to the domination of their authoritarian rulers ("I was only obeying orders"). Apparently Adolph Hitler once said, "How fortunate for the rulers that people do not think"!

Underlying this is probably a profound fear of the unknown. Many people (and in the pre-scientific age it must have been most people) have a sense of dark, probably sinister forces 'out there' which they do not understand, but get a glimpse of from time to time. Coincidences sometimes send a chill down the spines of those who encounter them. Was that really a coincidence or could it be that some force, some power was taking charge of those events?

For many people, having grown up in a society where for thousands of years a belief in the existence of an all-powerful punitive God, who 'knows our innermost thoughts', and from whose judgement we can never run away has been inculcated, the unknown feels like a constant lurking threat which is a source of great anxiety. Being good is the only protection we can get from punishment for any wrongdoing we get involved in. The consequences of getting it wrong are too serious to permit any uncertainty of belief. Hence enforced rigid dogma and the sharing of that belief by a close-knit community of like-minded people is a great comfort – safety in numbers! From a position of fear of the retributive consequences of offending an all-powerful, all-knowing God if we 'get it wrong' in our life-decisions, the risks of acting on our own fallible judgements are too great to be taken. Many religious people feel they need the support of acting in concert with a group of like-minded persons to attain some measure of inner peace, and the more powerful the authority they have in that group, the more confident they feel in the correctness of their opinions and judgements.

Final thoughts

In a nutshell the difference between the religion which is constituted by the humanistic face of Christianity, and that which is constituted by its authoritarian face, is that the former is predominantly a religion of the heart, while the latter is first and foremost a religion of the head, of cognition, of intellectual understanding and the formulation of dogma. The intellectual component of humanistic Christianity is a matter of providing guidance in the spiritual life, of recommendations as to how to behave in order to experience deep inner harmony and peace.

Cause and effect reigns supreme throughout the universe. Everything happens for a reason: as Einstein said, "God does not play dice". Under any particular set of conditions, certain events and certain actions have certain specific consequences. This is as true of the psychological and spiritual side of life as it is of the physical. Jesus' teachings are a set of statements about religious psychology – "If you do X, you will experience Y. If you pass judgement on others, your own standards of judgement will be revealed, when you forgive others for their wrongdoing, you will experience forgiveness for yours." Christian ethics are not a set of rules that have to be obeyed because they are 'true' or better than any other rules, but rather they are a tool for transforming human relationships. They are a set of windows into some fundamentally important cause-effect relationships in human behaviour and experience.

Where wrongdoing is concerned, the ethical principles identified by Jesus are not about the suppression of 'bad' behaviour, nor are they about the punishment of it. They are about a compassionate, non-judgemental understanding of what we see as being wrong so that we can help wrongdoers to discover a better way of achieving their objective of being a happier person. We all seek maximum joy in our lives, and to "live, move, and have our being" in the Kingdom of Heaven, is to experience the joy of living life to the full.[140]

For reasons explained earlier in this book, there is a constant adversarial undertone to the positions taken, and the statements made by those who find their spiritual home in the authoritarian face of Christianity. A split between our 'spiritual mind' and our 'carnal mind', and constant conflict between the two of them is taken as a fact of nature. This endemically adversarial way of looking at the human psyche (beloved of Paul and many others powerful in the Christian Church, past and present), colours every aspect of the beliefs of those who make up the authoritarian face of Christianity. From their concept of God and the relationship between God and humankind, to the predominantly negative, conflict-creating, "Thou shalt not" demand for obedience to authority, a sense of adversarialness is never far away. By contrast the emphasis on the 'Power of the Positive', joyful acceptance of diversity, and a compassionate, forgiving, but honestly assertive response to wrongdoing[141] permeates the thinking and behaviour of those who situate themselves in the humanistic Christian camp.

For authoritarian Christianity, the acceptance of the absolute rightness of the beliefs and theological niceties it proclaims, are the important issues. Its primary concern seems to be with obtaining uniformity of belief and practice among its members in respect of 'obedience to the will of God' in order to escape the punishment for their sins which awaits them in the next life (despite the often simultaneously held totally contrary belief that Jesus' death 'purchased' for us freedom from that terrible fate). It is clear that within very large segments of the Christian Church there is a deeply embedded controlling power hierarchy whose presence and influence defines the authoritarian face of Christianity. To the extent that any branch of any religion falls into this category, very prominent in its message to the world will be the twin concepts of obedience and punishment.

What it all comes down to is that the humanistic face of the Christian Church is concerned with making the world a kinder, happier, more loving, and more compassionate place in which God and each human being are seen to be united as two aspects of a single, indivisible whole. The humanistic Christian is optimistic that a state of bliss can be reached through each individual's living his or her life to the greatest possible extent in harmony with the ethical principles outlined in the teachings of

Jesus. From this perspective, the Christian Church's task is to help its members to better understand those guidelines for virtuous behaviour, and their implications for all aspects of our lives.

The future

As it stands Christianity is a house divided against itself, and its declining numbers in Europe, and the discovery at last by the world at large of the cancer of sexual depravity which has been eating away at the heart of the largest single Christian denomination, the Roman Catholic church, for centuries could well be the first signs of the sort of the 'great fall' which Jesus predicted for houses divided against themselves. There is good reason to believe that the Christian Church faces a stark choice between reform of some of its fundamental concepts and extinction. For those who have suffered under the cruelties inflicted on humanity by some of those who have made up its authoritarian face, it must have seemed in their agony, as though the religion which they may once have believed was the home of love, compassion and healing had indeed already become extinct. Humanity urgently needs the Christian Church as a whole to rediscover its humanistic face, but in order to do so it will need to realise, and abandon, at least something of the gross psychopathologies at the core of its authoritarian face.

In so far as those making up the authoritarian face of Christianity define moral virtue as obedience to the demands of any power hierarchy in any church, rather than acting with authenticity in terms of their own conscience, they have completely lost touch with one of the key elements in the ethical teachings of Jesus. This key element has been echoed from time to time in the visionary insights of those Christian thought-leaders like Thomas Aquinas who were occasionally capable of flashes of penetrating spiritual insight. Unfortunately, despite the great respect accorded Aquinas, his views in this matter have

315

not yet made a significant impact on the attitudes of the Vatican-based Catholic Church. The authoritarian corruption of Christianity has done much to undermine the respect of many in the modern world for the religion as a whole. It is a situation which does not have to continue to exist. As the great American Anthropologist Margaret Mead reminded us,

Never doubt that a small group of thoughtful, committed people can change the world; indeed it is the only thing that ever has.

Chapter 9

Why has the Christian Church been so spectacularly successful in establishing itself as a world religion?

People prefer to believe what they prefer to be true. – Anon

According to the *adherents.com* database, Christianity, with 2.1 billion people claiming some form of connection with it, is by far the world's most populous religion.[142] There are four primary reasons for this state of affairs.

Firstly, the ethical teachings of Jesus of Nazareth resonate in a very profound way with some innate sense of 'the rightness of things' in the human psyche. Seeking the welfare of others, and enhancing our own sense of well-being in the process, is not something we do because of being forced to do so by the weight of Jesus' authority, or the threat of eternal punishment if we do not. It is a core part of the way that that Mind-Body-Spirit unity which is the human being works, and which is of great adaptive value for the human race. The principle embodied in Rudyard Kipling's aphorism that the strength of the wolf is the pack, and the strength of the pack is the wolf, applies to a significant extent to human beings as well. We are nothing without at least some other members of the human race. We would not have survived more than a few hours in infancy if at least one of them had not attended to our needs as a neonate. Although we become less and less absolutely dependent on others as we grow older (until we reach a point at which we can no longer look after ourselves adequately), interaction with some select group of other people is a necessity for our sense of well-being throughout our lives. As John Donne reminded us, "No man is an island", and doing what we can to enhance the welfare of others is a good investment in ensuring that others invest at least some time, trouble, and love in doing what they can to ensure our welfare.

The idea of 'being good' in terms of this and the other ethical principles enunciated in what we know of the teachings of Jesus, is natural to the human being, at least until, for some of us, the negative experiences of child and adult life brutalise us. Any teachings which inspire us to try to live our lives in accordance with those ethical principles will be sought after by many people for whom they have an immediately obvious face validity. The principle that, "As ye sow so shall ye reap" (Galatians 6:7), is a fundamental law of the universe, part of the way the world works. That being so, working to make the world a better place for others makes sense from an evolutionary perspective. The more we live our lives in such a way as to maximise the conditions for others to find the right balance between the satisfaction of their own needs and helping the rest of nature to find the satisfaction of its needs, the more we shall find ourselves living in a world in which we enjoy that same benefit – a self-sustaining cycle of mutual helpfulness.

Secondly, but very differently, the development of the theology of the redemption of humankind through the sufferings and death of the 'Son of God' (to which St Paul made a major contribution) was a master stroke of public relations promotion of a 'Path to Salvation' which made the religion a powerfully appealing one to the very large number of people carrying a heavy load of guilt in respect of their shortcomings. Indeed for many Christians, it is only their fervent belief that Jesus 'has paid the price' for their sin, and that they are therefore safe from having to pay that price for themselves (provided they 'believe in Him'), that makes them able to live a reasonably happy life without being overwhelmed by terror at the thought of what might be awaiting them in that great unknown which lies beyond death. Offering a cast-iron guarantee of future immunity from punishment in return for unquestioning obedience to the dictates of church leaders may be a superb sales technique for recruiting new members to the organisation, but in manipulating people's feelings of guilt and fear to create a willingness, indeed an eagerness, to accept the pre-packaged formulas of its salvation theology, the Christian Church has lost its soul. That soul lies in the ethics of Jesus, not in the theology of the Christian 'Saint' Paul.

Thirdly, and closely related to the above, constructing a theology at the heart of which lies the concept of an omnipotent, omniscient God, one of the flaws in whose 'perfect' nature is his impotence to change that law of nature, of the universe which he created, that wrongdoing in this world has to be atoned for by pain and suffering on the part of either the wrongdoer or some proxy scapegoat, plays to all the fears generated by childhood experiences of punishment, unnecessarily and often irrationally visited upon us. Of course the belief in the real existence of such a being, and the need to sacrifice living creatures (sometimes human and sometimes animal) to propitiate it, existed many centuries before the Christian era, but its importation into the Christian religion has more to do with the psychopathologies of that troubled man St Paul than with any objective spiritual reality.

Pushing a concept of God as a cruel, punitive tyrant is bound to raise the temperature of people's anxieties about potential punishment awaiting them in the afterlife, and to make them even more receptive than they might otherwise have been to the offer of a proffered escape route from that awful fate. For those who can be persuaded to believe that the church's offer comes with a cast-iron guarantee, there can be only one conclusion to be drawn from a cost/benefit analysis of the relatively low cost (both financial and in terms of giving up the pursuit of certain worldly pleasures) as against the huge benefit of remission of punishment in the afterlife. The real winner in this transaction is of course the Church, the number of whose members worldwide has been steadily growing over the past two thousand years.

Fourthly, and again very differently, a major factor in the growth of Christianity has been something in which St Paul again played a major role, but this time a very positive one – making membership of the early Christian Church available to Gentiles as well as to Jews. Jesus seems to have aimed his message primarily at his fellow Jews ("I am not sent but unto the lost sheep of Israel" [143] (Matthew 15:24)). St Paul, in one of his more inspired contributions to his chosen religion, had a vision of a universal church and worked hard to persuade his co-religionists to open up membership of the Christian church to Jew and Gentile alike. Certainly Christianity would never, could never have become a world religion on the scale that it has if this opening up had not taken place.

In an increasingly educated world, in which thinking for oneself rather than simply accepting the vociferously expressed ideas of others is being more and more encouraged, the ragbag of conflicting fundamental concepts (which is what many people who have any significant contact with Christianity find it to be) is, in many parts of the Western world at least, slowly but surely losing its power to impress, and with it the position of authority which it once commanded. It is not surprising, given the above, that although still growing globally, Christianity is now experiencing declining numbers in some parts of the world, notably in Western Europe and North America.[144] This book has been written in the hope that it may make a significant contribution to strengthening the hand of those who find much that is powerfully good and of lasting value for humanity in the ethics of Jesus, and to cause those whose brand of Christianity is of the authoritarian kind, to think again about their attachment to ideas about the nature of God, and humankind's relationship with that being, which are fundamentally at variance with the ethics of Jesus.

Chapter 10

The difficulties many Christians will have in constructively hearing what I am saying in this book

There is nothing more difficult to take in hand, more perilous to conduct, or more uncertain in its success, than to take the lead in the introduction of a new order of things.[145]
– Niccolò Machiavelli. *The Prince*

Probably one of the greatest difficulties many people will encounter in allowing themselves to seriously consider the possibility that the views I express in this book have some truth in them, is that they may fear that all their Christian beliefs will collapse like a pack of cards if they agree with any of my criticisms of the religion. But that is a needless fear. I write this book as a Christian, with a deep affection for the Christian Church with several branches of which I have been actively involved ever since my early teenage years. In particular I identify very strongly with the ethical principles articulated by that charismatic Jewish teacher of two thousand years ago, Jesus of Nazareth. For me, the institution of the Christian Church has the potential to make a very significant contribution to bringing about the coming of the Kingdom of God on earth, making our planetary home a beautiful paradise.

I believe that any of us who criticise any aspect of any religion need to be at pains to affirm what we believe to be the good in it. Critically evaluating our beliefs and becoming even more committed to those we feel are true, but rejecting those we believe are inadequate or downright wrong, can only strengthen our convictions and our depth of spiritual understanding. As Albert Schweitzer once said, "No one can have a significant faith if they have not passed through a period of doubt". The need to critically evaluate, and if necessary reject, any ideas which we believe are no longer valid (or perhaps never were), is not applicable to just our religious thinking, but to every aspect of our life, whether it be in the field of politics, relationships, financial investment strategies, or anything else. The more thoroughly we do this, the more successful we shall be in all areas of our lives, and the more of a thrill we shall find living a life of liberated freedom to be.

Another thing which will make it difficult for some people to even entertain some of the ideas I put forward in this book is the amount of energy authoritarian church leaders have put into indoctrinating their flock, overtly or covertly, with the idea that everything in the bible is "the inspired word of God" which must not be subject to any sort of critical analysis. This is absolute nonsense. The bible is a historical document compiled from translations of translations of copies of documents which themselves were often copies of copies of translations. It contains, amongst other things, a record of many different people's ideas about the nature of God and the relationship between God and humanity. To try to critically evaluate the truth, validity, or usefulness of anything in the bible is not to 'argue with God'. All anyone is doing in that process is to challenge the interpretations of powerful authorities within the church of some aspects of the biblical record, a process which God, if he were a being with a face and facial expressions (which he/she is not), would undoubtedly smile upon.

One thing which I know will disturb some people, but hopefully disturb them in a constructive manner which will open the way to ever deeper, more profound spiritual insights is the fact that I am not treating important figures like St Paul with reverential deference, but as the ordinary human beings they were – human beings who had a mix of strengths and weaknesses, and were no less troubled by psychological problems and inadequacies than the rest of us, indeed sometimes much more so than many of us. In no other area of life than the religious one are the wise words of the twentieth-century Swiss psychiatrist Carl Gustav Jung and the eighteenth-century English poet Alexander Pope more relevant than in the religious field. Jung pointed out to us that, "Our greatest strengths, taken to excess, become our greatest weaknesses", and Alexander Pope amusingly, but perceptively, reminded us that,

For virtue's self may too much zeal be had;
The worst of madmen is a saint run mad.[146]

There is an old joke about the reaction to new ideas of the once-upon-a-time strongly-influenced-by-Calvinist-religion Scots peoples, which is a humorous reminder of the negative effects authoritarian religion can have on the processing of new ideas. According to this joke there are three stages to a Scotsman's response to a new idea: 1 "It's ridiculous," 2 "It's contrary to scripture," and 3 "Of course, I knew it all the time". Of course, this is a gross calumny on a minority group. It does not reflect the truth about the Scots people in general, but does demonstrate an insightful understanding of the reaction to new ideas of many people who have been brought up within the boundaries of the authoritarian face of Christianity.

It is my earnest hope that those who are scandalised by my analysis of the current state of Christianity and immediately go off in search of bible quotations to justify their rejection of the position I have taken on a number of theological issues, will eventually come to the point of saying, "Of course he is making some valid points. I've half suspected that something like this was true for some time". It is a happy thought, but my anticipation of that outcome is tempered by my awareness that, as an anonymous wise person once remarked, "Obstinacy is ever more positive when it is in the wrong". In particular, for those in leadership positions within the church who have devoted much of their lives to trying to persuade themselves and others of the absolute truth of their religious beliefs, discarding some of those which I criticise in this book would seem less like a liberation than an admission that a significant part of their lives has been valueless, or perhaps in some sort of face-saving way, the temptation to let go of some of them will be dismissed as the work of the Devil. It need not be so. Changing one's mind when one's knowledge of relevant facts changes is not a sign of weakness, but rather of courage and honesty.

But perhaps the thing which will present the greatest obstacle to many Christians in considering the points of view I express in this book, are my beliefs about the nature of that entity which lies at the heart of all religious thinking – God. I believe that Freud was right, and that Richard Dawkins and his fellow travellers are right in regarding the idea of the existence of some sort of invisible superman controlling the destiny of each human being as a delusion. But as I hope I make clear in this book, this most certainly does not mean that I regard those who believe in 'the existence of God' as deluded or suffering from some sort of mental illness. Whether or not anyone who believes in the existence of God is in or out of touch with reality depends very much on the concept of the nature of God which they hold, and to which they apply the verbal label 'God'.

I shall return to this fundamentally important topic in the last chapter of this book, but for now let me just state my own belief that God is a spiritual entity, a property of the universe, not an invisible controlling superman, and to paraphrase the words of Albert Schweitzer already quoted, fundamental to the nature of God is some sort of amalgam of the Will to Live and the Will to Love. God is neither male nor female. We feel the existence of that entity when we have various different types of experience which include amongst others, feeling the flow of compassionate, affirming love for all living creatures, and contemplating beauty, either in nature or in the artistic creations of the human mind. I know of no better capturing of the specifically Christian contribution to our understanding of the nature of God than those profound words of A. N. Whitehead already quoted,

> (God is) that function in the world by reason of which our purposes are directed to ends which in our own consciousness are impartial as to our own interests. He is that element in life in virtue of which judgment stretches beyond facts of existence to values of existence. He is that element in virtue of which our purposes extend beyond values for ourselves to values for others. He is that element in virtue of which the attainment of such a value for others transforms itself into value for ourselves.[147]

What Whitehead has to say in that paragraph is certainly not easy to understand at first, but it is by no means beyond human comprehension. The idea of God as an invisible superman may be easier to imagine, but leads us to a dead end. Wrestling with more demanding abstract concepts may be more difficult, but is ultimately more rewarding in finding a satisfying understanding of the nature of God, of spiritual reality, and of what is of permanent value in the Christian religion.

Chapter 11

Does it all matter anyway?

For it is not true that there is easy apprehension of the great formative generalities. They are embedded under the rubbish of irrelevant detail. ... The great intuitions, which in their respective provinces set all things right, dawn but slowly upon history.[148]
– Alfred North Whitehead. *Religion in the Making*

Does it all matter anyway? YES IT DOES. Aren't the religious beliefs of the individual a private matter? Yes and No. Those beliefs are a private matter, but the way people act on the basis of their beliefs is usually much more than a private matter. Their behaviour often impacts very powerfully on the physical, mental and spiritual health and well-being of those individuals with whom they interact.

Some of us were naïve enough to believe that the impact of Christian ethics over the past two thousand years, together with other developments in society, such as a greater respect for individual human rights, had created a situation in which Christian and even post-Christian societies had developed some sense of a baseline of agreed minimum standards of humane conduct, even in that most inhumane sphere of activity: war. The Geneva Conventions and the development of various human rights treaties seemed to indicate that civilisation, at least in some significant parts of it, was leaving behind some of the barbarities which have marked its past.

There is one good thing which might emerge from the wreckage of that illusion occasioned by recent revelations of vicious cruelty, overtly or covertly sanctioned at the highest levels by at least two countries which have been strongly characterised by the number of adherents to the Christian religion they contain, Britain and the United States. That one good thing might be that leaders of the various branches of the Christian Church might start to pay more attention to Christian ethics and what their religion is doing to address the reduction in the amount of cruelty and suffering in the world.

The twentieth century saw the development within "Western Christian civilisation" of not just poison gas, but of landmines, cluster bombs, nuclear bombs and a steady increase in the power and accuracy of traditional military weapons. Even more disturbing has been the emergence over the last few years of an attitude to torture by many both inside and outside the political establishment, as an acceptable weapon of war. For those of us who believed that, at least in the Christian West, such an attitude was an aberration of just a few seriously disturbed psychopathic individuals; this came as something of a shock. Even more of a shock has been that for many in the Christian Right (particularly in America), approval of torture seemingly is quite compatible with being a Christian.

With hindsight, this ethical decline is hardly surprising, given the amount of time and energy which has been put into trying to persuade the world of the truth of the theology of authoritarian Christianity. At the heart of that theology lies the concept of a Supreme Being who decrees and implements punishment as a necessary consequence for wrongdoing. His methods are brutal. We find this concept of God in both the Old and the New Testaments of the Christian Bible. In the Old Testament we read of God's commands to his faithful subjects to wipe out indigenous peoples, to use rape as a weapon of war, and to murder men, women, and children.[112]

Scarcely less morally repugnant is the New Testament's repeated references to an image of God as a cruel psychopath who decreed the suffering and death of his 'dearly beloved son'. Constant exposure to that version of Christianity, congenial to many of those with an authoritarian personality structure, must seep into the soul of those who have the misfortune to be indoctrinated into such beliefs. Many of those subject to such treatment will have had little or no exposure to the radically different ideas of the nature of God and Christian ethics which lie at the heart of the humanistic face of Christianity. Although by no means solely responsible for it, St Paul in particular bears a heavy burden of responsibility for this state of affairs, as do we if we adopt an attitude of resigned apathy towards it, and do not allow ourselves to critically evaluate received wisdom in whatever branch of the Christian Church we have been nurtured. As Einstein reminded us about every aspect of life, "The important thing is to not stop questioning".

In contrast to the behaviour of Jesus, whose professional life was devoted to the compassionate reduction of human suffering, both physical and psychological, the Christian Church as a whole has not only put minimal effort into that task, but some of its branches have at times been enthusiastically energetic in increasing the total amount of suffering in the world. Guilt is a major and sometimes intense form of psychological suffering, and the prescription of penances for wrongdoing which some branches of the church feel to be a necessary part of their activities is, if it has any purpose at all, designed to bring about a certain amount of suffering. In other branches of the church, the endless rabbitting on about the sinfulness and worthlessness of human beings causes gloomy self-loathing in many people, which drains much of their lives of joy, and causes them to reach for the bottle of, if not alcohol, then the more socially respectable anti-depressant or tranquilliser pills.

The Medieval Roman Catholic Inquisition is by no means the only activity of the Christian Church through which the amount of physical suffering in the world has been dramatically increased – holy wars, crusades and the colonial conquests of empire-building aggression have all played their part. Such activities have been initiated and fuelled by men (and it is nearly always *men*) with un-Jesus-like attitudes in some way similar to those of Archdeacon William Paley (1743-1805) who, in writing, *On Crimes and Punishments*, expressed his belief in the absolute incorrigibility of all criminals and in the futility of trying to reform them. Some of them, he averred, ought to be thrown into dens of wild beasts to perish, in "...a manner dreadful to the imagination yet concealed from the view".[149]

In some ways almost as shocking as the suffering the church has caused to its 'enemies' have been the attempts by some misguided Christians, mostly pain-free at the time of their outbursts, to thwart the attempts of compassionate persons to minimise, and if possible to abolish the experience of pain. Two examples from the world of medicine must suffice to make this point.

Chemical anaesthesia and hypnosis have been the two major routes modern medicine has followed in trying to eliminate the pain their patients suffer, either as a result of disease or in the course of the treatment of it. Many brilliant minds and highly skilled clinicians have developed modern anaesthesia to the point where it must be regarded as one of the greatest blessings of the modern world. Its development has not always had the unreserved backing of all Christians, as is shockingly illustrated by the history of medical attempts to relieve pain in childbirth.

In 1591 an Edinburgh woman named Euphanie Macalyane, unable to bear the thought of the pain of childbirth, asked the midwife, Agnes Sampson, to give her a remedy to relieve her suffering. At that time James VI (1566-1625) was the King of Scotland. (This was the same James who upon becoming king of England in 1603 authorized the English translation of the Bible known today as the King James Version.) King James, upon hearing of this, was reportedly furious and ordered Euphanie to be burned alive for daring to try to evade 'the curse of Eve', as recorded in Genesis 3:16: "The Lord God said … to the woman

....I will greatly increase your pangs in childbearing; in pain you shall bring forth children" (Genesis 3:16).

The discoverer of reliable anaesthesia for women in labour was the Scottish doctor, James Baker Simpson (1811-1870); in his post as a chief obstetric assistant he often witnessed the terrible suffering of women for whom labour did not proceed smoothly. Simpson became convinced that no woman ought ever to suffer such agony, and began working to develop an analgesic that would help to alleviate that suffering. After lengthy research he finally discovered that the pain could be reduced by the use of chloroform. He tested his discovery on women in labour with astounding success. On November 10th 1847, in an address to the Edinburgh Medico-Chirurgical[150] Society, Simpson reported that he had tested the analgesic thirty times and met with success every time.

The Scottish Calvinist Church decried this development as a 'Satanic invention', and some preachers warned pregnant women that should they allow this devilish treatment to be administered to them, their newborns would be denied the sacrament of baptism, and circulars were sent to all doctors in Edinburgh containing the following words,

> To all seeming, Satan wishes to help suffering women but the upshot will be the collapse of society, for the fear of the Lord which depends upon the petitions of the afflicted will be destroyed.

In defence of his use of anaesthesia Simpson cited Genesis 2:21 where God put Adam to sleep before taking out one of his ribs to make Eve. The riposte of his religious opponents was that that argument had no validity because Adam's 'operation' was done *before* the Fall while the curse on Eve was pronounced after it. Sophistry of this sort, which one encounters all too often in arguments with Christian conservatives, call to mind the comment made by Arthur Koestler in connection with the mid-twentieth century debates in Britain about the abolition of the death penalty, "The history of English criminal law is a wonderland filled with the braying of learned asses."[149]

It was six years before Queen Victoria (1819-1901), the nominal head of the Church of England, tipped the balance of the argument in Simpson's favour when she accepted the use of an anaesthetic for the birth of her son prince Leopold.

The mysterious case of hypnosis

Perhaps even more bizarre than the Scottish Calvinist church's reaction to Dr Simpson's invention was some of the opposition aroused by the medical use of hypnosis, the most effective pain-killing technique available to doctors before the advent of reliable chemical anaesthesia.

Although the hypnotic trance phenomenon has probably been around even longer than *Homo sapiens*, the word 'hypnosis' is relatively new. Derived from the Greek word 'Hypnos' (meaning sleep) it was first used in 1853 by James Braid, a Manchester physician, who used the phenomenon in carrying out painless operations. The first serious medical use of the phenomenon for which Braid coined the word, had been made by Anton Mesmer (1734 –1815), an Austrian physician who created a considerable stir in Paris with his dramatic cures of a range of medical and psychological conditions using a hypnotic phenomenon which he called 'animal magnetism'.

Before the word hypnosis was coined, this phenomenon was called mesmerism, because of Anton Mesmer's pioneering work in this field. Probably at least partly because of Mesmer's antics as something of a showman, the phenomenon was viewed with some suspicion, if not with downright anxiety and antagonism in some quarters. In 1837 John Elliotson (the first Professor of Medicine at London University and one of the founders of University College Hospital) started using 'mesmerism' with certain 'nervous conditions'. His methods were attacked in *The Lancet*, and the council of University College passed a resolution forbidding, "the practice of mesmerism or animal magnetism within the hospital". For the work of a medical man of such stature as Elliotson to be dismissed in this way is astonishing. In response he resigned in disgust.

Around the same time another English surgeon, James Esdaile, was performing hundreds of operations in India using 'mesmeric anaesthesia'. Hostile and sceptical reaction by officialdom caused his Calcutta hospital to be closed, despite a petition from a large number of ex-patients. In 1842, W. S. Ward amputated a leg of a mesmerised patient, who apparently felt no pain. He reported the case to the Royal Medical and Chirurgical Society in London, who refused to believe his report and ordered the record of his paper to be struck from the official minutes. Even more unbelievable is the fact that this extremely prestigious society, situated at the heart of the medical establishment in the capital city of what was at the time one of the most committedly 'Christian' countries in the world, could hold the view which it expressed on this occasion, that, even if Ward's account were true, surgery without pain would be immoral: "Patients ought to suffer pain while their surgeons are operating". The addiction of those making up the authoritarian face of Christianity to belief in the positive benefits conferred on humanity by the experience of punishment, pain, and suffering has had a deeply corrupting effect on the ethical sensibilities of those living in so-called 'Christian' societies, and has seriously interfered with the spread of those ethical principles of compassionate love embedded in the heart of the humanistic face of Christianity.

Practical applications

Child rearing

Amongst many other opportunities to inject more of the compassionate attitudes of Jesus enshrined in the humanistic face of Christianity into modern society, four stand out as needing particularly urgent attention by the Christian Church.

The first of these provides a wonderful opportunity for the church to co-operate with those with some sophistication of psychological insight (who by no means need to necessarily be persons who have studied the subject of psychology in any formal academic way) to be proactive in reducing the number of hurt, angry, and rebellious adults in the world. So many people are at greater risk of engaging in cruel behaviour towards other humans and animals than they would have been had they not been to a greater or lesser extent brutalised in childhood by harsh child-rearing experiences. One hears far more sickeningly aggressive warnings about the dangers of, "Sparing the rod and spoiling the child", from ardent 'Christians' than one hears of attempts by members of that group to promote enlightened, compassionate, and self-esteem-building child-rearing habits in those concerned with the upbringing of children. There are of course many Christian parents whose behaviour towards their children is marked by gentle, caring compassionate love, but sadly an appallingly large number who behave in a very different way. Adolph Hitler is but one example of the terrible consequences that can result from a parent's treating their child with unforgiving cruelty. One organisation which Christians of a humanistic persuasion might like to explore in this respect is the Aware Parenting Institute, based in California in the USA, but which operates internationally. Its website is to be found at www.awareparenting.com.

Contraception

The other three issues mentioned above as requiring urgent attention by the Christian Church are closely interrelated: Contraception, Abortion, and Euthanasia. They are all areas in which some parts of the Christian Church have been very active in trying to influence public opinion negatively. In a world in which the alarmingly accelerating rate of population growth is rapidly leading to a situation where the ability of the earth to provide for the needs of everyone living on it will be totally swamped by the magnitude of those needs, putting any economic, legal or religious barriers to the free availability for those who desire them, of Contraception, Euthanasia, and Abortion, is to say the least of it, highly irresponsible. Blanket rejection of these interventions is tantamount to being complicit in preparations for the mass suicide of the human race. But that is by no means the only or the most powerful reason why it is natural for those who espouse the values of humanistic Christianity to do what they can to counter the efforts of author-itarianly-minded Christians to ban the use of these options. Too many times the denial of their use results in an increase in the amount of suffering in the world.

Contraception is the simplest case for the application of humanistic Christian ethics since it does not involve the termi-nation of any life. There is absolutely no ethical or spiritual reason, and should be no religious reason, why preventing conception is an undesirable behaviour. The real reason under-lying the antagonism of some people within the Christian Church to it is doubtless the Pauline anti-sex stance which lingers in the unconscious, if not in the actual consciousness of those Christians. For them, the psychopathological beliefs of Paul have never been carefully and critically thought about, and so the general flavour of Paul's ideas about sex, instead of being decisively accepted or rejected, hang about like some all-pervading, brooding, guilt-inducing, disapproving presence conveying the message, "Don't enjoy yourself too much. You are not in this world to enjoy yourself. You are here to do God's will, not your own".

It seems logical, and no cause for alarm, that the more freely contraception is available, the more sexual encounters there will be between men and women. But far from being something undesirable, if both parties to such an encounter are well-informed about the health issues involved, and both desire it, the sexual encounter should not be regarded with grudging toleration, but rather as a cause for celebration. When such experiences are positive ones for all concerned, in both the short- and the long-term, we can only be glad that they happened. Adding to someone's pleasure and happiness without causing pain or unhappiness to anyone else is an unambiguously good thing from the perspective of humanistic Christianity.

Abortion

Abortion is the least straightforward case, but no physical suffering need be involved in the termination of pregnancy. Of course there are complex issues which need to be considered before any decision to have an abortion is made, and the experience of having one, especially without adequate emotional support, can be traumatic. The last thing any pregnant woman who is considering having an abortion needs is to be treated in such a way that she feels guilty if she chooses that option. Her decision needs to be made on the basis of a rational consideration of the physical and psychological consequences for both mother and foetus, of either course of action. To deny a pregnant mother the right to terminate the life of her unborn child for which she knows she cannot adequately care is cruel – to her, and even more so to the child. To try to rule that option out on legal or religious grounds regardless of the mother's feelings in the matter, is a highly uncompassionate act. A major part of the solution to the problems posed by abortion lies in more education about, and encouragement of the use of reliable contraception.

Important among the emotional issues which often cloud rational thinking about whether to have an abortion or not, is the widespread belief, particularly among religious people, that the preservation of life is a non-negotiable duty we all have which must override all other considerations – that just to be alive, happy or not, is an unambiguous good, or more frequently, is 'God's will', with which we must not try to interfere. For those who identify with the humanistic face of Christianity, it is not the preservation of life at all costs which is their ethical imperative, but rather the reduction as far as possible of the pain and suffering of all living creatures.

Euthanasia

The obsession of many authoritarian Christians with prolonging life and delaying death, even if it means increasing someone's suffering, is a curious aberration of Christian thought. St Paul was by no means alone in the Christian community in proclaiming that, "For me living is Christ and dying is gain" (Philippians 1:22), but there is a complete disjunction between the longing for death so frequently expressed in much Christian literature (and manifest in the behaviour of the Christian martyrs), and the efforts of so many Christians of an authoritarian persuasion to delay the advent of death, even for those who desperately desire it. It is death which such Christians fight against, not pain, the crusade against which marked Jesus' healing ministry.

Such effort on the part of Christians is misplaced. It is not death which is the terrible enemy of humanity and the animal world; it is pain and suffering, to the reduction of which all humanitarian effort needs to be directed. To fail to help any suffering person to gain release from a situation they find intolerable is to forget Jesus' dictum that, "The Sabbath was made for man, not man for the Sabbath", in other words that we should, "never sacrifice a person to a principle," as Schweitzer put it.

John Humphrys ends the deeply moving book which he wrote with Dr Sarah Jarvis on the subject of euthanasia entitled *The Welcome Visitor*[151] with an account of the death of his younger brother from incurable cancer. He wrote,

> I wish his final few days had been different. When I held his hand in his bedroom and we had our last real conversation and he told me what he feared, I wish I had been able to say to him: 'You are in control. We both know you are dying. It is for you and nobody else to decide how and when your life comes to an end. If you want help to die, we will give you that help.'
>
> But I could not – any more than I could help my father to die – and I shall never forgive myself for that. I let them down. I believe that the dying have at least the same rights as the living: above all the right to make their own decisions, to take control of the end of their lives in the way they wish. Anything less is a form of betrayal.

John Humphrys' words resonate strongly with my own experience of my involvement with my mother in the last six months or so of her life. Unable to stand straight up because of advancing osteoporosis, and suffering from Parkinson's Disease and some degree of Dementia she was virtually bedridden for the last year of her life and required fairly constant nursing. One day about six months before her death, having struggled to get her to sit up to take a little food and something to drink she lifted her eyes to me and with the most pathetic look said, "I wish I could die, Richard". What did I do? I put my arms around her and gently hugged her, telling her how much I loved her and how important she had been in my life, and how much I appreciated all she had done and been for me. And I totally ignored what she had said about wishing she could die.

How beautiful it would have been for all of us if in that tender moment had I been able to give her something delicious to drink with the pleasant flavour of which lingering in her mouth, she could have slipped away into peaceful oblivion. It would have been right for her, right for me, and right for humanity. As it was she battled on for several months, her speech gradually disintegrating into a few isolated words, and then for the last few weeks, nothing. Worst of all was the deterioration in her ability to eat even soft foods and eventually even to drink. For her last few days resting a small wet sponge on her tongue many times a day always left us anxious as to whether we had done enough to slake the thirst she must have felt at times.

It should not have been like that. The laws of the land should have been such that it would have been easy to get medical help to assist her to an easy transition out of this life. I should have been better prepared to find a way out for her. Looking back now, twelve years later I am appalled by how easily I acquiesced in a situation in which my mother endured, for at least six months, so much unnecessary suffering from which she obviously desperately wanted release. I think I must have been in a state of prolonged shock. What I did, by doing nothing to help her get her wish, was not the right thing for her. Indeed it was just not the right thing to have happened, and the fact that a major factor in my inaction was my deep love for my mother which made the idea of playing any part in bringing about her death almost unthinkable, does not make it any less wrong. One of the very important tasks which any humanistically-oriented religious institution could perform for humanity is to help prepare us all for taking compassionate action to reduce any suffering which anyone endures in the last months or years of their life, and if that means shortening their life, so be it.

Inconsistent ideas about the rightness or otherwise of taking the life of others

Authoritarian Christianity is not known for its promotion of pacifist ideas, and there is an element of hypocrisy in those who hold to a version of Christian principles which will not allow them to countenance the taking of steps to terminate the suffering of those seeking euthanasia, or to prevent the future suffering of an unwanted unborn child, but can rejoice in the death of enemy combatants in war. Opponents of euthanasia and abortion need to reflect on how they feel about that situation, and on how they feel about those compassionate souls who on the battlefield bravely act to put an end with a bullet to the sufferings of anyone, friend or foe, who is in extreme pain, and whose chances of getting swift pain-relieving medical attention before their death are negligible. How we feel about judicial murder, euphemistically usually referred to by the sanitised term, 'Capital Punishment', is also something we need to reflect on before trying to outlaw the compassionate medical procedures of euthanasia and abortion.

Not only is authoritarian Christianity very often characterised by apathy towards the reduction of human and animal suffering[152], it is often within that framework that the puritanical and really perverted view that "Suffering is good for you," is expressed. The words of Pope John Paul II that, "Suffering, particularly in the later years of life, is part of God's saving plan for humanity"[39] already quoted, reflect an attitude which is not uncommonly encountered in the authoritarian face of Christianity. That such a view flies in the face of everything Jesus taught and did, rarely if ever seems to occur to such people. When a choice has to be made between death and present or future suffering, the choice of death is entirely consistent with the ethical principles of humanistic Christianity.

Chapter 12

Epilogue

To-day there is but one religious dogma in debate: What do you mean by "God"? And in this respect, to-day is like all its yesterdays. This is the fundamental religious dogma, and all other dogmas are subsidiary to it.[153]

– Alfred North Whitehead. *Religion in the Making*

When I am asked, "Do you believe in God?", my reply, using C. M. Joad's apposite catchphrase is, "It all depends on what you mean by 'God'". If the questioner means (to quote the Shorter Oxford Dictionary), "Do you believe in the existence of God, 'The One object of supreme adoration; the Creator and Ruler of the Universe'", then my answer is "NO" – except in the sense in which I believe that the Force of Gravity, the Electromagnetic Force, and the Strong and Weak Nuclear Forces identified by physicists exist. If they did not, neither we nor anything else in the world would exist. The reality of those forces needs to be acknowledged and taken account of in our everyday behaviour, but we don't feel any need to adore and worship them, even though our continued physical existence is totally dependent on them.

So it is with God. If any one feels such a need it strongly suggests that their concept of God contains more than a little of the projection of the image of an idealised parent which Sigmund Freud somewhat simplistically believed was the only concept to which the label 'God' was universally applied. Expressions like, "You are so clever", "You can do anything", "I'm so lucky to have you", "Thank you for being so kind to me", "You're great", "You know everything", and "You are so powerful", may perhaps sometimes be appropriate to say to an earthly parent at some very early point in our development. It is, however, no more appropriate to address such remarks to God than it would be to address them to the Force of Gravity, although both these entities are fundamental properties of the universe, harmonising ourselves with which can greatly enhance the quality of our lives.

John Cleese's brilliant send-up of a school chaplain in the Monty Python film *The Meaning of Life* is a timely reminder of the truth contained in those wise words of one anonymous priest who started one of his prayers with the words, "God, who is beyond the vulgarities of praise and power". Perhaps vulgar is a very apt word to apply to many of those effusive eulogies to God, reminding him (somewhat unnecessarily one would think in view of his status as 'all-knowing') that his "is the Kingdom, the Power and the Glory", and that we grovel at his feet in adoration and abject submission, not a posture which his 'only begotten son' ever encouraged in his disciples and audiences.

If the questioner means, "Do you believe that there is some property of the universe which A. N. Whitehead partially defined as,

that function in the world by reason of which our purposes are directed to ends which in our own consciousness are impartial as to our own interests. He is that element in life in virtue of which judgment stretches beyond facts of existence to values of existence. He is that element in virtue of which our purposes extend beyond values for ourselves to values for others. He is that element in virtue of which the attainment of such a value for others transforms itself into value for ourselves.[145]

then my answer is a resounding, "YES", and more than that, echoing Jung's famous simple answer in a BBC interview to that question, "It's not a matter of belief so much as of knowledge: I have found that life works that way". My daily experience of life is that I live in a universe which, besides having the physical characteristics which are being understood in increasing detail by scientists, has a property which psychologists have barely begun to explore, the quality that, "It is in giving that we receive", "It is in forgiving others that we ourselves experience forgiveness".

Powerful though Whitehead's 'definition' of the nature of God is, he would almost certainly have been the last person to claim that he had said the last word on the subject. Fuller discussion of the question, "Who or what is God?", needs its own book, but for now suffice it to say that for me, Whitehead's words above, and Albert Schweitzer's musing to the effect that, "the relationship between the Will to Live, the Will to Love, and God is the most profound problem to which Philosophy can address itself", provide a broad framework within which all my experiences of the beautiful in art and nature, the pleasures of touch and other sensual and sexual delights, the experience of all forms of compassionate love whether expressed by myself or others, and all that I can understand of the work of scientists and mathematicians are integrated in a way which induces in me a deep sense of calm, peace and joy, and a profound awareness of the powerful positive forces at the heart of the universe.

That awareness makes all intellectual questions about 'the meaning of life', and what happens after death irrelevant. Ultimately all will be well. But I want, and I want to join with others who want all to be well for all, long before any 'ultimate end' of my life is reached. I identify myself as a Christian because the ethical principles laid out by Jesus provide for me one indispensable guide to achieving that aim of bringing about the Kingdom of Heaven on earth. The gems of psychological insight which now abound in the field of psychology (amongst much that is totally irrelevant to most human and animal lives) provide another.

I more than half suspect that no 'ultimate end' of anyone's life will ever be reached, the end of our physical lives being only a mini-ending of one part of a much greater whole; that the universe always has been and always will be. In the 'here and now' we experience part of not only the ever-changing ebb and flow of the surface of life but beneath that, contact with those everlasting, timeless spiritual entities which are (or should be) the stuff of religion. To quote again Emerson's provocative thought, "Other world? There is no other world! Here or nowhere is the whole fact." Spiritual entities do not exist in some realm outside ourselves with which we can only make contact with the help of religious rituals supervised by religious professionals, be they Popes, Archbishops, Priests, Ministers, Pastors, Rabbis or Imams. Such bits and pieces of human organisations *can* be helpful in deepening our contact with spiritual truths, but the sad reality is that they are more often than not, more of a hindrance than a help.

And when the body dies? I am indebted to an Anglican priest, the Reverend Harry Wiggett, for drawing to my attention a most beautiful symbolic description of that event, created by some unknown writer.

We are all like ice-blocks slowly melting into the most unbelievably warm and welcoming ocean of eternal Love and Light. ... as we slowly melt, absolutely nothing will be lost; all will be perfectly absorbed into the oneness of the All – a unity of Love beyond our wildest imaginings.

I should be sorry if anyone who has read this book feels more dismissive of the Christian Church than they were before reading it. That church has some appalling skeletons in its cupboards, but it is an institution that can provide some powerful spiritual experiences. For me, the music and the physical environment provided by the services of Evensong at places like the chapels of King's and St. John's Colleges in

Cambridge, and the warm silences, punctuated by the occasional sharing of inspiring thoughts of a simple Quaker meeting, have provided some of the peak experiences of my life. For that I am deeply grateful. They are a constant reminder of A. N. Whitehead's profound vision of the long-term history of the Universe, expressed in connection with his comments on the concept of Entropy – a measure of the ever-increasing degree of disorder in the physical universe.

The faith in the order of nature which has made possible the growth of science is a particular example of a deeper faith. This faith cannot be justified by any inductive generalisation. It springs from direct inspection of the nature of things as disclosed in our own immediate present experience. There is no parting from our own shadow. To experience this faith is to know that in being ourselves we are more than ourselves: to know that our experience, dim and fragmentary as it is, yet sounds the utmost depths of reality: to know that detached details merely in order to be themselves demand that they should find themselves in a system of things: to know that this system includes the harmony of logical rationality, and the harmony of aesthetic achievement: to know that, while the harmony of logic lies upon the universe as an iron necessity, the aesthetic harmony stands before it as a living ideal moulding the general flux in its broken progress towards finer, subtler issues".[154]

The universe shows us two aspects: on one side it is physically wasting, on the other side it is spiritually ascending. It is thus passing with a slowness, inconceivable in our measures of time, to new creative conditions, amid which the physical world, as we at present know it, will be represented by a ripple barely to be distinguished from non-entity.

The present type of order in the world has arisen from an unimaginable past, and it will find its grave in an unimaginable future. There remain the inexhaustible realm of abstract forms, and creativity, with its shifting character ever determined afresh by its own creatures, and God, upon whose wisdom all forms of order depend.[155]

A final thought

I started Chapter 1 of this book by quoting Thomas Hardy's bitter assessment of the ineffectiveness of the currently more than 2 billion strong Christian community (about a third of the world's population), in promoting world peace on any significant scale.

"Peace upon earth," the angels sang.
We pay a thousand priests to ring it.
And after 2000 years of Mass
We've got as far as poison gas.

I end this book with a reflection by the Nobel prize-winning economist J. K. Galbraith on a not dissimilar theme. He concludes his little book, *The Economics of Innocent Fraud*, with the words:

We cherish the progress in civilization since biblical times and long before. But there is a needed and, indeed, accepted qualification. As I write, the United States and Britain are in the bitter aftermath of a war in Iraq. We are accepting programmed death for the young and random slaughter for men and women of all ages. So, overwhelmingly, it was in World Wars I and II. So more selectively since, and still at this writing in Iraq. Civilized life, as it is called, is a great white tower celebrating human achievements, but at the top there is permanently a large black cloud. Human progress dominated by unimaginable cruelty and death.

The facts of war are inescapable – death and random

cruelty, suspension of civilized values, a disordered aftermath. Thus the human condition and prospect as now supremely evident. The economic and social problems here described, as also mass poverty and starvation can, with thought and action, be addressed. So they have already been. War remains the decisive human failure.[156]

For this sad situation the authoritarian face of Christianity, with its delusion of the existence of a God who is an autocratic and sometimes harsh and cruel ruler in control of the universe, is to a significant extent responsible. As argued earlier in this book, 'Saint' Paul, because of the prominence given to his views in the New Testament of the Christian Bible, has played a pivotal role in importing into Christianity the pre-Christian idea that, "The Lord is a man of war" (Exodus 15:3), who has at times commanded his subjects (Joshua 10:40) to slaughter thousands upon thousands of indigenous peoples, "both men and women, young and old" (Joshua 6:21). That 'God', according to Paul, apparently approves of the emotion of hatred (Romans 12:9), and approves of, and indeed participates in the infliction of suffering, death, and destruction on human beings. (Romans 2:9, I Corinthians 3:17 and 5:5).

Such a God is a fantasy figure derived from some of the worst aspects of human psychopathology, which ultimately spring from the unforgiving, punitive behaviours of harsh child-rearing practices. Belief in the existence of such a being is totally incompatible with the view of the nature of God which underlies Jesus' vision of the power of compassionate, forgiving love which lies at the heart of the universe.

If the Christian Church ever plays any effective role in putting an end to war and all the suffering it causes, it will be because of the passionate beliefs and compassionate behaviour of those who make up the humanistic face of the religion. One of those beliefs was beautifully expressed by Albert Schweitzer when he wrote:

All ... violence produces its own limitations, for it calls forth an answering violence which sooner or later becomes its equal or its superior. But kindness works simply and perseveringly; it produces no strained relations which prejudice its workings; strained relations which already exist it relaxes. Mistrust and misunderstanding it puts to flight, and it strengthens itself by calling forth answering kindness. Hence it is the furthest-reaching and most effective of all forces.[77]

It would be difficult to improve on that masterly, succinct summary of the ethics of Jesus once made by some anonymous person, and quoted in Chapter 5, "If it comes to a choice between being right or being kind, choose kind".

Of course it is not just in the field of religion that we too often find a disregard for the wisdom in that ethical principle of Jesus to the effect that, in Schweitzer's paraphrase, we should, "Never sacrifice a person to a principle". The historian Paul Johnson, in his survey of the lives and work of 20 intellectuals such as Rousseau, Shelley, Marx, Brecht, and Bertrand Russell (all but one of them male), who have tried to change the way human society functions, provides a chilling picture of the disjunction between their utopian visions for the future of humankind if their advice were to be followed, and the way in which most of them behaved towards others, particularly towards the women and children in their lives. Paul Johnson ends his book with the words,

Above all, we must remember what intellectuals habitually forget: that people matter more than concepts and must come first. The worst of all despotisms is the heartless tyranny of ideas.[157]

If Christian theology does not embrace the principle embedded in Jesus' belief that, "The Sabbath was made for man, not man for the Sabbath", Christianity will end up having been more of a curse than a blessing to humankind. All religious persons, whatever their creed, could with advantage share with Thomas Aquinas his fervent hope that, "In my zeal for truth, let me not forget the truth about love".

May nothing I have said in this book, (or anywhere else for that matter) in any way undermine the wonderful work that those who "live and move and have their being" in the humanistic face of Christianity are doing. But it is my earnest hope that what I have written here will make some contribution to bringing about in the future the sort of Christian Church envisaged by the Unitarian hymn writer Marion Franklin Ham (1867 – 1956) when she wrote,

> As tranquil streams that meet and merge
> And flow as one to seek the sea,
> Our kindred hearts and minds unite
> To build a church that shall be free.
>
> A freedom that reveres the past,
> But trusts the dawning future more,
> And bids the soul, in search of truth,
> Adventure boldly and explore.
>
> Free from the bonds that bind the mind
> To narrow thought and lifeless creed,
> Free from a social code that fails
> To serve the cause of human need.
>
> Prophetic church, the future waits
> Your liberating ministry,
> Go forward in the power of love,
> Proclaim the truth that makes us free.

The School

He always wanted to say things.

But no one understood them.
He always wanted to explain things
But no one cared.
So he drew.
Sometimes he would draw and it wasn't anything.
He wanted to carve it in stone or write it in the sky.
And it would be only him and the sky
And the things inside of him that needed saying ....
And it was after that, that he drew the picture.
He kept it under his pillow and would let no one see it.
It was a beautiful picture and he would look at it every night
    and think about it.
And when it was dark and his eyes were closed he would still
    see it.
And it was all of him and he loved it.
And when he started school, he brought it with him –
Not to show anyone, but just to have it with him like a friend.
It was funny about school.
He sat in a square brown desk, like all the other square brown
    desks,

And he thought it should be red.
And the room was a square and it was tight and close and
    stiff.
He hated to hold the pencil and chalk with his arms stiff.
With the teacher watching, watching, watching –
And then he had to write numbers

And they weren't anything.
They were worse than the letters that could be something if
    you put them together.
And the numbers were tight and square.
And he hated the whole thing.

The teacher came and spoke to him
She told him to wear a tie like all the other boys.
He said he didn't like ties, and she said it didn't matter.
After that they drew.
And he drew all yellow and it was the way he felt about the
    morning.
And it was beautiful.

The teacher came and smiled at him. "What's this?"

She said, "Why don't you draw something like Jen's
    drawing?"
Isn't that beautiful?
It was all questions.

After that his mother bought him a tie.
And he always drew planes and rocket ships like everyone
    else.

And he threw the old picture away.

And when he lay out looking at the sky, it was big and blue.
And all of everything, but he wasn't anymore.
He was square inside and brown.

His hands were stiff and he was like everyone else.

And the things inside that needed saying

Didn't need saying anymore.
It had stopped pushing.
It was crushed.
Stiff.

Like everyone else.

Anonymous

Appendix 2

Paradise Lost

Clancy Sigal writing of growing up on Chicago's West Side, says in an article entitled "The Heart that Failed" published in The Guardian some years ago:

"... Like looming locomotives bearing down on us, jobs, sex and war were inescapable. Some time around my twelfth year I had an eerie feeling of having joined an invisible marathon racing toward a vaguely unattractive goal: adulthood. Even at the time I sensed it was a hard road to go. I didn't know why but there was *something* wrong with it. Whenever I questioned the process, usually in a silly, offhand or embarrassed way, the predictable sneer was: "Aw, grow up!" Ah, but what if, on the basis of a strong hunch, you didn't want to?

"Too late. Parties, spin-the-bottle and kissing games, led to real sex; age led to the military draft; the first shave to rejecting kid's stuff in favour of the real thing; making money or in other ways getting on in the world. Or simply, as with so many of us on Chicago's West Side, surviving.

"I'm not sorry I missed being a teenager. However, I deeply regret having lost sight of the golden city, a place of the individual imagination beyond the first fears of childhood. When that special landscape of a child's heart misted over, when I grew tough and "realistic", I'm sure I began the process that landed me in intensive care.

"The case is unprovable. I'm still doing the conventional expected things,. I diet, exercise properly and listen to my friends' and doctors' advice. But, behind their backs as it were, sometimes at night when the light is out, I snap open my imaginary telescope and scan the turreted battlements of a far-gone time which, if I don't relocate it fairly exactly, surely will finish me off as efficiently as a fat-clogged artery.

"Even now, in hindsight, as I write about "growing up into a man", the process seems so universal and natural that to question it, let alone momentarily reverse the flow, feels grotesque.

"But I wonder how many of us keel over with heart attacks as an inner protest against all this adult male stuff that nobody exactly forced on us, indeed seemed at the time a positive and necessary good in our lives?

"Second thoughts like this, jogged by trauma and medication, can be wonderfully therapeutic as well as chilling as the gallows. We cannot abolish manhood as we know it. (Why, a child's voice within wants to know.) And I'm not even sure that, if we cancelled most of the obnoxious macho aspects, it would still erase the terrible rush to self-judgement that becoming a man, at least in America, entails.

"We leave behind too much in the scramble to sit at the adults' table. By wiping themselves out with "cardiac events" in such massive numbers, men may be voting with their hearts to get out of the trap at whatever cost. If untended, the child within us becomes a terrible and terribly powerful enemy."

A Brief Account of Albert Schweitzer's Ethical Principle of Reverence for Life

The starting point for Schweitzer's development of his principle of Reverence for Life is the acceptance of two aspects of the realities of human experience.

1   A fundamental property exhibited by all living things is the will-to-live. When a plant or animal suffers damage to its normal healthy functioning, it responds by devoting as much of its resources as possible to the preservation of its existence. The extent to which, after injury, living things are often able to recover at least enough of their normal functioning to continue to live, is sometimes quite remarkable. The way in which bodies mangled by physical disasters or overrun by destructive bacteria and viruses fight against the odds to continue to live at all costs, is a fundamental aspect of the way things happen in the universe. Nevertheless there are limits to how far this process can go, and sooner or later, whether the process is accelerated by injury and disease or not, the aging process takes its toll on every living thing and death supervenes.

2   Unfortunately, with the energies of all living things, both human other animal, and plants all directed to the same end of survival and growth, at least some degree of conflict for resources will inevitably be a constant theme in nature. Very often that conflict will result in the termination in death of the will-to-live of some living things in response to the demands of other living things. The continued life of humans is bought at the expense of the death of many creatures, and the same situation exists at every level of

complexity in nature, down to at least the level of unicellular organisms. Although the decisions of some humans to be vegetarian, and even more so those who choose to be vegan, do very significantly reduce the total amount of death and suffering in the world, the continued life of every human being does necessarily involve the death of some living creatures, even if only at the level of insects and microbes. To refuse to use medication to combat some bacteria and viruses when they attack us can be tantamount to committing suicide.

An attitude of *Reverence for Life* refers to the conviction that notwithstanding the inevitability of death for some living things in order to support the continued life of others, all life has the right to exist and we have a fundamental ethical obligation to keep the amount of pain, death, and destruction in the universe to that absolutely unavoidable minimum which is essential for the continuation of any organism's life. We should never arbitrarily terminate the life of any living thing just because we have the power, and feel the impulse, to do so. For Schweitzer, holding to the principle of Reverence for Life means,

> experiencing the compulsion to show to all will-to-live the same reverence as I do to my own. There we have given us that basic principle of the moral which is a necessity for thought. It is good to maintain and to encourage life; it is bad to destroy life or to obstruct it.[158]

Of course this applies to humans, but equally to all living creatures. Schweitzer writes movingly of the attitudes and behaviours towards the 'lower animals' of those imbued with the spirit of Reverence for Life.

A man is truly ethical only when he obeys the compulsion to

help all life which he is able to assist, and shrinks from injuring anything that lives. Life as such is sacred to him. ... If he walks on the road after a shower and sees an earthworm which has strayed onto it, he bethinks himself that it must get dried up in the sun if it does not return soon enough to ground into which it can burrow, so he lifts it from the deadly stone surface, and puts it on the grass. If he comes across an insect which has fallen into a puddle, he stops a moment in order to hold out a leaf or a stalk on which it can save itself.[159]

Of course simply trying to prolong life by fighting disease is not sufficient. Without the widespread use of both human and animal contraception nature will use its own effective, but often cruel tactics to keep animal populations, human and otherwise, within the limits that the earth's resources can support, no matter what strategies we adopt to prolong the individual's lifespan.

In Schweitzer's thinking the attitude of mind of *Reverence for Life* extends beyond merely preserving the life of as many organisms as possible. It extends to preserving the individual's pain-free health and happiness in a richly fulfilling life. He writes:

As in my own will-to-live there is a longing for wider life and for the mysterious exaltation of the will-to-live which we call pleasure, with dread of annihilation and of the mysterious depreciation of the will-to-live which we call pain; so it is also in the will-to-live all around me, whether it can express itself before me, or remains dumb.[158]

For Schweitzer the principle of *Reverence for Life* extends to keeping to an absolute minimum the destruction of beauty, man-made or in nature. Contemplating and preserving such beauty provides a powerful enhancement of the ability of all of us who have a deep *Reverence for Life*, to enjoy the lives, our own and those of the other creatures, we so passionately seek to preserve.

Schweitzer, who lived through two world wars, was well aware of the strength of the societal forces individuals experience to suppress many aspects of their instinctual compassionate impulses. The operation of the defence mechanism of *Reaction Formation* leads many people who are embarrassed by the stirrings of tender feelings within themselves to react with apparent scorn towards the behaviours and beliefs of those who feel deeply for the sufferings of others. Towards the end of his book *Civilization and Ethics* Schweitzer writes of those who embrace the principle of Reverence for Life,

> He is not afraid of being laughed at as sentimental. It is the fate of every truth to be a subject for laughter until it is generally recognized. Once it was considered folly to assume that men of colour were really men and ought to be treated as such, but the folly has become an accepted truth. Today it is thought to be going too far to declare that constant regard for everything that lives, down to the lowest manifestations of life, is a demand made by rational ethics. The time is coming, however, when people will be astonished that mankind needed so long a time to learn to regard thoughtless injury to life as incompatible with ethics. Ethics are responsibility without limit towards all that lives.[160]

The rootedness of an attitude of *Reverence for Life* in the ethical principles espoused by Jesus which provide the bedrock on which humanistic Christianity rests will not have escaped the reader. In Schweitzer's words,

> The ethic of Reverence for Life is the ethic of Jesus brought to philosophical expression, extended into cosmical form, and conceived of as ethically necessary.[161]

Appendix 4

Some of Paul's Psychopathologies not Unique in the New Testament

To be fair to Paul, it must be realised that he is by no means the only New Testament writer to display some of the sort of psychopathological ideas which I have been discussing in Chapter 7. Much of the whole Judeo-Christian tradition is permeated by authoritarian attitudes which often in one way or another corrupt the spiritual truths which lie at the heart of the religions. The subject is worthy of much more thorough treatment, but just two examples of other New Testament manifestation of these attitudes must suffice for now. The author of John's gospel puts into Jesus' mouth the words, "Ye are my friends, if ye do whatsoever I command you" (John 15:14), words which Jesus almost certainly never uttered, but which would be natural to many of those who successfully jockeyed for positions of power in the early Christian Church. The other brief example is the New Testament First Epistle of Peter which is replete with examples of psychopathological authoritarian and often misogynistic thinking. This Epistle is addressed,

> To the exiles of the Dispersion in Pontus, Galatia, Cappadocia, Asia and Bithynia, who have been chosen and destined by God the Father and sanctified by the Spirit to be obedient to Jesus Christ and to be sprinkled with his blood (I Peter 1:1-2).

In it the author shows (amongst other things) the same male chauvinist attitudes towards women as inferior beings that Paul does. For example, in I Peter 3:1, he commands, "Wives ... accept the authority of your husbands", and two verses later proceeds to lay down the law about how wives should (or should not) adorn themselves, arrogantly claiming to know God's views on the subject.

> Do not adorn yourselves outwardly by braiding your hair, and by wearing gold ornaments or fine clothing; rather let your adornment be the inner self with the lasting beauty of a gentle and quiet spirit, which is very precious in God's sight. It was in this way long ago that the holy women who hoped in God used to adorn themselves by accepting the authority of their husbands. (I Peter 3:3-5).

And in the next verse, the writer of the epistle follows up this blatant attempt to bully women into conforming to his will by quoting with approval as a model for male-female relationships, the fact that, "Sarah ... obeyed Abraham and called him her master."

But women are not the only targets of Peter's autocratic edicts. Closely paralleling what Paul wrote in Romans 13:1-6, he also orders his readers to, "Fear God. Honour the emperor" (I Peter 2:17), and, "For the Lord's sake accept the authority of every human institution, whether of the emperor as supreme, or of governors as sent by him" (I Peter 2:13). He tells slaves that they must accept the authority of their masters, "with all deference, not only those who are kind and gentle but also those who are harsh" (I Peter 2:18). He rounds it all off by telling those who are younger that they must "accept the authority of the elders" (I Peter 5:5).

If the writer of this Epistle was indeed, "a witness of the sufferings of Christ" as he claimed to be in the last chapter of this Epistle (I Peter 5:1), then he very probably is indeed the apostle Peter. If so it is clear that it was not just Jesus' philosophy of non-violence that he had totally failed to absorb. Had Jesus known what he was going to write in this New Testament Epistle he would have had more to rebuke Peter about than just his violent act of cutting off the ear of the High Priest's servant in the Garden of Gethsemane, and it is vanishingly unlikely that the words attributed to Jesus in Matthew 16:18, "And I tell you, you are Peter, and on this rock I will build my church, and the gates of Hades will not prevail against it", would ever have been uttered by Jesus.

Even as it is, given Peter's dismal performance in the Garden of Gethsemane it is almost certain that those words were in fact an interpolation into the gospel record made by someone in the early church, possibly orchestrated by Peter himself. An additional, particularly compelling reason to doubt the authenticity of those words is that Jesus himself never founded any church, Christian or otherwise, nor ever talked about doing so. He saw his life's work as being to inaugurate the Kingdom of God on earth, and even after his death, the body of people who later became the early church were expecting Jesus' imminent return to earth as the Messiah who would do just that. It was only as the days of waiting for that eschatological event, the Parousia (the second coming of Christ), turned to weeks, and months and eventually to years, that that dream gradually faded and the remnants of the group of disciples came to realise that Jesus' prophecy that "This generation shall not pass, till all these things be fulfilled" (Matthew 24:34), was not going to come true. Eventually realising this, they gradually resigned themselves to keeping Jesus' memory and vision alive through a church committed (at least officially) to that end. Unfortunately that church has so far proved a pretty poor substitute for the Kingdom of God.

Notes

1   Kahlil Gibran, *The Prophet*, London: Heinemann, 1926.

2   Alfred North Whitehead. *Religion in the Making*, Cambridge: Cambridge University Press, 1926, p. 79.

3   This idea was by no means universally accepted in the early Christian Church. We have to thank the politically-motivated ambitions of the fourth-century Roman Emperor Constantine, for the dominance of this belief in later Christian thought. See Chapter 3 for further discussion on this point.

4   Alfred North Whitehead. *Religion in the Making*, Cambridge: Cambridge University Press, 1926, p.131.

5   Richard Webster. *Why Freud was wrong: Sin, Science and Psychoanalysis*, London: HarperCollins, 1995.

6   Erich Fromm. *Psychoanalysis and Religion*, New York: Bantam Books, 1950.

7   Ibid, p. 34.

8   Alfred North Whitehead. *Religion in the Making*, Cambridge: Cambridge University Press, 1926, p. 149.

9   Amy Tan. *Saving Fish From Drowning*, New York: Harper Perennial, 2006.

10   The other two are classical conditioning (learning by association) and modelling (learning by imitation).

11   A. A. Milne. *The House at Pooh Corner*, London: Methuen, 1950, pp. 129-130.

12   Fundamentalism is not an attitude to religious texts found only within the Christian tradition. It was present in Judaism long before the Christian era and is probably to be found in every religion with a significant number of adherents. Trevor Ling in his *A History of Religion East and West* discusses the 'glamour' which for many people hangs over the written words of religious scriptures, ascribing this to "the idea that these writings were divinely inspired down to the last jot and tittle; a view which was fostered

by the Jewish scribes from Ezra onwards".

13   Of course this clearly implies that for the writer of this particular part of the book of Genesis, God is both male and female, or more accurately, that the totality of the characteristics of males and females as a collective are contained in the Godhead – male characteristics have no priority over female ones, a very different picture from that contained in the second Genesis Creation story in which the creation of man came first, and the creation of woman a poor second.

14   Geza Vermes. *The Authentic Gospel of Jesus,* London: Penguin, 2004.

15   Trevor Ling. A *History of Religion East and West,* London: MacMillan, 1968, p. 290.

16   CE = In the Common Era (formerly AD = *Anno Domini,* being the Latin for, 'In the year of the Lord'). Similarly BCE = Before the Common Era (formerly BC, an abbreviation for, 'Before Christ').

17   Ian Wilson. *Jesus: The Evidence,* London: Book Club Associates, 1984, p. 164.

18   Ibid, p.157.

19   Ibid p.160.

20   Ibid p.165.

21   We believe in one God, the Father Almighty, Maker of heaven and earth, and of all things visible and invisible. And in one Lord Jesus Christ, the only-begotten Son of God, begotten of the Father before all worlds, God of God, Light of Light, Very God of Very God, begotten, not made, being of one substance with the Father by whom all things were made; who for us men, and for our salvation, came down from heaven, and was incarnate by the Holy Spirit of the Virgin Mary, and was made man, and was crucified also for us under Pontius Pilate. He suffered and was buried, and the third day he rose again according to the Scriptures, and ascended into heaven, and sitteth on the right hand of the Father. And he shall come again with glory to judge both the quick and the dead, whose kingdom shall have no end.

And we believe in the Holy Spirit, the Lord and Giver of Life, who proceedeth from the Father and the Son, who with the Father and the Son together is worshipped and glorified, who spoke by the prophets. And we believe in one holy catholic and apostolic Church. We acknowledge one baptism for the remission of sins. And we look for the resurrection of the dead, and the life of the world to come. Amen.

This statement of faith exists in several different variant forms, some churches favouring one of these and some another, but all saying essentially the same thing, and all totally lacking any reference to the ethical principles which Jesus urged upon his followers, or indeed to anything that happened between his conception and the trial before Pontius Pilate which immediately preceded his crucifixion.

22   Ian Wilson. *Jesus: The Evidence*, London: Book Club Associates, 1984, p. 168.

23   Ibid.

24   Ibid.

25   Diarmaid MacCulloch. *The History of Christianity: The First Three Thousand Years*, London: Allen Lane, 2009, p. 218.

26   David Barrett, George Kurian, and Todd Johnson. *World Christian Encyclopaedia: a comparative survey of churches and religions in the modern world*, Oxford: OUP, 2001. See also www.religioustolerance.org.

27   Alfred North Whitehead. *Religion in the Making*, Cambridge: Cambridge University Press, 1926, p. 144.

28   Geza Vermes. *The Changing Faces of Jesus*, London: Penguin Books, 2000.

29   A form of printing press using movable wood or ceramic type was known in China from 1040, and in Korea an important innovation was made with the invention of movable metal type in c. 1230, but these developments seem to have remained unknown to the Western world for many centuries.

30   These verses amplify the very much more sketchy account given in the other two synoptic gospels of reported sightings of Jesus after

his death. The fact that they did not appear in, "The most reliable early manuscripts," is of considerable interest because of the way in which they bolster the case made out in Matthew and Luke for belief in the reality of the Resurrection of Jesus.

31   Charles Freeman. *A New History of Early Christianity*, New Haven: Yale University Press, 2009.

32   Wycliffe was a prominent theologian who was dismissed from his position at the University of Oxford in 1381 for criticisms he was making of the pre-reformation Catholic Church (the one undivided branch of Christianity in Europe at the time). A particular target of his criticism was the Roman Catholic doctrine of the Eucharist, and especially its doctrine of Transubstantiation – the idea that in the Mass the bread and wine become the actual body and blood of Christ. This doctrine demonstrates in an extreme form, the fundamentalist tendency present in large parts of Christianity to favour literal over metaphorical interpretations of the words of scripture.

33   In a number of his writings that profound-thinking Jewish scholar, Geza Vermes, has a highly illuminating discussion of the original meaning of the gospel words on which the belief that Mary was a virgin when she gave birth to Jesus, are based.

34   As reported in *Christian Century*, November 16, 2010.

35   Similarly Paul's epistles were written for the edification of specific churches at a specific point in their early history, and Paul doubtless had no idea of the central place they were to occupy in the Christian Bible many centuries later.

36   Scholars believe that each of the Synoptic Gospel writers had access to some earlier account of the life and teachings of Jesus. This hypothesised document is referred to as 'Q', the first letter of the German word Quelle, which means 'source'. If such a document did in fact ever exist, no copies of it seem to have survived.

37   Stephen Mitchell. *The Gospel According to Jesus*, New York: HarperCollins, 1991.

38   Geza Vermes. *The Authentic Gospel of Jesus*, London: Penguin, 2004,

p. 371.

39   Karen Armstrong. *The Spiral Staircase*, New York: Harper Collins, 2004.

40   There are subtle differences between the concepts underlying different Christians' use of the terms, "The Kingdom of God" and, "The Kingdom of Heaven", but going into these would lead us too far from the main thrust of this book. For present purposes I shall simply use the two terms more or less interchangeably.

41   Quoted by Ludovic Kennedy in his book, *All in the mind: a farewell to God*, London: Hodder & Stoughton, 1999.

42   What Jesus says here about what constitutes the "first and great commandment" (as reported in Matthew 22:37-40) is an almost exact quote from Deuteronomy 6:5, variant forms of which are to be found at Deuteronomy 10:12; 11:1, 13, and 22; 19:9; and 30:6. His statement of what constitutes the second most important commandment is an exact quote from part of verse 18 of Chapter 19 of the book of Leviticus, "Thou shalt love thy neighbour as thyself". As Jesus said, "Think not that I am come to destroy the law, or the prophets: I am not come to destroy, but to fulfil". (Matthew 5:17).

43   "Disinterested" = "not interested for personal gain", as opposed to "uninterested" = "having no interest in something".

44   See also Matthew 18: 1 – 4; Mark 9: 35 – 37; Luke 9: 46 – 48; and 22: 24-26.

45   Interestingly, although the idea is implicit in much of what Jesus is reported to have said, there is no record in any of the four gospels of his having spoken these words. The quote actually comes from Acts 23:35, where it is written that Paul urged his audience, "to remember the words of the Lord Jesus, how he said, It is more blessed to give than to receive".

46   As Karen Armstrong points out in her *Twelve Steps to a Compassionate Life*, the influential Chinese philosopher Confucius also taught the Golden Rule, saying, "Never do unto others what you would not like them to do unto you", while much the same

idea was expressed by the prophet Muhammed when he said, "Not one of you can be a believer unless he desires for his neighbour what he desires for himself".

47   Amusingly illustrated in the (doubtless apocryphal) story of the two boy scouts who when asked why they had returned so late from an excursion to 'do a good deed', said they had been helping an old lady to cross the road. To their scoutmaster's astonished, "But why did that take you so long?", they replied, "Well she didn't want to go"!

48   "If there be among you a poor man of one of thy brethren within any of thy gates in thy land which the Lord thy God giveth thee, thou shalt not harden thine heart, nor shut thine hand from thy poor brother: but thou shalt open thine hand wide unto him, and shalt surely lend him sufficient for his need, in that which he wanteth".

49   "He coveteth greedily all the day long: but the righteous giveth and spareth not."

50   As in, "But who indeed are you, a human being, to argue with God? Will what is moulded say to the one who moulds it, 'Why have you made me like this?'" (Romans, 9:20-21).

51   Tradition has it that this phrase was first uttered by John Bradford (1510-1555). He was a highly regarded reforming Anglican priest who fell out of favour with the current political establishment, was imprisoned in the Tower of London, and subsequently was burnt at the stake. He reputedly uttered the words, "There but for the grace of God goes John Bradford," when, as a prisoner in the tower, he saw one of his fellow-prisoners led away to execution.

52   The Pharisees were part of a movement that arose within Judaism in approximately the third century BCE and gradually became absorbed into mainstream Judaism, upon the development of which it exerted considerable influence. As one would expect over the hundreds of years the movement existed, and given the thousands of people who were part of it, its character changed as the years went by, being at times almost something of the nature of

a political party, at others more a social movement, and sometimes just a school of thought among the Jews. At the time of the writing of the Gospels the Pharisees seem to have been particularly noted for the importance they placed on the strict observance of Jewish religious rites and ceremonies.

53 Almost exactly the same wording occurs at Luke 14:11 in the context of the parable of choosing a seat at the wedding feast, and again almost exactly the same words, but spoken in a quite different context are to be found at Matthew 23:12.

54 Dag Hammarskjöld in his diary, comments on this incident in the gospel record: "Jesus' 'lack of moral principles'. He sat at meal with publicans and sinners, he consorted with harlots. Did he do this to obtain their votes? Or did he think that perhaps he could convert them by such 'appeasement'? Or was his humanity rich and deep enough to make contact, even in them, with that in human nature which is common to all men, indestructible and upon which the future has to be built?" p. 134.

55 Echoing the words of verse 11 of Psalm 37, "But the meek shall inherit the earth; and shall delight themselves in the abundance of peace".

56 Matthew 6:1-8 reads: 1 Take heed that you do not your alms before men, to be seen of them: Otherwise ye have no reward of your Father which is in Heaven. 2 Therefore when thou doest thine alms, do not sound a trumpet before thee, as the hypocrites do in the synagogues and in the streets, that they may have glory of men. Verily I say unto you, They have their reward. 3 But when thou doest alms, let not thy left hand know what thy right hand doeth: 4 That thine alms may be in secret: and thy Father which seeth in secret himself shall reward thee openly. 5 And when thou prayest, thou shalt not be as the hypocrites are: for they love to pray standing in the synagogues and in the corners of the streets, that they may be seen of men. Verily I say unto you, They have their reward. 6 But thou, when thou prayest, enter into thy closet, and when thou hast shut thy door, pray to thy Father which is in

secret; and thy Father which seeth in secret shall reward thee openly. 7 But when ye pray, use not vain repetitions, as the heathen do: for they think that they shall be heard for their much speaking. 8 Be not ye therefore like unto them: for your Father knoweth what things you have need of, before ye ask him.

57 The practical application of this principle in everyday life is no simple matter. The problems are obviously ones which that deeply spiritual former Secretary-General of the United Nations, Dag Hammarskjöld was wrestling with when he wrote in his diary, "Your position never gives you the right to command. It only imposes on you the duty of so living your life that others can receive your orders without being humiliated." (Dag Hammarskjöld. *Markings,* London: Faber & Faber, 1964, p. 96).

58 Contrast this with Jesus' complaint against the Scribes and Pharisees at Matthew 23:4, "They tie up heavy burdens, hard to bear, and lay them on the shoulders of others; but they themselves are unwilling to lift a finger to move them".

59 When I became old enough to legally drive a car, it was required of those applying for a driver's licence in South Africa where I lived, to study a slim little booklet called 'The Highway Code'. It started off with an amusing verse, the wisdom in which extends far beyond what is appropriate for good motor vehicle driving practice – in life both inside and outside the motor car we often need something more that just being in the right, virtuous though that state generally is.

Here lies the body of Jonathan Gray,

Who died maintaining his right of way.

He was quite in the right as he sped along

But he's just as dead as if he'd been wrong.

60 Geza Vermes in his *The Authentic Gospel of Jesus,* London: Penguin, 2004, has an enlightening discussion on Jewish attitudes towards work on the Sabbath on pages 44-50.

61 In response to those legalistic religious extremists who disapproved of his carrying out acts of healing on the Sabbath, Jesus

injected a little commonsense practicality, "Doth not each one of you on the Sabbath loose his ox or his ass from the stall, and lead him away to watering?' (Luke 13:15), and, "Which of you shall have an ass or an ox fallen into a pit, and will not straightway pull him out on the Sabbath day?" (Luke 14:5, and Matthew 12:11).

62   William Temple. *Mens Creatrix*, London: McMillan, 1917, p. 206.

63   Joseph Fletcher. *Situational Ethics: The New Morality*, London: SCM Press, 1966.

64   John Robinson. *Honest to God*, London: SCM Press, 1963.

65   A. N. Whitehead. *Modes of Thought*, Cambridge: Cambridge University Press, 1938.

66   Joseph Fletcher. *Situational Ethics: The New Morality*, London: SCM Press, 1966, p. 13.

67   Ibid, p. 20.

68   "Other world? There is no other world! Here or nowhere is the entire fact." Ralph Waldo Emerson. *Uncollected Lectures. Natural Religion*, New York: W. E. Rudge, 1932.

69   John de Gruchy. *Being Human: Confessions of a Christian Humanist*, London: SCM Press, 2006.

70   W. Hoffmann. *A Sporting Life – with a Happy Heart. A Training guide for those with Coronary Heart Disease and those who wish to avoid it*, Cologne: Bayer Pharmaceuticals, 1983.

71   Of course there may sometimes be other, less high-minded reasons which motivate our forgiveness of others for hurting us. With typical impish irreverence, Oscar Wilde once advised: "Always forgive your enemies – nothing annoys them so much".

72   Accounts of this event are also given in Mark 11:15-17; Luke 19:45-46; and John 2:13-16.

73   It is also worth noting that what Jesus is reported to have said to those he drove out of the Temple were not ideas of his own creation, but paraphrases of words from the Hebrew Bible, "My house shall be called the house of prayer," from Isaiah 56:7, and from Jeremiah 7:11, "Is this house, which is called by my name, become a den of robbers in your eyes? Behold, even I have seen it,

saith the Lord".

74 Albert Schweitzer. *My Childhood and Youth*, London: Unwin, 1924, pp. 92-3.

75 Harold Loukes. *The Quaker Contribution*, London: SCM Press, 1965.

76 Another example of Jesus' humanistically-orientated sensitivity to the real life consequences of following (or not following) the ethical principles he believed were an important aspect of being in the Kingdom of God, is demonstrated in his advice, reported in Luke 14:8-11. Delivered in the context of his belief that humbling ourselves brings greater benefits to us than exalting ourselves, he reportedly said, "When thou art bidden of any man to a wedding, sit not down in the highest room; lest a more honourable man than thou be bidden of him; And he that bade thee (and him) come and say to thee, Give this man place; and thou begin with shame to take the lowest room. But when thou art bidden, go and sit down in the lowest room; that when he that bade thee cometh, he may say unto thee, Friend, go up higher: then shalt thou have worship in the presence of them that sit at meat with thee. For whosoever exalteth himself shall be abased; and he that humbleth himself shall be exalted."

77 Albert Schweitzer. *My Childhood and Youth*, London: Unwin, 1924, p. 94.

78 Geza Vermes. *The Authentic Gospel of Jesus*, London: Penguin, 2004, p. 65.

79 Ibid p. 403.

80 The last four lines of *Little Gidding*, the fourth of T. S. Eliot's *Four Quartets* read:

> We shall not cease from exploration
> And the end of all our exploring
> Will be to arrive where we started
> And know the place for the first time.

81 There are good ways and there are destructive ways of expressing our anger and our sexuality – the emotions themselves, however, are neither good nor bad, they 'just are', like hunger and thirst. A

much fuller account of the concept of our Shadow and the potential for good of making friends with it, and for ill by trying to deny its existence, is to be found in Chapter 9 of my *Achieving Our Full Potential*.

82 Matthew 23:25-26. See also Luke 11:39-40.

83 It is virtually certain that these seven items of wrongdoing are not exactly the ones that Jesus mentioned, but a mixture of what the gospel writer remembered of what Jesus said and his own views of what constitutes 'wrongdoing'.

84 Geza Vermes. *The Authentic Gospel of Jesus*, London: Penguin, 2004, p. 370.

85 For those of us without inside knowledge of the Catholic priesthood, Bernãrd Lynch's, *If It Wasn't Love: Sex, Death and God*, published by Circle Books in 2012 contains some real surprises, amongst which his statement (on page 52) that "Gay priests, as is well reported and documented, constitute forty to fifty percent of Catholic clergy", must be one of the more astonishing.

86 Ted Honderich (Ed). *The Oxford Companion to Philosophy*, Oxford: Oxford University Press, 1995.

87 As is his prayer, "Lord, in my zeal for the love of truth, let me not forget the truth about love".

88 Melanie Parry (Ed). *Chambers Biographical Dictionary*, Edinburgh: Larousse, 1997.

89 The Cape Times. Thursday, November 25, 2010, p. 6.

90 Those words were prophetic. The latest eruption into the public arena of the ongoing battle between conservatives and those in the Vatican of a more liberal disposition, was occasioned by the newly appointed (as of March 2013) Pope Francis' highly controversial (in Roman Catholic circles at least) assertion that, "Everyone! ... Even the atheists. Everyone!" has been "redeemed" by the "Blood of Christ".

91 The Vatican's underlying thinking here seems to be that using a condom to stop HIV infection is a good thing because it means a reduction in the death rate. Using them to prevent pregnancy is a

bad thing because that will mean a reduction in the birth rate. The implications of increased survival and birth rates in further overburdening a grossly overpopulated planet seems to be the last thing the Vatican has any plans to address.

92   It is within this tradition that this book is being written.

93   The description of his world-view given by a former Prime Minister of India, Pandit Nehru, "In terms of culture I am an Indian, in terms of religion, a Hindu, and in terms of ethics, a Christian", is an inspiration to those of us who enthusiastically support the implementation of Karen Armstrong's vision that gave birth to her Centre for Compassion.

94   Ralph Waldo Emerson, *Uncollected Lectures. Natural Religion*, New York: W. E. Rudge, 1932.

95   At the opposite end of the control spectrum lie the Quakers who have minimal organisational structures, but who have had an influence on the world out of all proportion to their relatively small numbers. Administrative leadership of the groups making up the Quaker movement is in the hands of an annually elected clerk who has no special authority over other members, none of whom claim to have any special monopoly of the truth, either in matters of belief or control of the movement. It is no coincidence that the very unauthoritarianly organised Quakers have minimal interest in doctrinal matters, and devote most of their time and energy to the practical manifestations of the importance they place on Jesus' prime ethical principle of compassion.

96   A striking example of this is the substantial, and growing number of Roman Catholics who disregard their church's rulings, issued with all the intimidating weight of the concept of papal infallibility, forbidding the use of contraceptives, the practice of abortion, and even, most courageously, the ordination of women priests. Apparently a recent survey of lay Roman Catholics in the United States found that 57% of their sample was in favour of such a development.

97   For example: the Inquisition, the judicial torture and killings of

heretics, the reign of terror unleashed on those accused of witch-craft (which according to one estimate led to the deaths of around two million people in Europe between the fourteenth and eighteenth centuries), and the wholesale persecution of Jews and other minority groups in Europe over the past thousand years. The pattern continues down to the present day with the allowing, contrary to the Geneva Convention, of the torture of suspected terrorists by some of the major leaders of twenty-first century 'Western Christian Civilisation'.

98   In the place of God, as in the phrase *in loco parentis*, describing the powers, rights, and duties of those entrusted with the carrying out of the duties of parents in their absence.

99   The COED defines atonement as, "Reparation for a wrong or injury".

100   Opus Dei, formally known as The Prelature of the Holy Cross and Opus Dei, is a highly controversial organization within the Catholic Church. A predominantly lay organisation, founded in Spain in 1928, in 2009 it had 90 000 members, of whom almost 2000 were priests. About 70% of Opus Dei members live in their private homes, leading traditional Catholic family lives with secular careers, while the other 30% are celibate. Brought to the attention of a wider public by the publication of Dan Brown's best-selling *The Da Vinci Code*, criticisms of the movement have centred around (amongst other things) its secretiveness, its recruiting methods, the strict rules governing members, its perceived elitism and misogyny, the right-leaning politics of most of its members, and the practice by celibate members of mortification of the flesh. In 2002, the founder of the movement was canonised by Pope John Paul II, becoming St Josemaría Escrivá.

101   "By one man sin entered into the world." (Romans 6:12).

102   It is interesting to compare this belief that we are all (for even thousands of generations since Adam) born guilty of original sin, with the statement in both versions of the 10 Commandments which limits the inheritance of guilt (or at least God's punishment

for it) to the fourth generation at most. "I the Lord thy God am a jealous God, visiting the iniquity of the fathers upon the children unto the third and fourth generation" (Exodus 20:5 and Deuteronomy 5:9). Even more absolutely contradictory is the assertion by the biblical prophet Ezekiel that, "The son will not bear the punishment for the father's iniquity, nor will the father bear the punishment for the son's iniquity; the righteousness of the righteous will be upon himself, and the wickedness of the wicked will be upon himself" (Ezekiel 18:20). So much for the idea of "original sin" and the inheritance of guilt! It is astonishing how Christian fundamentalists who believe that every word in the Bible is literally 'the word of God', can reconcile Ezekiel's words with the supposed 'words of God' in Exodus 20:5 and Deuteronomy 5:9, and both of them with that fundamental assumption of Paul and his co-workers in the field of Atonement theology that the whole human race is tainted by Adam's sin of disobedience. Not that Paul himself was a believer in the literal truth of every religious text in the bible. For one thing, as a generator of new religious writings (many of which eventually found their way into the Christian bible) he, admittedly only *occasionally*, but very appropriately acknowledged the fallibility of his intellectual understanding of religious matters. For another, Paul was, to say the least of it, very open to the adoption of a metaphorical rather than a literal interpretation of biblical writings, as illustrated later in this book. In the next chapter I shall suggest a tentative hypothesis as to what it is which sustains the very unhumanistic idea of "original sin," and its transmission down through the generations.

103 Or in the Roman Catholic tradition, in a time-limited Hell called Purgatory, for a length of time individually determined by the number and seriousness of the sins committed since the last granting of absolution by a priest.

104 The December 2007 edition of Scientific American has an excellent article on psychopathy, a mental condition that was first described systematically by the American psychiatrist Hervey Cleckley in

1941. Superficially charming, psychopaths tend to make a good first impression on others and often strike observers as remarkably normal. However, largely devoid of guilt, empathy and love, they have casual and callous interpersonal relationships. Psychopaths routinely offer excuses for their reckless and often outrageous actions, placing blame on others instead. They rarely learn from their mistakes and they have difficulty in inhibiting their impulses.

105 There are many reasons for doubting that Jesus actually said these words. For one thing there was no "New Testament" (or "New Covenant" as some translations have it) when Jesus was alive. The concept was only developed by the early church after Jesus' death, and so those words could not possibly have been spoken by him, and must have been inserted into the gospel record after his death. But see also the very helpful discussion of this topic by Geza Vermes in his *The Authentic Gospel of Jesus*, pp. 301 to 307.

106 "Verily I say unto you, Except ye ... become as little children, ye shall not enter into the kingdom of heaven" (Matthew 18:3), and "Suffer the little children to come unto me, and forbid them not: for of such is the Kingdom of God" (Luke 18:16; Mark 10:14; and Matthew 19:14).

107 Which is the ridiculous peg upon which many fundamentalist Christians hang their rejection of tentative scientific attempts to understand the evolution of the universe and everything in it to the state it is in today.

108 Alfred North Whitehead, *Religion in the Making*, Cambridge: Cambridge University Press, 1926, p. 129.

109 Robert Louis Stevenson's novel *Dr Jekyll and Mr Hyde* is one of the outstanding characterisations of this disorder in fiction.

110 Those who believe that every word uttered by Paul in his biblical epistles is divinely inspired, forget that Paul himself was well aware that he did not always live up to his strivings in respect of 'doing good'. What we say is an important part of what we do, so Paul's 'admission of guilt', to the effect that the way he behaves is

not always right, implies that he sometimes said things he regrets and wishes he hadn't. His expressed wish that some of his religious opponents would castrate themselves (discussed a little later in this chapter), may well be just one of an unknown number of things that fall into that category. To regard everything Paul wrote and said as 'the word of God,' does neither Paul nor God any favours at all.

111 Romans, I and II Corinthians, Galatians, Philippians, I Thessalonians, and Philemon. These were written between roughly 50 and 62 CE, to various branches of the Christian Church, in the founding of which he had played a pivotal role.

112 See for example, Numbers 31:7-18; Deuteronomy 20:10-14; and perhaps the most bloodthirsty of all, the Old Testament Book of Joshua wherein the slaughtering of thousands upon thousands of indigenous peoples, "both men and women, young and old" (Joshua 6:21) was carried out "as the Lord God of Israel commanded". (Joshua 10:40).

113 "I actually hear reports of sexual immorality among you, immorality such as even pagans do not tolerate: the union of a man with his father's wife" (I Corinthians 5:1). Presumably the woman in question was his father's second (or subsequent) wife, not the man's mother, which Oedipal situation would presumably have called forth even more violent condemnation from Paul.

114 This last arrogant statement suggests that Paul sometimes forgot his purely human status, and thought of himself as no less than God himself.

115 These are two of the foundation texts relied on for the doctrine of Predestination – the belief that God destined people for an eternity in either heaven or hell at or before their birth. Never widely believed by Christians (despite the considerable biblical support which has been adduced for the idea), this doctrine is particularly associated with the name of John Calvin (1509-1564), a French theologian and pastor who played an important part in the development of the Protestant Reformation.

116 Dag Hammarskjöld, *Markings,* London: Faber & Faber, 1964, p. 69.

117 The way in which Paul seems to have destroyed his close relationship with his friend Barnabas when they were about to set out on a missionary journey together, does not suggest a Jesus-like approach to conflict resolution. Barnabas wanted to take his cousin John Mark with them on this journey, but Paul disagreed, "And the contention was so sharp between them, that they departed asunder one from the other" (Acts 15:39). There is no evidence in the biblical record that the two ever saw each other again.

118 It is interesting that in verse 35 of Chapter 20 of the New Testament book of Acts (probably written by Luke, and certainly not by Paul), we find Paul reportedly talking about "the words of the Lord Jesus, how he said, It is more blessed to give than to receive". One swallow doesn't make a summer of course, but this suggests that Paul knew very well the original source of the original ethical principles he expounded (often in a corrupted form), as discussed in the previous section of this chapter. When talking to people knowledgeable about Jesus' teaching, Paul would have known that he would do himself no favours by not acknowledging the source of the idea he was promoting. However, when communicating in his epistles with gentile audiences who lacked this background knowledge, he did not acknowledge Jesus as the source of the ethical principles he propounded. This looks suspiciously as though he was trying to claim all the credit for the formulation of those principles for himself. It may be too far-fetched a speculation, but considering this lack of transparency on Paul's part in the context of his fantasy about becoming the father-in-law of Jesus Christ discussed later in this chapter, the possibility presents itself that part of Paul's fragmented mind might have been jealous of Jesus, and his reputation as a spiritual leader. If there is any truth in this speculation it might also shed some light on Paul's apparent total lack of interest in Jesus' life, and his obsession with "preaching only Christ crucified". A dead Christ may have been experienced by Paul as much less of a threat to his

masculinity than a living, highly charismatic man.

119 That claim is one which most adherents of the Jewish and Muslim religions do not accept, (and without a significant modification of the traditional Christian "supreme ruler" concept of what constitutes Messiaship and the Kingdom of Heaven, nor do some Christians). For those of us making up the humanistic branch of Christianity, what the Saviour Jesus saved us from, was a militaristic view of the longed-for Messiah and the associated Kingdom of God.

120 Tarsus, the birthplace of the Saul who was later to become known as St Paul, lies on the Mediterranean south coast of what is now Turkey.

121 Paul entertained no illusions about his limitations as a public speaker. In I Corinthians 2:1 he describes the input he gave the Corinthians when he was with them as having been without "excellency of speech or of wisdom," and three verses later says of himself, "My speech and my preaching were not with enticing words." In II Corinthians 10:10 he reports that some people say of him, "In person he is unimpressive and his speaking amounts to nothing", without making it clear whether or not he agrees with that assessment, while in II Corinthians 11:6 he rather defensively asserts, "I may not be a trained speaker but I do have knowledge".

122 Kephas, the Hebrew for 'rock,' was translated into Greek as Petros (which means 'stone'), into Latin as Petrus, and into English as Peter.

123 Paul obviously saw the physical abuse he had suffered at the hands of various authorities as having a very positive side. He seems to have felt that the sufferings he endured gave him an unassailable status in the Christian hierarchy. As an argument stopper he proclaimed with some irritation (in Galatians 6:17), "From now on let no one make trouble for me; for I carry the marks of Jesus branded on my body".

124 In the seven epistles which modern biblical scholars fairly unanimously accept as genuinely written by Paul, there is a very uneven

distribution of verses dealing with sex. There are no verses devoted to that subject at all in the single chapter of Philemon, only one verse in each of Philippians and I Thessalonians, six verses in each of Galatians and Paul's second Epistle to the Corinthians, and twenty four in his Epistle to the Romans. The overwhelming majority of what Paul has to say on the subject is to be found in his first Epistle to the Corinthians which contains no less than seventy-six verses devoted to sexual issues. Reading between the lines of his two epistles to the Corinthians it would seem that by no means all the members of that church were successfully intimidated into accepting Paul's teachings on the subject, and, perhaps for this reason, he was not as warmly and as universally welcomed back into that church as he would obviously like to have been. The way in which he dealt with that church's treatment of him, by turns self-pitying and aggressively threatening, are not the most impressive parts of Paul's written output.

125 The words, "It is well for a man not to touch a woman," in I Corinthians 7:1 appear to come from an enquiry that the Corinthians were making of Paul as to what he felt about that statement. Paul does not explicitly give his opinion as to whether or not he agrees with that view, but from the fact that the next verse starts with "Nevertheless" it is quite clear that he does agree with it. The fact that there is no explicit recommendation that it is best that a woman should not touch a man says a lot about Paul's attitude in regard to the relative importance of men and women.

126 Perhaps when Paul wrote his second Epistle to the Corinthians he had forgotten that in his first Epistle to them he had said, "He who marries his fiancée does well; and he who refrains from marriage will do better". Paul seems to have never given a thought to how the fiancée might have felt about either situation, and was presumably quite unconscious when he wrote his second Epistle to the Corinthians of the implication for what he was writing there of what he had previously written in I Corinthians 7:38 to the effect that if Christ accepted Paul's offer of a bride then he would

be doing well, but could be doing better. Paul would doubtless have been horrified had he realised that in offering a bride to Christ he could be seen as trying to tempt Christ to engage in a less than perfect behaviour, and so reveal himself as a less than perfect being, even if, should things turn out that way, the effect on Paul might be to allow himself to feel a little better about his own imperfections.

127 Sometimes there are multiple factors involved in the causation of malfunctioning things in the physical world, but in everyday life we more commonly find a single cause. However, in the psychological realm it is almost always the case that multiple factors are involved in the causation of any strange or pathological behaviour. If one's car will not start it would be highly unusual if the reason was that the battery was flat AND an electrical wire had been snapped AND the car had run out of petrol. Much more usually it is only one of these factors (or some other single factor such as a breakdown in functioning of the petrol pump) that has caused the problem. With psychological issues such as Paul's obsession with suppressing sexual behaviour, there is almost certainly at least one, if not many more additional factors all partially responsible for this psychological abnormality.

128 www.glamour.com/sex-love-life/2007/01/purity-balls

129 www.time.com/time/magazine/article/0,9171,1823930,00.html# ixzz1nxBQeldi

130 The Anglican Church has been quicker 'to see the light' in the matter of the ordination of women priests than the Vatican-controlled Roman Catholic church. The Anglican Church is now ordaining women priests (there is even an Anglican female presiding bishop in the United States) without the feared split in that church happening around this issue. By contrast, the refusal of the Vatican-based Roman Catholic Church to change its entrenched positions on a number of issues (including that of the ordination of women) has already led to the splitting off of the 'Old Catholic Church' in Europe and a potential split in the Austrian Church is

threatened as a result of the *Priests' Initiative* as discussed at the end of Chapter 5.

131 Sufism is the mystical branch of Islam. Rumi was a thirteenth-century Persian poet, jurist, theologian and Sufi mystic.

132 Matthew 16:28. But see also Matthew 23:36 ("All these things shall come upon this generation"); and Matthew 24:34 ("This generation shall not pass, till all these things be fulfilled"); Mark 9:1 ("There be some of them that stand here, which shall not taste of death, till they have seen the kingdom of God come with power"; and Luke 9:27 ("There be some standing here, which shall not taste of death, till they see the kingdom of God.")

133 Sigmund Freud. *The Future of an Illusion,* London: Hogarth Press, 1927.

134 i.e. ascribing human qualities to non-human things.

135 Aaron Emmanuel Suffrin in James Hastings (Ed). *Encyclopaedia of Religion and Ethics,* Edinburgh: T. and T. Clark, 1913.

136 It must be borne in mind that although most mainstream Christians seem to be content to have vague, confused, and not seriously thought-through ideas about whether or not God has a physical body, it is one of the articles of belief of the 13 million strong Mormon 'Church of Jesus Christ of Latter Day Saints' (to give it its official name), that "God the Father has a body of flesh and bones", as their nineteenth-century founder Joseph Smith put it. In the United States, the Mormon Church, with its 5.5 million members is the fourth largest individual Christian denomination.

137 Just how far the restrictions of those functioning within the world view of authoritarian Christianity extend, is amusingly illustrated by an 'Ordinance' issued by one of the synodal gatherings of the early Christian Church, the 'Second Council of Carthage' in 256 CE: "If any clerk or monk utters jocular words causing laughter, let him be excommunicated". How widespread the support for that view was is unknown, but the churchly disapproval of laughter was not a new thought which entered the church at that Council. More than a hundred year earlier Clemens of Alexandria (c. 150

CE – c. 215 CE), a second-century leader of one of the splintered factions of Christianity at that time, had written, "Laughter does not become a Christian".

138　Newman had something else other than an acceptance of the institution of slavery in common with St Paul. He committed himself to a life of celibacy at the age of 15, but his diary around this time expressed concern about the temptations awaiting him when he returned home from boarding school and met girls at Christmas parties, and as an adult, Newman wrote about the deep pain of the 'sacrifice' of the life of celibacy.

139　It is interesting that popular opinion has it that it is women far more than men who are likely to adorn themselves in an inappropriately extravagant fashion, and distract the minds of worshippers away from the contemplation of purely spiritual things if this female 'weakness' is not kept firmly in check. Not surprisingly the misogynistic St Paul did not hesitate to throw the weight of his spiritual authority into keeping women in their place in this respect. But it is doubtful whether any woman (even royalty) has ever attended a church service as extravagantly dressed as the Pope and his all male entourage regularly are. Perhaps it is not too fanciful to suggest that part of the terror the thought of having women priests (and even more so women bishops) inspires in some male breasts, is that priestly robes will bestow an air of even more unseemly attractiveness and/or power on the woman, thereby tempting male worshippers to think wicked thoughts and/or to undermine the male-dominated power balance within the church.

140　See Albert Schweitzer's very appropriate description of pleasure as a "mysterious exaltation of the Will-to-Live," in Appendix 3.

141　The Quaker maxim about the good which can flow from 'speaking truth to power,' captures one aspect of this way of being.

142　The next five most numerically strong world religions are Islam, 1.5 billion, the grouping of secular/non-religious/Agnostic and atheist persons, 1.1 billion, Hinduism 900 million, Buddhism 376 million, and Chinese traditional religion 294 million.

143 It is possible that Jesus expressed this view, but at least equally possible that these words were interpolated into the early gospel text by some person or group of persons who belonged to that faction within the early Christian church which was opposed to opening up membership of the religion to non-Jews.

144 The American magazine *Newsweek*, in its cover story in the issue of 13 April 2009 entitled *The Decline and Fall of Christian America*, claims that the number of Americans who consider themselves Christians has fallen ten percentage points in two decades.

145 Niccolò Machiavelli. *The Prince*, Gutenberg.org, 1532.

146 Alexander Pope. *To Murray*. Ep. VI. of *Horace*. L. 26.

147 A. N. Whitehead. *Religion in the Making*, Cambridge: Cambridge University Press, 1926, p. 158.

148 A. N. Whitehead. Ibid, pp. 133-4.

149 Arthur Koestler. *Hanged by the neck*, Harmondsworth: Penguin, 1961, p. 53).

150 Chirurgical = Surgical

151 John Humphrys and Dr Sarah Jarvis. *The Welcome Visitor*, London: Hodder and Stoughton, 2010.

152 The ethical issues involved in meat eating are rarely addressed by the Christian Church. The fact of the matter is that the slaughter of animals for food does often involve appalling suffering for the animals concerned. The role of religion in this process is another of the terrible blots on its reputation. Christianity as a whole is by no means alone among the world's religions in that respect, but this book is about Christianity and the inhumanity of so much of the behaviour of humankind towards animals should feature in any consideration of the contradictory trends within that religion.

Although there are not lacking large numbers of Christians, particularly those who make up the religion's humanistic face, who are horrified that the Christian bible contains the claims it does about the nature of the God-ordained relationship that exists between humans and other animals, too few have done anything to challenge those barbarous ideas. As recorded in Genesis 1:28, God "told" humanity to "subdue the earth", and to "have dominion over the fish of the sea, and over the fowl of the air, and over every living thing that moveth upon the earth". Even more horrifying is that eight chapters later it is claimed (in Genesis 9:2-3) that God proclaimed to humanity that, "the fear of you and the dread of you shall be upon every beast of the earth, and upon every fowl of the air, upon all that moveth, and upon all the fishes of the sea; into your hand are they delivered. Every moving thing that liveth shall be meat for you".

Such a monstrous concept of God, is of a piece with the one that sees God as a being who created a universe with a property which left him with no alternative but to condemn his 'dearly beloved son' to a painful death. Belief in the existence of such a being lies at the base of the sophistry beloved of some of the fundamentalist Christians to be found in the ranks of the authoritarian branch of the religion, to the effect that it is our Christian duty to eat meat, and not to do so is 'sinful'.

Four particularly valuable internet websites for those who want to seriously face the issue of animal suffering are to be found at www.ifaw.org, www.spcai.org, www.Care2.com, and www.animal saustralia.org. These sites provide a wonderful vehicle for those wishing to do something to reduce the amount of animal suffering in the world.

153 A. N. Whitehead, *Religion in the Making*, Cambridge: Cambridge University Press, 1926, p. 67-68.

154 A. N. Whitehead. *Science and the Modern World*, Cambridge: Cambridge University Press, 1926, p. 20.

155 A. N. Whitehead. *Religion in the Making*, Cambridge: Cambridge University Press, 1926, p. 160.

156 John Kenneth Galbraith. *The Economics of Innocent Fraud*, London: Penguin, 2005, pp. 55-56.

157 Albert Schweitzer. *Civilization and Ethics*, London: Adam and Charles Black, 1923, p. 242.

158   Ibid pp. 243.

159   Ibid p.243-4.

160   Quoted in George Seaver. *Albert Schweitzer: The Man and his Mind.*
      London: Adam and Charles Black, 1955, p. 309.

161   Paul Johnson. *Intellectuals*, London: Orion Books, 1994, p.342.

Bibliography

Karen Armstrong. *The Spiral Staircase,* New York: Harper Collins, 2004.

Karen Armstrong. *Twelve Steps to a Compassionate Life,* London: The Bodley Head, 2011.

David Barrett, George Kurian, and Todd Johnson. *World Christian Encyclopaedia: a comparative survey of churches and religions in the modern world,* Oxford: OUP, 2001. See also www.religious tolerance.org.

Richard Dawkins. *The God Delusion,* London: Bantam Press, 2006.

Antoine de Saint- Exupéry. *The Little Prince,* New York: Reynal and Hitchcock, 1943.

John de Gruchy. *Being Human: Confessions of a Christian Humanist,* London: SCM Press, 2006.

Ralph Waldo Emerson. *Uncollected Lectures. Natural Religion,* New York: W. E. Rudge, 1932.

Joseph Fletcher. *Situational Ethics: The New Morality,* London: SCM Press, 1966, pp. 13 and 20.

Charles Freeman. *A New History of Early Christianity,* New Haven: Yale University Press, 2009.

Charles Freeman. *The Closing of the Western Mind,* London: Pimlico, 2003.

Sigmund Freud. *The Future of an Illusion,* London: Hogarth Press, 1927.

Erich Fromm. *Psychoanalysis and Religion,* New York: Bantam Books, 1950.

Kahlil Gibran, *The Prophet,* London: Heinemann, 1926.

Trevor Greenfield. *An Introduction to Radical Theology,* Winchester, UK: O-Books, 2006.

Dag Hammarskjöld. *Markings,* London: Faber & Faber, 1964.

W. Hoffmann. *A Sporting Life – with a Happy Heart. A Training Guide for those with Coronary Heart Disease and those who wish to avoid it,* Cologne: Bayer Pharmaceuticals, 1983.

Paul Johnson. *Intellectuals,* London: Orion Books, 1994.

Ludovic Kennedy. *All in the Mind: A farewell to God,* London: Hodder &

Stoughton, 1999.

Arthur Koestler. *Hanged by the neck,* Harmondsworth: Penguin, 1961, p. 53).

Trevor Ling. *A History of Religion East and West,* London: Macmillan, 1968.

Harold Loukes. *The Quaker Contribution,* London: SCM Press, 1965.

Diarmaid MacCulloch. *The History of Christianity: The First Three Thousand Years,* London: Allen Lane, 2009, p. 218.

Niccolò Machiavelli. *The Prince,* Gutenberg.org, 1532.

A. A. Milne. *The House at Pooh Corner,* London: Methuen, 1950, pp. 129 - 130.

Stephen Mitchell. *The Gospel According to Jesus: A New Translation and Guide to his Essential Teachings for Believers and Unbelievers,* New York: HarperCollins Publishers, 1991.

Richard Oxtoby. *Achieving Our Full Potential: Towards More Effective Living,* Cape Town: New Voices, 2009.

Elaine Pagels. *The Gnostic Gospels,* London: Penguin, 1979.

John Robinson. *Honest to God,* London: SCM Press, 1963.

John Robinson and David Edwards. *The Honest to God Debate,* London: SCM Press, 1963.

Bertrand Russell. *Why I am not a Christian,* London: Watts, 1927.

Albert Schweitzer. *Civilization and Ethics,* London: Adam and Charles Black, 1923, p. 242.

Albert Schweitzer. *My Childhood and Youth,* London: Unwin, 1924.

George Seaver. *Albert Schweitzer: The Man and his Mind,* London: Adam and Charles Black, 1955.

Aaron Emmanuel Suffrin, in James Hastings (Ed). *Encyclopaedia of Religion and Ethics,* Edinburgh: T. and T. Clark, 1913.

Amy Tan. *Saving Fish From Drowning,* New York: Harper Perennial, 2006.

William Temple. *Mens Creatrix,* London: McMillan, 1917, p. 206.

James Matthew Thompson. *The Synoptic Gospels Arranged in Parallel Columns,* London: Oxford University Press, 1910.

Geza Vermes. *The Changing Faces of Jesus,* London: Penguin Books, 2000.

Geza Vermes. *The Authentic Gospel of Jesus,* London: Penguin Books,

2004.

Geza Vermes. *The Nativity: History and Legend,* London: Penguin, 2006.

Geza Vermes. *Christian Beginnings: From Nazareth to Nicaea, AD 30 –325,* London: Allen Lane, 2012.

Richard Webster. *Why Freud was wrong: Sin, Science and Psychoanalysis,* London: HarperCollins, 1995.

Alfred North Whitehead. *Modes of Thought,* Cambridge: Cambridge University Press, 1938.

Alfred North Whitehead. *Religion in the Making,* Cambridge: Cambridge University Press, 1926.

Ian Wilson. *Jesus: The Evidence,* London: Book Club Associates, 1984.

Additional Relevant Reading

Gordon Allport. *The Individual and His Religion,* New York: Macmillan, 1967.

Karen Armstrong. *The Bible: The Biography,* London: Atlantic Books, 2007.

Michael Baigent. *The Jesus Papers,* London: HarperElement, 2006.

Colin Bower. *Open Minds, Closed Minds and Christianity,* Valyland, South Africa: Aardvark Press, 2005.

Thomas Dormandy. *The Worst of Evils: The Fight against Pain,* New Haven: Yale University Press, 2006.

Timothy Freke, and Peter Gandy. *The Jesus Mysteries,* London: HarperCollins, 1999.

Colin Hart. *The Ethics of Jesus,* Cambridge: Grove Books, 1997.

Colin Hart. *The Ethics of Paul,* Cambridge: Grove Books, 1999.

David Hart. *Faith in Doubt,* London: Mowbray, 1993.

David Hart. *One Faith?,* London: Mowbray, 1995.

David Hart. *The Story of Christianity,* London: Quercus, 2007.

Christopher Hitchens. *God is not Great,* London: Atlantic Books, 2008.

Peter Hitchens. *The Rage against God,* London: Continuum Books, 2010.

John Hogue. *The Last Pope: The Decline and Fall of the Church of Rome,* Shaftesbury: Element, 2000.

John Humphrys. *In God we Doubt: Confessions of a Failed Atheist,* London: Hodder & Stoughton, 2007.

William James. *The Varieties of Religious Experience: A Study in Human Nature,* New York: Longmans, Green and Co.,1929.

Jonathan Kirsch. *The History of the End of the World,* New York: HarperSanFransisco, 2006.

Hans Kung. *On Being a Christian,* London: Continuum, 2008.

Bernãrd Lynch. *If it wasn't Love: Sex, Death and God,* Winchester: Circle Books, 2012.

Brian Mountford. *Christian Atheist: Belonging without believing,* Winchester: O Books, 2011.

Albert Nolan. *Jesus Today: A Spirituality of Radical Freedom,* New York: Orbis Books, 2006.

Elaine Pagels. *The Origin of Satan,* London: Penguin, 1995.

Elaine Pagels. *Adam, Eve, and the Serpent,* London: Penguin,1988.

Philip Pullman. *The Good Man Jesus and the Scoundrel Christ,* Edinburgh: Canongate, 2010.

Jonathan Schell. *The Unconquerable World,* London: Penguin, 2004.

Albert Schweitzer. *The Mystery of the Kingdom of God,* London: Adam & Charles Black, 1950.

Bishop Spong. *Eternal Life: A New Vision,* New York: HarperOne, 2009.

Bishop Spong. *Rescuing the Bible from Fundamentalism,* New York: HarperOne, 1991.

Geza Vermes. *The Religion of Jesus the Jew,* London: SCM Press, 1993.

Geza Vermes. *Jesus in His Jewish Context,* London: SCM Press, 2003.

Geza Vermes. *The Passion,* London: Penguin, 2005.

Geza Vermes. *The Resurrection,* London: Penguin, 2008.

Geza Vermes. *Who's who is the age of Jesus,* London: Penguin, 2005.

Keith Ward. *A Vision to Pursue,* London: SCM Press, 1991.

Richard Webster. *A Brief History of Blasphemy,* Southwold, Suffolk: The Orwell Press, 1990.

A. N. Wilson. *Jesus,* London: HarperCollins, 1992.

Colin Wilson. *Religion and the Rebel,* London: Victor Gollancz, 1957.

Gary Wills. *Papal Sin: Structures of Deceit,* Image (Random House), New

York, 2000.

Gary Wills. *Why priests? A failed tradition*, Viking Adult (Penguin), New York, 2012.

David Yallop. *In God's Name*, London: Jonathan Cape, 1984

Acknowledgements

I must first and foremost thank my family, wife Colleen and sons Chris, Oliver, and Sven for their interest in and constant support, help, and encouragement of my writing of this book. As regular editorial readers of various drafts of sections of the book, their comments and advice have been invaluable to me.

A number of other friends and colleagues have been generous with the time and trouble they have taken with reading and discussing various parts of the book. Corinna Arndt, Valda Bedford, Kit Hodge, Adam Struben, and Dr Roger Teichman have all in different ways been immensely helpful to me. A special word of thanks to Louise-Mary Alexander, Marcelle Boshoff, Candice Edmunds, and Karla Hugo who have acted as my research assistants at various times over the past 5 years that I have been particularly focussed on writing this book.

Most gentlemen of the cloth to whom I have shown parts of the manuscript as it was written have clearly felt uncomfortable with it. In marked contrast, Rev Gordon Oliver and Rev Harry Wiggett have been generous with their praise and enthusiasm for what I have been doing.

Among the voices from the past whose writings have inspired and educated me I must particularly mention the powerful influences of Albert Schweitzer and A. N. Whitehead. Very much somebody of the present, to whose copious writings and several conversations with whom I owe a significant debt, is the late Geza Vermes, a former Professor of Jewish Studies at Oxford University. His work and ideas really opened my eyes in a highly significant way to the wider Jewish context in which Jesus lived and thought. No profound understanding of the spiritual depths of Jesus' life and work can be achieved, I believe, without at least some such knowledge, and I have found Dr Vermes' work enormously valuable in that respect.

Finally I must thank John Hunt publishers, and my editor there, Trevor Greenfield, for their far-sightedness in seeing value for the future of humanity in the publishing of this book. Thank you John and Trevor.

Richard Oxtoby,
Constantia,
Cape Town.

CHRISTIAN
ALTERNATIVE

Throughout the two thousand years of Christian tradition there have been, and still are, groups and individuals that exist in the margins and upon the edge of faith. But in Christianity's contrapuntal history it has often been these outcasts and pioneers that have forged contemporary orthodoxy out of former radicalism as belief evolves to engage with and encompass the ever-changing social and scientific realities. Real faith lies not in the comfortable certainties of the Orthodox, but somewhere in a half-glimpsed hinterland on the dirt track to Emmaus, where the Death of God meets the Resurrection, where the supernatural Christ meets the historical Jesus, and where the revolution liberates both the oppressed and the oppressors.

Welcome to Christian Alternative... a space at the edge where the light shines through.